PROSPECTIVE TEACHERS

PROSPECTIVE TEACHERS

Aptitude, Intelligence and Morality

(A Study in Andhra Pradesh)

C. Siva Sankar

SP SHIPRA

SHIPRA

₹ 1250; US$ 50
ISBN: 978-93-91978-06-8

First Published in India in 2023

Prospective Teachers: Aptitude, Intelligence and Morality

Published by:
SHIPRA PUBLICATIONS
LG 18-19, Pankaj Central Market
I.P. Ext., Patparganj, Delhi 110092, India
Tel.: +91 11 2223 5152/6152; 96500 28065
E-mail: info@shiprapublication.com
www.shiprapublication.com

Contents

List of Tables

Preface

Teaching is a set of activities intended to produce learning in desired manner. Through teaching, teacher motivates and directs student behavior towards learning objectives or goals. Effective teacher can create a positive learning environment by providing suitable learning experiences and resources with a view to make the students as active participants in learning process. With her/his teaching competence, s/he will make students as meaning makers in the light of inquiry based learning, project based learning, evidence based learning, situated learning and blended learning. Effective teacher always promotes students' creative, critical, reflective and meta-cognitive skills.

If any prospective teacher wants to become as an effective teacher, s/he needs teaching aptitude, sufficient intellectual level and morality. These qualities are the greatest ornaments for becoming as a reflective practitioner in teaching learning process. This book provides empirical evidences on teaching aptitude, sufficient intellectual level and morality of prospective teachers. This book should pave the way for teachers to be and to become as an effective teacher with pragmatic findings and implications.

I express my gratitude to Dr. D Srinivas Kumar, Head, Department of Education and HRD, Dravidian University, Kuppam, who helped me with his guidance, suggestions and constant encouragement in completing this study successfully. I thank Prof. G. Lokanadha Reddy, Dean, School of Education & HRD, Dravidian University, Kuppam, A.P. for his support and valuable suggestions.

I express my indebtedness to my parents C. Venkata Subbaiah and C. Eswaramma, my grandmother C. Seethamma and my uncles and cousins for their constant encouragement and cooperation. I extend my sincere thanks to my grandfather C. Subba Rayudu for his moral support. Finally, I thank to all my colleagues, friends, well-wishers and those who have helped me directly or indirectly in this work.

1

Effectiveness of Teachers
Teaching Aptitude, Intellectual Level and Morality

Concept of Education

Education connotes 'modification of human behaviour' and it is a life long process. It affords opportunities to the individual to develop physically, intellectually, socially and morally. Education makes a man rational, self-reliant, civilized and sociable. Education has been defined as a process directed to the all-round development of personality of the learner. True education, therefore, is not to furnish a lot of information but to facilitate learning and ultimately culminate into wisdom. Wisdom comes only through morality and intellectuality (Singh, 1996; Dhar, 1996).

As Gandhiji wrote in his autobiography "By education, I mean an all-round drawing out of the best in child and man-body, mind and spirit". Dewey defines education as reconstruction or reorganization of experience which adds to the meaning of experience, and which increases ability to direct the course of subsequent experience.

National Policy on Education (NPE, 1986) adds, "Education is a unique investment in the present and future that develops manpower". Every individual should be a moral and intellectual being. If there were no such sound moral and intellectual vision, a proficient individual could produce some powerful means of destructions against the development of society. Therefore, Education is an intrinsically intellectual as well as moral idea and act (Lickona, 1991; Wynne and Ryan, 1993; Hawkridge David, 1995; Dhanavel, 2000).

National Education Policy 2020 in its Introduction writes that Education is fundamental for achieving full human potential, developing an equitable and just society, and promoting national development.

Concept of Teacher

In any educational system, teacher is the fundamental element that determines school performance and students' achievement. The International Commission on Education (1973) has rightly observed that teacher is an important agent to re-think and change the criteria and basic situation of the teaching profession. Teachers are the major agents in delivering educational reform. Teacher is both recipient and deliverer of improvement and expansion of education. S/he is the custodian of future. S/he is the man of inner integration of mind and heart and is the torch-bearer of race (Woldetsdik, 2005).

National Commission on School Teachers (1983-87) says, "If a nation's teachers are **C3**, the nation itself cannot but be **C3**. And let there be no doubt about this - if we wish to be A**1** nation, our teachers have to be A**1**". It is fact that the teachers cannot be A**1** without aptitude towards teaching profession, intellectuality and morality. If teacher has righteous aptitude towards teaching and sufficient intellectual level, s/he will be well-informed with latest trends, techniques, methods, approaches, theories, principles, skills, abilities, levels, variables, technologies regarding teaching. Raj (1999) stressed that the teacher is put on the highest pedestal along with one's parents and even higher than the God one worships.

Teacher's role as planner, decision maker and implementer in the emerging and futuristic society assumes great importance. Teachers play many different roles such as demonstrator, dispenser of information, task master, disciplinarian, model, mediator, surrogate parent, therapist, midwife, evangelist, persuader or propagandist, stimulator of inquiry, valuable professional colleague, manager of students' well-being, real change leader, conveyor of knowledge, an agent of social change, a national builder and the maker of man (Naik, 2000; Agarwal, 2002 and Rai, 1999).

As a conveyor of knowledge, it is the task of the teacher to escort the learner in an appropriate path and teacher must be capable of cultivating the habits and values by whatever stratagem s/he can. S/he should keep the fund supplied regularly by new experiences, new thoughts and discoveries, by reading and moving around with people from whom s/he can acquire such things (Rai, 1999). As a mediator, the teacher sets the stage for learning process, s/he provides children with meaningful opportunities to acquire skills and concepts, s/he makes open-ended plans to fulfill broad educational purposes or goals and he interacts with children to help them develop their thinking powers. (Whitehead, 1979).

Teacher is the manager of self-directed and interactive learning which promotes independence, interaction, communication, leadership, teamwork and responsibility for one's own work and continued learning of the students. As manager of students' well-being teachers, should provide students with a safe, secure and emotional learning environment. Teachers as managers need to be clear communicators, good listeners, good organizers, and good motivators and to be able to deal fairly and equitably with parents and people (Meera Joneja, 2008).

Teacher is expected to be a role model for young children. Children imitate their teachers, so they should represent a model of behaviour. As a therapist, teacher's preparation should consist in large part of psychological or psychiatric training. As a surrogate parent, teacher is responsible for child's health, social adjustment, emotional health and character development. As a disciplinarian, teacher must accept a considerable amount of responsibility for curbing mischievous behaviour. Teacher has to assign tasks, ask questions and correct answers as task master, and imparting information as a dispenser of information (Naik, 2000).

The responsibilities of teachers are (Krishanaji, 1994):

- To produce ideal, humane and enlightened future citizens of the nation.
- To provide environment in which the child will be able to lead a contented, fearless, happy and peaceful life and help others to lead the same kind of life.
- To train them in developing the capacity of observation, comprehension assimilation, analysis, differentiation, integration and creativity.
- To imbibe the qualities of self- confidence, honesty, love, tolerance, service, justice, fearlessness and freedom among the children.
- To make the child to be simple, normal, dignified, firm and polite.
- To strengthen the bonds between the child and her/his family, mother tongue, culture and the soil and to evolve suitable programmes such as learning by doing and earn while you learn.
- To make children learn reading, writing, speaking, calculating and doing thinks effectively.

Qualities relating to personality such as physical appearance, good vitality, good voice, character, expression, zeal of missionary, humour, laughter, impartiality, social and emotional stability and patience etc. are necessary for teachers. Ryburn says, "Self-analysis on the part of teacher is a necessary equipment and the teacher must acquire a moral alertness. Qualities relating to human relationships such as co-operative attitude, democratic attitude, religious tolerance etc are needed to teacher.

Teacher is a valuable professional college because s/he shares her/his ideas, vision, work and goals; s/he trains her/his students to take part in various inter-house and inter-school complementation. As a teacher, s/he has to learn how to help problematic children and tackle problems through dialogues and discussions. S/he should be able to communicate, motivate and inspire others (Meera Joneja, 2008)

Nayar (1994) depicts that teacher is a motivator and facilitator of learning, achievement, progress and growth inside and outside the classroom as well. Besides, s/he is a curriculum planner, collector, producer and user of teaching-learning resources and an evaluator of students' capacities and tendencies. As a teacher, s/he has to

- maintain a proper psycho-social climate,
- contribute to the guidance and counseling,
- maintain healthy relationship with students, colleagues, management, parents and the community as a whole,
- contribute to the societal endeavors like awareness generation, public education programmes and constructive social service projects,

- promote self-goal getting, self-direction, self-evaluation and self-improvement, and
- emphasize critical approach and openness, freedom and flexibility, innovation and methods.

For fulfilling teachers' roles, responsibilities and developing essential qualities, they primarily should have teaching aptitude and intellectual capacities.

Teachers are accountable to the teaching profession to maintain their personal, mental health to enable themselves to do the best what they are called upon to do in the teaching profession. They should accept accountability in their profession forthwith and maintain their record of humble services to the nation straight and above board (Gibson, 1976). National Commission for Teachers (1983-85) stressed that the teacher had to struggle for the propagation of moral values.

Concept of Teacher Education

For the development of nation, it is important to have effective teachers, and these effective teachers can be produced only through good system of teacher education which creates awareness among the teachers about their roles, functions and responsibilities and is meant for human resource development and manpower planning (Das, 1997; Pande, 2004). Education is a process of human enlightenment and empowerment for the achievement of better and quality of life. Teacher Education is one of the linkages between the education and society (Sarani, 2006). Teacher Education is the process of professional preparation of teachers. It means acquisition of knowledge, skills and ability which helps a teacher to discharge her/his professional duties and responsibilities effectively and also reshaping the attitudes, habits and personality of teacher (Deb, 2004).

As per NCTE Act 1993, "Teacher Education means programmes of education, research and training of persons for equipping them to teach at pre-primary, primary, secondary and senior secondary stages in schools and includes non-formal education, part-time education, adult education and correspondence education". Having delved so far into various aspects related to education and teacher, it is better equipped to perceive purposefully the important aspects related to teacher education. Teacher Education is to empower a teacher to integrate them thoughtfully in her/his diverse chores of professional activities (Singh, 1996).

According to *Good's Dictionary of Education,* "Teacher Education means all the formal and non-formal activities and experiences that help to qualify a person to assume responsibilities of a member of the educational profession or to discharge her/his responsibilities more effectively". Teacher Education is not only meant for teaching the teacher how to teach but also to kindle her/his initiative to keep it alive to minimize evils of the "Hits and Miss" process and to save time, energy, and money of the teacher and the taught.

According to the *International Encyclopedia of Teaching and Teacher Education*, "Teacher Education or Teacher Development can be considered in 3 phases: Pre-service, Induction and In-service. The three phases are considered as parts of continuous process". Challenges of Education (India, 1985), A Nation at Risk (USA, 1985), Learning to Succeed (UK, 1993), Learning to Be (UNESCO, 1973) and so on have looked critical at their national and International System of Education. Teacher Education under this multi-cultural, dynamic and universal background has to be re-constructed and revamped to meet the new challenges of the 21st century and to play its role more effectively. They emphasize that teacher education should produce qualitative prospective teachers.

Delors Commission says that teachers have always been valued in the society as major agents in individual and social development and teacher education is essential to provide professional and academic opportunities to teachers to acquaint themselves with the changes in the scientific and technological areas, social, moral, intellectual and cultural contexts. Teacher Education seeks to prepare good teachers providing them with a sound foundation of the theoretical knowledge, understanding, skills, attitude and interests. It enables the trainees to acquire knowledge, skills and techniques for effective teaching and to inculcate in the trainees the desired ideals and behavioural patterns of the society. It develops certain attitudes, values and interests in conformity with ideals of democracy, socialism and secularism.

Teaching Education: Concerns and Commitments

Challenges of Education: A Policy Perspective (1985) mentions that the teacher performance is the most crucial input in the field of education. Whatever policies may be laid down, in the ultimate analysis, these have to be interpreted and implemented by teachers as much through their personal example as through teaching-learning processes. NEP (1986) has similarly said, "The status of the teacher reflects the socio-cultured ethos of a society". So, the education system cannot become a suitable and potential instrument of national development without committed and capable teachers are produced through Teacher Education.

University Education Commission (1949) has rightly observed, "Teacher acts as pivot for the transmission of intellectual traditions and technical skills from generation to generation and helps to keep the lamp of civilization burning". The Secondary Education Commission (1952) stressed that the teacher's personal qualities, her/his educational qualification, her/his professional training and the place that s/he occupied in the school as well as in the community are the most important factors in the contemplated educational reconstructions.

The Education Commission (1964) pointed out, "For the qualitative improvement of education, a sound programme of professional education of teacher is essential". Committee on plan project (1964), in their "Report on Teacher Training" referred that Teacher Training is well-informed with latest trends, approaches, techniques, skills, standards, attitudes and values which are most useful for teachers and prospective teachers. NPE (1986) and Revised NPE (1992) laid emphasis on improving and revamping Teacher Education through a sound programme of professional education for bringing about qualitative improvement in education.

As a concrete step towards this end, the National Council of Teacher Education (NCTE) was setup by an Act of Parliament (1993) which came into existence with effect from 17th August 1995. NCTE (1998) has rightly elicited that Teacher Education is not only meant for teaching the teacher how to teach but also to minimize her/his troubles and to discharge her/his responsibilities with efficiency and effectiveness. It is no longer a training process but an education strategy for enabling teachers to inspire and infuse the students with commitment and concern for their well-being.

In the view of specific concerns and issues of Teacher Education, NCTE (2004) has come out with a document in which general objectives of Teacher Education have been stated as:

- To empower the teachers to make synthesis between India and modern educational ideals and practices for removing the colonial impact.
- To enhance their professional commitments, competencies and performance skills for the implementation of curriculum of school education.
- To break the isolation of teacher education and develop the capacity for working with community.
- To reconstruct knowledge in the contemporary context and to utilize ICT for the improvement of teaching-learning process.
- To cultivate scientific and rational thinking among them and to develop capacities for value-oriented action.
- To acquaint teachers and students with new educational experiments and absorb them in educational practices including evaluation.
- To foster the desire among the teachers for lifelong teaching and strong desire for in-service education.
- To ensure all-round personality development of students and teachers.
- To integrate physical, yogic, aesthetic, moral and intellectual education.
- To empower teachers to undertake action research, case studies and field work etc.

From the historical background of teacher education in India, it is perceived that teacher and teacher education remained in focus. All commissions and committees recommended for the improvement of working conditions of teachers and their professional growth in independent India, for the qualitative improvement of teacher education and for ensuring the national goals of education.

Teacher Education: Programmes and Perspectives

Teacher Education is a continuous process and its pre-service and in-service components are inseparable (NPE 1986). In the light of the recommendations of NPE, a Centrally Scheme of Restructuring and Reorganization of Teacher

Education was taken up in 1987, to create a viable institutional infrastructure, academic and technical resources base for continuous up-gradation of knowledge, competence and pedagogical skills in school teachers by organizing orientation and training programmes (Singh, 1996; Yadav, 2000; Yadav, 2003).

The scheme proposed the setting up of one District Institute of Education and Training (DIET) in each district, 250 Colleges Of Teacher Education (CTEs) and 50 Institutes of Advanced Study in Education (IASEs) in the country. All these institutes have to organize both pre-service and in-service education programmes for teachers. At the national level, institutes like National Council of Educational Research and Training (NCERT), National Council for Teacher Education (NCTE), National Institute of Educational Planning and Administration (NIEPA) etc., have the mandate to provide academic resource support to the institutions comprising the training network at the state and district levels. Similarly, State Councils of Educational Research and Training (SCERTs)/State Institutes of Education (SIEs) also have the mandate to serve the school education from pre-primary to senior secondary state.

Keeping in view the existing institutional infrastructure and the large teaching community, the Teacher Education programmes need to be reviewed and strengthened.

Pre-Service Teacher Education Programme

The Pre-Service Teacher Education involves preparation of teachers for various levels of schooling. This programme provides the teachers with basic professional competencies in terms of content and process for effective transaction of curriculum. It is a stage of laying foundation for teaching.

The aim of this programme is to prepare professionals of required performances, commitments and competencies. This programme would indulge:

a) up-to-date knowledge of the subject, general as well as special teaching methods, psychological approaches, and an appropriate philosophy of life enabling teachers to cultivate proper attitude, values and skills.
b) devising learning experiences adopted to diverse situations and
c) coping with student relations analyzing their characteristics, recognizing their talents as well as identifying their difficulties and giving necessary measures.

The students of Teacher Education are known as student-teachers or pupil-teachers or prospective teachers. Prospective teachers are the key-agents in implementation of educational programmes at various stages after becoming teachers. They are required to participate in various activities related to the development of the individual and the society. They possess responsibility to acquire adequate knowledge, skills, interests, aptitude and attitude favourable to their teaching profession. They have to master the subject contents and also theories in various faculties and disciplines, besides the skills of using methods and materials for presenting the same effectively and efficiently. They have to gain proficiency in teaching and also in learning.

They are the caterers and catalysts in bringing out dynamic changes in all disciplines. Unless they are intelligent and moral beings, their work cannot be effective and meaningful and their commitments, competencies cannot be in active mode. Thus, they should have teaching aptitude, sufficient intellectual level and morality in teaching-learning process.

Concept of Teaching Aptitude

Teaching aptitude is a compound word consisting of two words i.e., teaching and aptitude. Teaching aims at helping learner to learn or change their behaviours in a relatively permanent manner or involves arrangement of situations for facilitating learning. Teaching has been regarded as a profession. It is a form of public service which requires of teachers' expert knowledge and specialized skills, acquired and maintained through rigorous and continuing study, it also calls for a sense of personal and corporate responsibility for the education and welfare of the pupils in their charge (ILO, 1984).

It is basic fact that teaching is the fundamental duty of a teacher. It is a unique, creative, rational and human activity. It is called not merely an art but the profound of all sciences. It is an intricate, complex and conscious activity. The major goal of teaching is maximizing teacher effectiveness which is quite pertinent to school effectiveness. It is rightly said that the more efficiencies the teacher has, the more effective in her/his teaching.

Effective teaching must ensure maximization of learning experiences. It aims at achieving the objective of education to the optimum. Effectiveness can be achieved with the help of skillful teachers, well-planned curricula, suitable infra-structural facilities and library personnel. Justice and impartiality are virtues which must be cultivated for effective teaching. Successful teaching must create a congenial atmosphere in the classroom for mutual interaction between the teachers and students. Successful teaching must develop initiative and independence in thoughts and actions of students in the classroom (White head, 1979; Mohanty; 2007).

Teaching is the stimulation, guidance, direction and encouragement of learning. Teaching is a communication between two or more persons who influence each other by their ideas and learn something in the process of interaction (Burton, 1978).

Robert Gagne (1965) defined teaching in a psychological manner as 'Teaching means arranging conditions of learning that are external to the learner. These conditions need to be constructed stage-by-stage; each stage is the just acquired capabilities of the learner, the requirements for retention for these capabilities. Kulkarni (1968) has defined teaching as the process wherein conditions are deliberately created to enable a specified learner to behave in a specified manner, to perform or to experience certain desired objectives.

The word 'aptitude' is derived from the word 'aptos' which means 'fitted for'. Thus, it is a present condition which is indicative of an individual's potentialities for the future. Aptitude is a unique combination of ability and personality characteristics which predisposes a person to do one kind of work better than another and increases her/his chances of success in it. It is a combination of characteristics indicative of an individual's capacity to acquire some specific knowledge, skill or set of organized responses such as the ability to become an artist or to become a teacher etc.

Bingham (1939) defined aptitude as a condition symptomatic of a person's fitness, of which one essential aspect is her/his readiness to acquire proficiency – her/his potential ability and another is her/his readiness to develop an interest in exercising her/his ability. Aptitude includes both inborn capacity and effects of environment on the individual. It is a measure of the probability of the success of an individual with training, in a certain type of situation – a job, in school or learning a language. It is linked with specificity, unitary composition, facilitation of learning activity and constancy. Current research studies support the thesis that both factors innate and acquired, interact and contribute are involved in aptitude. The aptitude is pluralistic rather than unitary.

An aptitude test is designed to discover what potentiality the person has for learning some particular vocation or acquiring some particular skill. According to Bingham (1939), aptitude tests measure present performance, then, in so far as behaviour, past and present, is known to be symptomatic of future potentialities, the test data supply a means of estimating those potentialities. The estimate is necessary in terms of probabilities only. Aptitude tests can be used for the purpose of guidance in selecting subjects for studying in colleges. They can be used for helping the individual to select the profession of her/his choice. They can also be used in selecting the candidates for admission into various training courses. In the present study teaching aptitude test prepared by Dahiya and Singh (2004) is used.

NPE (1986) has placed immense trust in the teaching community, teacher competency, teaching aptitude and favourable attitude to the teaching profession are to be ensured before training or recruitment of teachers takes place. Ramamurthy Committee (1992) recommended that selection of student-teachers should be regulated through stringent aptitude. Effective steps have to be taken so as to develop qualities such as empathy, positive attitude, aptitude towards teaching profession and society and other cherished moral values.

Therefore, in the interest of a successful, meaningful and developing educational system for the country, it is absolutely essential that the choice of the teachers is made properly, scientifically and objectively. If the desirable characteristics are to be developed in teacher-trainees, the trainees need to have the aptitude for these characteristics. In the absence of the aptitude, these may not be developed to the required levels.

Teaching aptitude is a person's potential for teaching, the total of all the traits and abilities which are needed for success in teaching. A person, who has a good proportion of the traits and abilities required for becoming a successful and effective teacher, has high mental caliber, real interest in the profession, an adequate grounding in the subject matter, willingness to improve professionally, skill in experimentation, thirst for knowledge, creativity, interest in reading and love for children. These qualities indicate teacher's aptitude for teaching.

In view of the urgent need for revamping the educational scene, recruitment of teachers with high aptitude for teaching assumes great importance. It may be possible for teacher training institutions to do better job if candidates with high aptitude for teaching enter their portals. The knowledge of the specific aptitude factors that have strong influence on teacher behaviour may help the training institutions in their selection process.

The aptitude of teacher towards teaching is an important aspect that helps him/her to feel well in her/his job. Teaching aptitude is likely to prove helpful to teachers in maintaining harmonious relations with their pupils, characterized by mutual affection and sympathetic understanding. Teaching aptitude focuses on high sense of duty and integrity. Selection of the right type of persons for the teaching profession is of utmost important for the progress of the educational system. Only right type of persons can perform the right type of work in any field.

The task before the teachers in modern society is very formidable and complex. The teacher has not only to equip the child with the tools of learning but has also to impart various skills as well as qualities so that the child is able to adjust himself/herself in the rapidly transforming society. Further, the teacher has to play a role by which s/he is able to help the child actively and intelligently participate in the cultural revolution of to-day. For these reasons, basically the teacher should have aptitude towards teaching so that s/he is able to play and perform important and helpful role in her/his professional task.

Teacher behaviour, Teacher performance, Teacher competencies and teacher effectiveness can be determined with the help of teaching aptitude. Proper selection of teachers and training of teachers are essential for improving teacher effectiveness (Adawal, 1973). Therefore, it is felt extremely necessary to measure the teaching aptitude of those prospective teachers who seek admission into college of education. The teaching aptitude of student teachers undergoing the B.Ed. programme should be measured so that in cases where negative aspects regarding teaching profession have been found in the training programmes and activities in the colleges of education could be so changed and so modified that aptitude towards teaching profession can be cultivated in them.

Teaching aptitude tests are helpful in measuring the probability of success of prospective teacher in teaching profession. Teaching aptitude tests may measure the teacher's aptitude towards children, attitude towards parents and community, skills in teaching, interest in reading, professional information regarding classroom and school activities, interest in the profession, educational, social and communicative aspects.

Need of Teaching Aptitude

Banerji (1956) stressed that successful teaching needed qualities like quick thinking, ready wit, easy adaptability and humour which go to making a teacher bright and smart in the classroom situations. Also, he stressed that successful teaching was associated with teaching aptitude of teachers. Sherry (1964) revealed that the success in teaching was related to teacher's aptitude towards teaching. Samantaroy (1971) investigated on the possible nature of relationship among teaching aptitude, teacher adjustment and teaching efficiency. He observes that teacher maintains adjustment with environment and improves her/his teaching efficiency through aptitude towards teaching and he found that there was positive relationship between teaching efficiency and teaching aptitude.

Teaching aptitude was to be sound predictor of teacher effectiveness (Sharma 1969). Teaching aptitude was significantly related to classroom teacher behaviour (Vijendra 1972). The most outstanding positive traits of the teachers having teaching aptitude as viewed by the pupils were good teaching, kind and pleasing manners, good advice and guidance to pupils, regular and punctual attendance and equal treatment to all (Thakur (1976).

Teachers with good teaching aptitude are significantly more expressive, co-operative, attentive, generous, bright and alert, fast in learning, efficient in abstract thinking, realistic about life, effective in adjustment, persevering, responsible and dominated by sense of duty, spontaneous and abundant in emotional responses (Mann 1980). He, also, mentioned that there was possible relationship between success in teaching and teaching aptitude. Jain (1982) studied the classroom behaviour patterns of teachers in relation to their aptitude and identified that both were significantly related to each other. Vyas (1982) reported that teaching aptitude had significant relationship with self-rating and the promotion of proficiency in teaching and was characteristically interrelated with intelligence of prospective teachers. Sundarajan, Sakthivel and Ponnalagoppan (1988) found that the student-teachers belonging to the formal system had favourable teaching aptitude than their counter parts in the distance education programme and teaching aptitude took significant role in gaining skills and interest in teaching profession.

Teaching aptitude influences the personality characteristics of teachers. Prasad (1970) identified that professional efficiency of teacher was connected with classroom teaching aptitude and organizing activities related to school and community.

Adval (1952) revealed that there was low aptitude on the part of prospective teachers towards teaching profession. Hence, the investigator has attempted a study on teaching aptitude as one of the important variables for prospective teachers in teaching-learning process. Jayamma (1962) indicated that professional knowledge, individual qualities of humour, patience, sympathy and aptitude in teaching were essential things for teacher. Kulanclaivel (1968) stated that good teachers having aptitude in teaching treat students alike, reprimand students for their follies then and there, try to act as friend, and guide and improve good qualities in students. Debnath (1971) said that knowledge of subject matter, sincerity in teaching, mastery of methods of teaching, qualification, sympathetic attitude towards children, friendliness, democratic behaviour, possession of all round information and teaching aptitude were related to teaching efficiency.

There is significant role of teaching aptitude of teachers in teaching-learning process. Hence, teaching aptitude is selected as one of the important variables for prospective teachers in his study.

Sources and Factors Associated with Teaching Aptitude

The sources of teaching aptitude include professional knowledge, attitudes towards children, school related information, educational aspects, social aspects and communicative aspects. These sources are derived from the research studies conducted by various investigators. Srivastava (1965) conducted a study on "teaching aptitude and its functional phenomena". The test included 10 personality traits such as cooperative attitude, kindliness, patience, wide-interest, fairness, moral character, discipline, optimum, scholarly taste and enthusiasm of student-teachers.

Pandey (1968) made a teaching aptitude test for selection purposes in the institutions of teacher education for primary level. It included 8 components. They are: 1) professional knowledge, 2) vocabulary, 3) inferential reasoning, 4) number series, 5) numerical reasoning, 6) logical selection, 7) general information and 8) reading comprehension. This test yielded the four factors viz., general educational factor, reasoning factor, numerical skill factor and reading comprehension factor. The main sources of this test were trainees at D.Ed level and their qualifications academically.

Pandey (1968) studied on teaching aptitude of teachers. For this, he constructed a test with 10 teacher's traits. They are – interest in the profession, attitude towards children, skill in teaching, ability to maintain discipline, health and interest in reading etc. Shah (1962) attempted a study on aptitude test for secondary school teachers. The battery of test was formed with 5 components. i.e., 1) mental ability 2) attitude towards children 3) adaptability 4) professional information and 5) interest in the profession. Sharma (1969) identified 21 factors contributing to success in teaching on the basis of job analysis at initial stage. Finally, five factors were included. There were as same as shah did in his test.

Sherry (1964) made a battery of psychological tests for prediction of success in teaching. Keeping in view of hypothetical factors, the formulated hypotheses were: 1) Teaching is associated with physical, intellectual, social and emotional equipment of the teachers. 2) Success in teaching is determined by a teachers' interest in the subject. 3) Success in teaching is related to teacher's attitude towards teaching. 4) Combination of measures of intelligence, personality and aptitude may give a better prediction of teaching efficiency.

Singh (1974) and Kulshrestha (1974) had designed an instrument to identify and measure the dominant and emerging values of teachers and their characteristics in the present socio-cultural environment of school. Bhattacharya and Shah (1967) developed teacher efficiency inventory which included the items related to teacher's attitude and teacher's resourcefulness. Anand (1961) tested the usefulness of projective tools in the assessment of qualities of teachers for gaining success in teaching.

Concept of Intelligence

A mere glance at the relevant literature will quickly show that intelligence is a technical term introduced to designate a technical concept. Observational Psychology, Introspective Psychology, Experimental Psychology, Business, Physiology and finally study of individual differences, each has contributed valuable evidence for clarifying intelligence. The words 'Intelligence' and 'Intelligent' are widely used in everyday language and in scientific disciplines. This use is polymorphous. Intelligence is the efficient use of cognitive, rational, mental resources, something which involves thinking, deliberation, reasoning, pondering, remembering, weighing, and alternative courses of actions (Anderson, 1992; Deese, 1993; Searle, 1980; James, 1983).

There is a corresponding variety of considerations and observations which backup ascriptions of 'intelligent' and 'intelligence': being well adopted; being adaptive; being flexible, versatile, quick, efficient; being able to make detours to reach a certain goal; coping successfully with an environment and with changes in an environment; maximizing survival chances, being able to deal with new situations; being able to look ahead (anticipation), making economic use of available resources; being able to learn etc., consequently, Intelligence is understood as the maximal application of available knowledge (Newell Simon, 1981) and intelligent behaviour is seen in terms of sensing-thinking-acting cycles (Mcfarland Bosser, 1993). Intelligent behaviour is produced or controlled by mental, rational and cognitive processes.

Concept of Intelligence in Psychology and Philosophy

Intelligence has played a significant role in the history of psychology and an even greater role in the history of humankind. There is no agreed upon definition of the concept of intelligence neither in psychology nor in philosophy. Experts' definitions differ widely. The study of experts' definitions of intelligence was done in 1986 by Douglas Detterman and Robert Sternberg, two leading figures in the psychological research on intelligence. They solicited two dozen definitions which were given by experts in the field of intelligence. Some of them are:

1. Intelligence is a very wide array of cognitive and other skills (Sternberg, 1986).
2. Intelligence is the power of good responses from the point of view of truth or facts (Thorndike, 1930).
3. Intelligence is the ability to carry on abstract thinking (Terman, 1916).
4. Intelligence refers to person's ability to learn, understand, and deal with novel situation (Kline, 1991).

5. Intelligence refers to an aggregate or global capacity of the individual to act purposefully, to think rationally and to deal effectively with her/his environment (Weschler, 1901).
6. Intelligence is the ability to undertake activities that are characterized by a) difficulty, b) complexity, c) abstraction, d) economy, e) adaptiveness to a goal, f) social value, g) the emergence of originals, and to maintain such activities under conditions that demand a concentration of energy and a resistance to emotional forces (Stoddard, 1943).

Kline (1991) reported that an intelligent person may be viewed as quick-witted, acute, keen, sharp, canny, astute, bright and brilliant. Robert Sternberg (1986) reported that characteristics of intelligent person include greater preference for, more attention to, and highly developed abilities for dealing with novelty; an ability to process information rapidly; an ability to ignore irrelevant information; and an ability to solve problem accurately. As a working definition, intelligence can be considered as the ability to acquire, re-call and apply knowledge to understand concrete and abstract concepts and the relationships among objects and ideas, and to use knowledge in a meaningful way.

Nickerson, Perkins and Smith have complied the following list of abilities that they believe and represent human intelligence as:

- The ability to classify patterns. All humans with normal intelligence seem able to assign non-identical stimuli to classes. This ability is fundamental to thought and language since words generally represent categories of information.
- The ability to modify behaviour adaptively to learn. Many theorists consider adapting to one's environment the most important mark of human intelligence.
- The ability to reason deductively. As we considered earlier, deductive reasoning involves making logical inferences from stated premises.
- The ability to reason inductively to generalize. Inductive reasoning requires that the person go beyond the information given. It requires the reason to discover rules and principles from specific instances.
- The ability to develop and use conceptual models: this ability means that we form an impression of the way the world is and how it functions and use that model to understand and interpret events.
- The ability to understand. In general, the ability to understand is related to the ability to see relationships in problems and to appreciate the meaning of these relationships in solving a problem. Validation of understanding is one of the most exclusive problems in intelligence testing.

Johri (2007) has identified the factors that are taken to be indicative of intelligence are ability for making use of symbols and abstract thinking, facility for fertile imagination, capacity to learn new tasks, ability to solve problems, being efficient to act purposefully and many more. The nature of intelligence is that it includes many kinds of abilities and varieties of capacities

Essential Features of Intelligence

a) *Intelligence as individual mental abilities:* Individual difference psychologists, from Binet (1905) to modern psychometricians, can be divided into two camps. One group of individual difference psychologists – Binet and Simon and Terman reported that Intelligence Quotient (IQ) was understood to point the differences in mental ability, not to social competence or performance. Another group of individual difference psychologists – Thorndike, Thurston, Carroll, Guilford, Sternberg and Gardner kept looking for differentiated components of intelligence using sophisticated techniques of factor analysis and cluster analysis. They treated intelligence as an attribute of the individual, not as a set of practices in which individuals adapt and tune their behaviours to immediate contexts of performance.

b) *Intelligence as structure for reasoning:* Piaget's interest in intelligence was entirely different from any of the measures. He proposed that humans are biologically prepared to develop certain logico-deductive structures. Piagetian theory holds that each individual develops these structures, along with certain fundamental mathematical and scientific concepts for which the logical structures are essential, through interactive engagement with the world. Doise and Mugery (1984) have argued that social interaction is an essential engine of the development of intelligence. However, they reported intelligence consisted of structures for reasoning.

c) *Intelligence as acquisition of cultural tools and practices:* Vygotsky (1978) is the first modern theorist of cognitive development to place social interaction at its heart. Many of Vygotsky's interpreters such as Cole and Scriber (1974), Wertsch (1985) have argued that learning and cognitive development are the matter of absorbing cultural practice through participation in activities in the society. Vygotsky proposed that the development of human mental functioning 'presupposes a specific social nature and a process by which children grow into the intellectual life. The process of socialization incorporates the acquisition and use of knowledge, ways of thinking and reasoning with that knowledge are the cultural tools. These tools might be said to constitute intelligence.

d) *Intelligence as habits of learning:* Pellegrino and Glaser (1982), Brown (1983) and Good now (1990) observe that learning affordance properties of objects, events and places require practice and experience that are gained through consistent encouragement and instruction from other individuals. They revealed that people's habits of thinking and learning are heavily influenced by their beliefs about intelligence.

e) *Intelligence as a social construction:* Goodnow has treated intelligence as a social construction. He observes that people acquire knowledge cognitive skills and strategies or learn to apply that knowledge or skill in problem solving. He notes that people who are intelligent in practice:

- Believe they have the right to understand things and make things work.
- Believe that problems can be analyzed and they are capable of that analysis.
- Know how to ask questions, seek help and get enough information to solve problems.
- Have habits of mind that lead them to actively use the tool kit of analysis skills and the various strategies for acquiring information.

Theories and Research on Intelligence

Most psychologists would define intelligence as a person's ability to learn and remember information, to recognize concepts and their relations, and to apply the information to their own behaviour in an adaptive way. Traditionally, psychologists have followed two major approaches in their study of the nature of intelligence. i.e., 1) Differential Approaches 2) Developmental Approach. The differential approach tries to devise tests that identify and measure individual differences in people's knowledge and abilities to solve problems. The developmental approach studies the ways in which infants learn to perceive, manipulate, and think about the world. In the past few years, cognitive psychologists have begun to use a third approach, the information-processing approach which is based on research methods that they developed to study the types of skills people use to think and solve problem. There are different theories to study nature of intelligence. The important theories have been explained as given below:

1. Spearman's Two Factor Theory: The first influential factor analyst was British psychologist Charles Spearman (1927). He proposed that person's performance on a test of intellectual ability is determined by two factors: 1) The 'g' factor which is a general factor and 2) The 's' factor which is a specific factor to a particular test. Spearman's (1927) identification of 'g' and 's' led his view to be called the two-factor theory of intelligence.

Spearman viewed 'g' as central and supreme. He defined the 'g' factor as comprising three qualitative principles of cognition. i.e., 1) apprehension of experience, 2) education of relations and 3) education of correlates (Sternberg, 1985). For instance, analogy problems require all three of spearman's principles of cognition. He concluded that a general factor 'g' accounted for the moderate correlations among different tests of ability. Thus, a person's score on a particular test depends on two things: the person's specific ability (s) on particular test and his or her level of the 'g' factor or general abstract reasoning ability.

2. Louis Thurstone's Group Theory of Intelligence: Louis Thurstone (1938), an American contemporary of spearman, performed a factor analysis and extracted 7 factors, which he labelled verbal comprehension, word fluency, number, spatial visualization, memory, reasoning and perceptual speed. These seven factors are termed as primary mental abilities. At first, Thurstone's results contradicted spearman's hypothesized 'g' factor. However, Eysenck (1988) suggested that the second factor analysis could be performed on Thurston's factors. If the analysis found one common 'g' factor, then spearman's 'g' factor would receive support. In other words, if Thurston's seven factors themselves had second order factor in common, this factor might be conceived of as general intelligence.

3. Cattell's Theory of Intelligence: Cattell (1971) was the most influential factor analyst. According to Cattell, in addition to 'g', intelligence consists of two factors i.e., 1) Crystallized Intelligence 2) Fluid Intelligence. Crystallized Intelligence consists of accumulated knowledge and skills and It depends on culture and learning opportunities. It includes word analogies, tests of vocabularies, general information, arithmetic problems and use of language. In contrast, fluid intelligence involves the ability to see relationships among stimuli and that depends on conditions in the brain.

Cattell regards Fluid Intelligence as closely related to a person's native capacity for intellectual performance; In other words, it represents a potential ability to learn and solve problems, where as experience with language and exposure to books, school and other learning opportunities develop crystallized intelligence. Thus, crystallized intelligence (g**c**) depends on fluid intelligence (g**f**). If two people have the same experiences, the one with the greater fluid intelligence (Cattell, 1987).

4. Carroll's Theory of Intelligence: Using improved factor analytic techniques, John Carroll (1997) re-analyzed hundreds of studies of relationships between mental abilities. His findings yielded three-stratum theory of intelligence that elaborates the models proposed by Spearman, Thurstone, Cattell and others.

Carroll (1997) represents the structure of intelligence as a pyramid, with 'g' at the top and eight broad abilities in the second stratum, arranged from left to right in terms of decreasing relationship with 'g'. Each broad ability is believed to be a basic and biological characteristic. At the lowest stratum are narrow abilities-specific manifestation of second stratum factors that result from experience with particular tasks. Carroll's model is the most comprehensive factor-analytic classification of mental abilities. It provides a useful framework for researchers seeking to understand mental test performance in cognitive processing terms.

5. Sternberg's Triarchic Theory of Intelligence: Sternberg (1985) has devised a theory of intelligence that derives from the information-processing approach used by many cognitive psychologists. His theory is known as triarchic theory of intelligence. It is based on componential analysis. This theory has three parts: 1) Componential Intelligence, 2) Experiential Intelligence and 3) Contextual Intelligence. He states that information-processing skills, prior experience with tasks, and contextual (cultural) factors combine to influence intelligent behaviour.

The componential sub theory spells out the information- processing skills that underlie intelligent behaviour. It relates with strategy application, knowledge acquisition, meta cognition and self-regulation. The experiential sub-theory states that highly intelligent individuals, compared with less intelligent ones, process information more skillfully in novel situations. In new task, the bright person learns rapidly by making strategies automatically. The contextual sub-theory proposes that intelligent people skillfully adapt their information- processing skills to fit with their personal desires and the demands of their everyday worlds. When they cannot adapt to a situation, they try to shape or change it to meet their needs. If they cannot shape it, they select new context that are consistent with their goals. Thus, Sternberg's, theory emphasizes the complexity of human mental skills and the limitations of current tests in assessing complexity (Sternberg, 1985, 2000).

6. Gardner's Theory of Multiple Intelligences: Howard Gardner's (1983, 1993) theory of multiple intelligence provides a view of how information-processing skills underlie intelligent behavior. Gardner defines intelligence in terms of distinct sets of processing operations that permit individuals to solve problem, create products, and discover new knowledge in a wide range of culturally valued activities. The multiple intelligences are a set of capacities that have traditionally been outside the scope of definition of intelligence. Originally, they included linguistic, logico-mathematical, musical, spatial, bodily- kinesthetic, naturalistic, interpersonal and intrapersonal. Later, Gardner (1993) added existential and spiritual intelligences to this set. Gardner argues that each intelligence has a unique biological basis, a distinct course of development and different expert, or 'end-state' performances. In sum, his list of abilities has yet to be firmly grounded in research.

7. Guilford's Theory of Intelligence: Guilford's (1959) theory of intelligence seems much closer to that of Bruner who is interested in complex mental process. Bruner has described the "act of discovery" where as Guilford has defined cognition as discovery and discussed divergent thinking. Skinner has seen the need to analyze thinking into its specific component behaviour in order to teach it more effectively.

The most significant outcome has been the development of a united theory of human intellect, which organizes the known, unique or primary intellectual abilities into a single system called the "structure of intellect". The discovery of the components of intelligence has been by means of the experimental application of the method of factor analysis. Each intellectual component or factor is a unique ability that is needed to do well in a certain class of tasks.

The first way of structure of intellect is classified according to the basic kind of process or operation performed. This kind of classification gives five major groups of intellectual abilities, viz., 1) Cognition 2) Memory 3) Convergent thinking 4) Divergent thinking and 5) Evaluation. Here, cognition means discovery to rediscovery. Memory means retention of what is cognized. In convergent thinking operation, the information leads to one right answer or to a recognized best conventional answer. In divergent thinking operation, we think in different directions, sometimes searching and seeking variety. In evaluation, we reach decisions as to goodness, correctness, suitability or adequacy of what we know, what we remember and what we produce in productive thinking.

The second way of classifying the intellectual factors is according to the kind of material or content involved. The content may be figural, symbolic or semantic. Figural content is concrete material. This is perceived through the senses. It does not represent anything except itself. Visual material has properties such as size, form, odour, location or texture. Symbolic content is composed of letters, digits and other conventional signs. Semantic content is in the form of verbal meanings or ideas, for which no examples are necessary.

When a certain operation is applied to a certain kind of content, as many as six general kinds of products may be involved. The six kinds of products are: 1) units 2) classes 3) relations 4) systems 5) transformations and 6) implications. The three kinds of classification of the factors of intellect can be represented by means of a single solid model. This model is referred as 'structure of intellect'. Each cell in the model calls for a certain kind of ability that can be described in terms of operation, content and product.

The above said theories of intelligence are taken as vital parts in identifying the concept, nature, types, principles and dimensions of intelligence. Most of the psychologists had constructed and standardized the tests of intelligence in the light of theories of intelligence.

Need of Intelligence

Intelligence is the functional component of human mind. Higher knowledge, pursuit of excellence and worthy of life are possible only through intelligence. Intelligence gets percolated into the system of public life. Bedi (1982) strongly confirmed that intelligence has a direct connection to the quality of life and he articulates that intellectual thinking is at the heart of our future and can deal with the change, the complexity and the interdependence that are inextricably part of the world.

Bhagoliwal (1982) reported that more effective teachers were characterized by higher level of intellectual capacity and intellectual functioning. Menon (1982) adds that good performance is depended on intellectual level regarding reasoning, numerical ability, general mental ability, logical and special ability. Kumar (1980) reported that intellectual person could possess leadership role as good nature, boldness, independence, alertness in supervision, impartiality, honesty and communicative skills. Dlima (1979) reported that intelligence was the base for social interaction, self-concept and academic achievement.

Mayer and Salovey (2003) have found empirically that there is positive correlation between intelligence and personality factors. Kumari, Padmini,

Tripathi identified that intelligents could get adjustment with their environment. Researches also reveal that intelligence is positively inter-related with creativity and intelligence is a significant factor which influences the achievement of an individual.

Intelligence had significant impact on learning Jogi (1987). Shahin investigated on intelligence and social behaviour and explained that they are positively corrected. Social maturity depends upon intelligence. Emotional maturity also depends upon intelligence (Agarwal, 1975). And also, there is significant positive relationship between morality and intelligence (Prahallada, 1982; Bandyopadhaya, 1981; Rani, 1968).

So, intelligence is a prominent agent in influencing the personality, learning ability, creativity, performance, achievement, adjustment, self-concept, social interaction, social and emotional behaviour, leadership and morality of an individual. Most of the researches have been done on testing the intellectual level of children in order to understand their behaviour and to take appropriate decisions for their educational guidance. Few researches are done on testing the intellectual level of teachers as well as prospective teachers who are undergoing the training in teacher education institutions.

Teacher Education Institution needs the intellectual trainees in order to make them effective teachers in all domains with the help of latest trends, tendencies, techniques, skills and strategies. If prospective teachers are well intellectual beings, they will train the children and themselves in developing good character and personality, good nature, desirable social and emotional behaviour, ability to adjust, ability to learn effectively and to achieve goals, ability to think creatively and act morally. Hence, intellectual level is selected as a dependent variable in this study.

Sources and Factors related to Intelligence

The first Indian doctorate in test construction was awarded to Desai (1954) for developing a battery of group tests of intelligence in Gujarat for the age group 12 to 18 years, studying in standards VII to XI of secondary schools. The investigation sought to prepare a tool to measure verbal ability, number ability, ability to perceive relations and follow directions, imagination, reasoning, judgment, memory, suggestibility and speed of response. Accordingly, the subtests included in the tests were: 1) following directions 2) opposites, 3) disarranged sentences 4) proverbs 5) reasoning 6) number sequence 7) analogies 8) similarities 9) narrative completion 10) memory and suggestification 11) synonyms and antonyms 12) classification 13) arithmetical problems 14) geometrical figures 15) family-tree 16) arranging in alphabetical order imagery tests 17) code language or foreign language tests 18) mirror images and 19) general information. The battery was standardized on a representative sample of 4735 boys and 4770 girls. The reliability of the test with test- retest was 0.77 and split-half was 0.94.

A revision of this test was attempted by Bhatt and Desai (1969) to standardize it for urban and semi-urban areas of Gujarat. It included 10 sub tests. They were: 1) following directions, 2) opposites, 3) disarranged sentences, 4) classification, 5) meaning of proverbs, 6) number sequence, 7) analysis, 8) differentiation, 9) arithmetical reasoning and 10) verbal reasoning. This was administered to a sample of 1106 boys and 897 girls (from VII to XI) from the schools selected by stratified sampling method. The reliability of the test with test-retest was 0.84 and split-half was 0.86. The correlation with the original test by Desai was 0.77.

Buch (1960) prepared a test for assessing the social intelligence of individuals quantitatively and to study the effect of environmental factors on social intelligence. The subtests included in the test were: 1) judgements in social situation (27 items), 2) memory for names and faces (12 items), 3) observations of human behaviour (33items), 4) recognition of the mental state of the speaker (19 items), 5) sense of humour (14 items) and 6) social introduction (22items). Reliability coefficients found by K-R formula 20 and 21, test-retest method were 0.92, 0.93 and 0.92. Concurrent Validity and Cross Validity were found in this study. Nayar (1980) also studied on social intelligence test construction in Mysore.

Bhavasar (1967) prepared a non-verbal group test of intelligence for high schools (IX, X & XI) of Gujarat. This test included similar figure test (14 items), classification tests (15 items), analogy test (17 items), mirror reflection test (18 items), series test (18 items) and completion test (18 items).

Pal and Mishra (2004) experienced the need for a suitable test for measuring the intelligence of students studying in graduate and post graduate classes. They constructed a test to measure intelligence of graduate and post graduate students. This test contained six subtests. They were: 1) Word Meaning, 2) Classification, 3) Number Series, 4) Analogy, 5) Code Transformation and 6) Syllogism. By studying and analyzing suitability and usability of various standardized tests of intelligence, this study adopts Pal and Mishra's Test of General Intelligence (PMTGI) to measure the intelligence of prospective teachers studying in Colleges of Education.

Concept of Morality

The first and foremost requisite for any society is that its members must be moral. It is not possible to expect good education or harmony in any society without morality. Morality is directly concerned with a certain range of actions: not only the manifest behaviour, but the thoughts, attitudes, motives, intentions, feelings and decision dispositions of the agent. Morality is linked with basic virtues like sincerity, simplicity, gentleness, modesty, compassion, humility, courtesy, co-operation, self-reliance, self-control, truthfulness, dutifulness, good conduct, courage, non-violence, non-stealing, endurance, knowledge, wisdom etc. (Prahallada, 2000; Rama Rao, 1992; Frankel, 1988; Crittenden, 1972).

Morality is essential to develop positive and healthy attitude towards life, to mould the balanced personality, to develop high degree of intellectual maturity and to learn adjustment with changing environmental conditions (Taneja, 1990). It gives directions and firmness to life. It is set of guiding principles of life and brings quality of life. It teaches us to preserve whatever is good and worthwhile in what we have inherited from our culture. (Joshi and Kireet). Morality is not a thing that simply 'radiates' from one person to another. It includes both thinking morally and behaving morally. Hence, it is needed to think of morality extensively in the field of Teacher Education for bringing out moralistic teacher to fulfill the aspirations of the nation.

The word "morality" is derived from the Latin words Moralis, Mos and Moris which mean manner, custom, habit, tradition, or the way of accomplishing things. Moral means dealing with, or capable of distinguishing between right and wrong. It is characterized by conventional virtues: trustworthy, kindly, courteous, respectable, proper, scrupulous, conscientious, good, truthful, decent, honourable, honest, high minded, saintly, pure, worthy, correct, seemly, dutiful, principled, conscientious, chaste and ethical (*Webster's New World Dictionary*).

Morality means the quality of being moral, which renders an action right or wrong. It also means the conformity to the moral code of the social group. Morality is concerned with those principles, rules, ideals and behaviour patterns that a man takes to be of overriding importance - *Encyclopedia of Values and Morality.*

Webster's Universal College Dictionary (1997) has rightly distinguished among the concepts of moral, morale and morality as under:

a) Moral means pertaining to or concerned with the principles of right conduct or the distinction between right and wrong; capable of recognizing and conforming to the rules of right conduct. Morals are principles, standards or habits with respect to right or wrong conduct.
b) Morale means emotional or mental condition with respect to confidence, zeal etc.
c) Morality means conformity to the rules of right conduct; virtuous conduct; a doctrine or system of morals.

Different faculties have viewed morality from different points of view. Philosophers, psychologists, educationalist, scientists and moralists have defined in various ways.

Concept of Morality in Philosophy, Sociology and Psychology

a) Philosophical conceptions of morality: According to the Rig Veda, the best basic moral principles were equality, mutuality and freedom. Rig Vedic morality is not a customary morality. It showed some awareness to universal principles (Sathaye, 1970). The Atharva Veda has given a wide description of dharma (morality). It says that the earth is upheld by dharma and dharma has six limbs. They are: 1) truth, 2) eternal cosmic order, 3) consecration, 4) austerity, 5) prayer and 6) sacrifice. Radha Krishnan (cited in Rama Rao, 1994) said that individual's life would be judged on the touch stone of morality. Morality saves man from worldly sorrows. It is base for good character and personality. Sacrificial action is a symbol of the offering of will and self, which is inner most and precious to us. Vivekananda (cited in Rama Rao, 1994) adds that to be selfless in our deeds is morality (dharma).

According to Heriyanna dharma (morality) is an innate in man. Man of dharma has the sense of discriminating between good and evil. The Charvaka hold that dharma could be known by common experience. They hold that seeing is believing. Hindu theists, Buddhists and Jains believed that dharma was something more than merely utilitarianism. They call this as Pramana (methods of verifications). According to Jewish thought, the fundamental rule of morality is self-evident. He expresses, "Do not do unto the neighbour, what you do not want him to do unto you".

There are three major theses in moral philosophy that attempt to say what it means to have a moral code: 1. Intuitionism, 2. Emotivism and 3. Prescriptivism. The first one holds that people know intuitively what is moral and good. However, intuitionists provide no rational basis determining what is moral. Emotivism holds that morality is an attempt to influence some one to behave in certain way. According to prescriptive view, morality consists of agreeing to certain basic principles about how to treat others (Sieber, 1980).

b) *Sociological conceptions of morality:* The most prominent among the sociologists who wrote on morality was Durkheim. (1925) viewed morality as a process of socialization. According to his conception, moral standards originated external to the subject and eventually were internalized by the subject. Psychologists also explained this internalization of cultural norms as values. Durkheim (1925) believed that morality resulted from social interaction or immersion in a group. He also believed that moral development was a natural result of an attachment which manifested itself in a respect for the symbols, rules and authority of group.

Morality, so far as it concerns an individual, includes her/his manners, habits and customs. It also includes the values s/he cherishes and the moral principles s/he has imbibed. Manners are concerned with how he/ she conducts himself/ herself in the company of others. Habits are concerned with such things which affect her/his health and hygiene. Values refer to end state of experience, desires and goals which can be achieved through learning, conditions and socialization.

Manners, traditions and customs differ from country to country and from one social group to another in the same country. There is always scope to change one's way of behaviour so as to obtain social approach in a new set-up. Hence, the proverb is "Be a Roman while in Rome". It is also possible to improve one's manners by looking at examples in a more civilized society. Habits are as important as manners. Manners can be learnt even after some age. But habits are to be acquired early in life. Habits form an important part of a disciplined life. Keeping the mind clean by daily prayer and meditation, being punctual in respect of food, sleep, duty and other engagements etc., constitute good habits.

Values refer to mode of conduct. They are conceptions of something that is socially preferable. They are aimed at perfection, satisfaction, self-realization, development, integrity and cohesion etc. They are influenced by philosophical, cultural and religious perspectives. Value system is a backbone of a unified society. Values help in developing good habits and manners. They are set of impressions which lead to character and personality (Rao, 2004).

Values are the essence of morality handed down by each human generation to the succeeding generation for the latter's own well-being. They are standards or ethics for moral behaviour conditioned by one's cultural tenets and guarded by conscience. Values relate to interests, pleasures, likes, preferences, duties, moral obligations, desires, needs and many other modalities of social orientation (William, 1968). Personal and social values lead to moral and spiritual values. Personal values include regularity, responsibility, self-respect, self-control, industriousness, truthfulness, honesty, trustworthiness, dutifulness, service-mindedness, integrity etc., whereas social values include patriotic look, egalitarianism, justice, equality, environmental protection, team spirit, leadership, friendship, accountability, freedom, good conduct, social service, scientific temper, co-operation, forgiveness, tolerance etc. Thus, moral values are unique, original and permanent (Rao, 1992).

c) Psychological conceptions of morality: McDougall may be considered as the first psychologist who dealt with morality in some detail. According to McDougall, every moral tradition embodies a great number of ready-made judgements formulated in words and every well-organised society imposes its moral traditions upon each of its members with tremendous force. The child simply learns to accept maxims simply through suggestion by her/his parents as well as by her/his teachers. So, Mc Dougall's explanation indicates the internalization of moral standards through suggestion. Psychologists explained morality in three modes. They are: i) psychological conception of morality, ii) social learning conception of morality and iii) structural developmental conception of morality.

i) Psychoanalytic Conception of Morality: According to Freudian theory (1933), moral standards are largely unconscious products of powerful irrational motives and are based on the need. For the Freudians, what is moral is that which is socially sanctioned and that which the individual internalizes through identification with his or her parents. Based on psychoanalytic tradition, flugel (1944) presented psychological characteristics of moral progress, which were a trend away from egocentricity and towards sociability. He said that moral judgement increasingly would be penetrated by intellectual understanding and morality would increase self-responsibility. The psychoanalytic perspective takes into account of interpersonal and socio-cultural influences on moral development.

ii) Social Learning Conception of Morality: Social learning approach regards moral development as a matter of internalization. According to this approach, to behave morally is to internalize the controls on behaviours that inhibit harmful acts and facilitate beneficial acts. Eysenck's (1976) definition of morality as 'conditioned reflex' is an example of this approach. Social learning theorists believe that children largely learn to behave morally through modeling, observing and imitating adults who demonstrate appropriate behaviour (Bandura, 1977; Sieber, 1980).

Thus, psycho-analytic and social learning theorists approached morality through the internalization (the process of adopting societal standards for right action as one's own), while the structural developmental theorists approached morality through the concept of a universal concern for justice and fairness.

iii) Structural Developmental Conception of Morality: Paiget and Kohlberg are two prominent persons who followed developmental approach to morality. Piaget began his search for stages in moral development with the notion that the care of morality is two-fold process. i.e., 1) Respect for the rules of the social order and 2) A sense of justice. According to Piaget, morality consists in a system of rules and the essence of morality is to be sought in the respect which the individual acquires for these rules.

Kohlberg (1968) believes that the essential structure of morality is the principle of justice and the core of justice is the distribution of rights and duties regulated by the concepts of equality and reciprocity. According to Kohlberg (1968), justice is not a rule or set of rules; it is a moral principle. By a moral principle, he means a mode of choosing which is universal and all people adopt it always in all situations. There are exceptions to rules, but no exception to principles. A moral principle is not only a rule of action, but also a reason for action. Kohlberg (1968) explained that principle of justice as respect for persons was "higher than law" because the claims of the law and social contract may be deduced from it.

Moral philosophy is thus used to define the end point of moral development as being justice and to analyze the observed developmental progress towards the highest form of justice. It may be seen that psychoanalytic and social learning literatures are far behind cognitive and structural developmental studies in attempting systematically to specify the stages of development that underly specific kinds of moral perspective, reasoning and capacity to act.

Essential Features of Morality

a) *Morality as rooted in human nature:* During the 1970's, biological theories of human social behaviour suggested that many morally relevant behaviours and emotions have roots in our evolutionary history (Wilson, 1975). According to socio-biologists, many morally relevant pro-social behaviours, such as helping, sharing and co-operating are rooted in the genetic heritage of our species (Trivers, 1971; Anderson, 1999). Still, the biological perspective reminds morality as adaptive value.

b) *Morality as the adoption of social norms:* According to Sigmund Freud's Psychoanalytic Theory, morality is strengthened by super ego in middle childhood. Guilt or conscience development is an important motivator of moral action. Recent psychoanalytic research underscores the importance of a positive parent-child relationship, emphasizing attachment as a vital foundation for acquire moral standards. Erik Erikson, in his Psycho-Social theory placed greater emphasis on the super ego as a positive, constructive force that leads to the development of morality.

   As per social learning theory, moral behaviour is acquired just like other set of responses through reinforcement and modeling. Social learning theorists believe that children learn to behave morally through modeling, observing and imitating adults who demonstrate appropriative behaviour (Bandura, 1977). Both psycho analytic and social learning theories view moral development as a process of adopting societal norms. Personal commitment to society is an essential aspect of moral development.

c) *Morality as social understanding:* According to the cognitive-developmental perspective, cognitive maturity and social experience lead to advances in moral understanding, from a superficial orientation to physical power. Piaget (1932, 1965) stated that morality was supported by cognitive maturity and peer interaction. The cognitive-developmental approach assumes that individuals develop morally through construction-actively attending to and inter-relating multiple perspectives on situations in which social conflicts arise. In sum, the cognitive developmental position on morality is unique in its view of the child as a thinking moral being who searches for moral truth.

Theories and Research on Moral Development

Historically, three philosophical doctrines have attempted to explain moral development of children. First one is the doctrine of 'original sin'. This doctrine is represented in modified form by psychoanalysis. They conceived the young child must be subordinated by adults to societal objectives. Second one is the doctrine of "innate purity". It places great emphasis on the role of higher mental processes in moral development. Piaget's cognitive developmental approach is a descendent of this doctrine. The third doctrine assumed that the infant is neither corrupt nor pure but an infinitely malleable "tabula rasa". Learning theorists followed this doctrine. There are many theories on morality. Among them, important theories are depicted as given below:

1. *McDougall's Theory of Morality:* McDougall (1908) may be considered as the first person who delineated four broad stages in moral development. They are 1. Anomy 2. Heteronomy 3. Sense of reciprocity 4. Autonomy. The child begins her/his life in a stage of anomy (lawlessness). Her/his

behaviour is not governed by any rules and s/he is at the mercy of instincts and impulses.

But, in second stage, the child is dominated by the rules imposed by others. Here, the rules are external to him/her and s/he inevitably interprets them within the narrow limits of her/his egocentric immaturity. Towards the age of eight, the child in developing relationship with peers, becomes conscious of give and take between them i.e., the sense of reciprocity develops in the child. At the age of 11 years, the child enters the stage of autonomy i.e., self-rule. It is marked by the progressive interiorisation of the rules learned under the way of heteronomy. At this stage the child develops her/his own ideals of conduct. S/he no longer development on fear of authority or fear of public opinion. Moral development culminates with the attainment of autonomy.

2. *Bull's Theory of Morality:* Norman J. Bull (1969) admits that moral knowledge and understanding are pre- requisites of moral action. He has recognized four stages of moral development. They are: A) Anomy, B) Heteronomy, C) Socionomy and D) Autonomy. These stages are in the order of chronological age development of the child. Each stage has its own characteristic features.
   a) Anomy: This is the stage of morality from birth to a few years of childhood. The child has not developed any sense of morality or immorality. The behaviour of the child is based purely on her/his instincts and controlled by pleasure or pain as a result of natural consequences. It is so to say 'amoral' with no capacity for moral judgment.
   b) Heteronomy: This stage is characterized by the child's obedience to external authority. The child's behaviour is controlled by the adult through reward and punishment and it is disciplined by artificial consequences. It is an essential stage for moral development. It is stronger between the ages 7 to 9. It should be treated as a stage at which the seeds of moral autonomy must be sown.
   c) Socionomy: During this stage, the child's moral judgement is shaped by social forces. The child becomes conscious of himself/herself and her/his self-respect, feels responsibility and likes to establish healthy relationship with others in the society. The measures of the society exercise control over the child through their remarks of praise or blame, approval or disapproval of her/his actions. At this stage, sympathy merges into reciprocity, reciprocity merges into conscience. Conscience becomes the dominant motivating factor in moral judgement.
   d) Autonomy: This is a stage of purely internal moral development, a period of self-rule for the individual who imposes moral codes on

himself/ herself by himself/ herself. Her/his actions are guided by her/ his conscience and the nature of discipline is self-discipline. It is the stage when an individual is capable of taking moral decisions on her/ his own without any fear or fervour. Her/his moral consciousness or conscience is aroused. According to Norman J. Bull, conscience is born out of emotions, trained by critical reasoning and the application of one's own moral principles to particular situations.

3. *Durkheim's Theory of Morality:* Durkheim (1925) viewed moral development as a process of socialization. According to him, moral standards originate outside the individual and are pressed upon him/her through social pressure and eventually get internalized by him.

   The first critical stage in moral development involves acquiring an unquestioning sense of respect for the rules of one's culture. The second critical stage of moral development entails adopting impersonal ends for one's actions. Development of empathy is the basic element in the second stage of moral development. The final stage of moral development is development of autonomy- the capacity to make moral decisions without being influenced by peer group pressure dictates of authority (Durkheim).

4. *Psycho-Analytic Theory of Moral Development:* Psychoanalysts explained the process of moral development through development of superego. Freud saw morality and justice as functions of the super age, that heir of the Oedipus Complex, which stemmed from identification with parental authority. Tice (1980) has postulated five stages in recent version of psychoanalytic theory of moral development.

   Stage 1: Primary Morality: The first moral stage is achieved through the formation of super-ego structures. In the first stage, which may stretch between 5-6 years of age, true morality begins with the internalized criticism and coincides with the ego's perception of its own fault. True autonomy is only possible through internalization of earlier identification with parents and their directives, criticism, prohibitions and ideas.

   Stage 2: Middle Childhood Morality: The second stage which stretches between 8-12years, is a period of elaboration and consideration and is brought about by the achievement of latency tasks. These tasks involve reality testing and abstract conceptual memory organization. In this stage, much greater competence is accrued in all six sets of moral capacities, viz., a) To be a moral agent, b) To take moral point of view, c) To attain moral values, rules, principles and ideals, d) To gain information relevant to moral decision making, e) To exercise moral judgment and f) To take moral course of action once it has been chosen.

   Stage 3: Adolescent Morality: This stage appears in early and middle adolescence i.e., 14-16 years of age. The pubertal child tends to want her/ his heroes to be actual people, although these heroes are projections of

Child's own trial fantasies. By middle adolescence, the child is capable of internalizing hero-images and making them into more abstract ideals. During this stage, the child is able to use verbal representations and symbolization to handle conflicts, to entertain hypothesis, to formulate generalization through thought and to engage in co-operative efforts.

Stage 4: Early Adult Morality: This stage appears between ages of 16-20 years. In late adolescence, a person builds on developing a sense of individual self-hood and identify. It is the time to reform old values, rules, principles and ideals and form new ones within freshly ordered structures of meaning, intention and primary action.

Stage 5: Late Adult Morality: In this stage, individual tries to attain long term relationships. He/ she frames professional commitments and sets priorities. S/he focuses on spiritual aspects. This stage is turning to high level morality with respect to righteousness, dutifulness, truthfulness etc. As one grows older, aging and death are bound to take on new significance.

5. *Peck and Havighurst's Theory of Morality:* Peck and Havighurst (1960) explained moral development through character development. Through longitudinal study, they classified 5 stages in character development. They were: A) Amoral Stage, B) Expedient Stage, C) Conforming Stage, D) Irrational- Conscientious Stage and E) Rational- Altruistic Stage.
    a) Amoral Stage: During the period of infancy, the child follows her/his whims and impulses without regard for how it affects other people. S/ he feels no need to control his/ her personal impulses and exhibits no controls. His/ her impulses may or may not be immoral, anti-social or destructive in intent but he/ she disregards the moral connotations and consequences of his/ her behaviour. He has no super-ego or conscience or internalized moral principles.
    b) Expedient Stage: In this stage, child considers other's people welfare and reactions only in order to gain her/his personal ends. S/he follows social rules only when it suits his/ her purpose. S/he exhibits correctly in the presence of adults. S/he has no internalized moral principles or conscience or super-ego.
    c) Conforming Stage: In the later childhood years, the child develops one general internalized principle i.e., to do what others do. S/he wants to conform to all the rules of the group. S/he is not consistently honest in all situations. The child in this stage has only a crude form of conscience.
    d) Irrational-Conscientious Stage: During adolescence or adulthood some persons behave according to their own internalized standards of right and wrong. Every act is judged according to her/ his own standards and s/he disregards the opinion of others around her/ him. Here, the 'blind' super ego is at work. There are the characteristics

of the children who have accepted and internalized the parental rules but have not attained the awareness that the rules are man-made and intended to serve a human and functional purpose.

e) Rational - Altruistic Stage: This stage is highest level of moral maturity. A person in this stage has a stable set of moral principles, by which s/he judges and directs his/ her own action. S/he objectively assesses the results of an act in a given situation and approves it on the grounds of whether or not it serves others as well as herself/ himself. S/he is altruistic because s/he is ultimately interested in the welfare of others. S/he is a rational because s/he is not following the rule for rule's sake, without regard to its human effects. S/he has a strong and firm conscience or super-ego.

6. *Loevinger Theory of Morality:* In contrast to psychoanalytic viewpoint that concentrates on super-ego, Loevinger (1970) explains moral development through ego developmental stages. He has proposed a theory of ego-development in six stages.

In the first stage, an infant construct a stable world for himself/ herself and separates himself/ herself as an object in that world. In the first stage (impulsive stage) the infant is governed by impulses. In this stage, punishment seems to be retaliatory and as immanent in things. The child is dependent and equates good and bad with clean and dirty. In the second stage (opportunistic stage), the child is capable of delaying her/his impulsive behaviour for her/his immediate advantages. S/he understands the concept of blame but uses it for blaming others or circumstances. S/he understands the rules clearly.

In the third stage (conformist stage), the child feels what is conventional and socially approved is right and what is disapproved is wrong. The child shows a sense of belongingness, a superficial niceness and also helpfulness. In the fourth stage (conscientious stage), self-evaluated standards and self-criticisms are developed. S/he feels guilt not for breaking rules, but for hurting another person. S/he is aware of choices and strives for long term goals and ideals.

In the fifth stage (autonomous stage), a sense of individuality and concern for emotional dependence are well developed. S/he can cope with conflicting inner needs with an increase in tolerance. S/he shows respect for autonomy in other people. In the last stage (integrated stage), the person shows a reconciling of inner needs and renunciation of unattainable goals and wishes. Here, the person cherishes individuality. This stage can be equated with Maslow's self-actualizing stage.

7. *Piaget's Theory of Morality:* Piaget's early work on children's moral judgment was the original inspiration for the cognitive-developmental perspective. To study the children's ideas about morality, Piaget relied on

open-ended clinical interviews, questioning 5 to 13 years old Swiss children about their understanding of rules in the game of marbles. He proposed a system of two major stages of moral development which encompass both respect for rules and sense of justice. One was heteronomous morality and another was autonomous morality.

a) Heteronomous Morality (about 5 to 10 years): Heteronomous means under the authority of another. The term 'Heteronomous morality' suggests, children of this stage view rules as handed down by authorities (God, parents and teachers), as having a permanent existence, as unchangeable, and as requiring strict obedience. In this stage, the child judges the rightness or wrongness of an act based on the magnitude of its consequences, the extent to which it conforms exactly to established rules and whether or not elicits punishment. In this stage, the moral understanding is characterized by realism.
b) Autonomous Morality (about 10 years to order): It is more advanced stage and also called as morality of co-operation or reciprocity. It is the stage in which children view rules as flexible, socially agreed-on principles that can be revised to suit the will of the majority. Duty and obligation for the autonomous child are more apt to revolve around conforming to peer expectations and considering their welfare, expressing gratitude for past affection and favours. S/he views that punishment should be reciprocally related to the misdeed. Here, the moral understanding is characterized by ideal reciprocity.

According to Piaget (1965), each stage is an integrated whole rather than simply the sum of ideas pertaining isolated bits of behaviour. Both stages differ qualitatively rather than quantitatively. Maturation and experience play a role in the transition from one stage to the next. Maturation is related with cognitive capacities and experience is related with peer interaction. Although Piaget repeatedly refers to the importance of cognitive development and peer interaction, s/he does not attempt a systematic explanation of the process by which these two factors interact to more the child through moral realism to moral autonomy.

In short, Piaget viewed moral development as the outcome of an active process, involving the development of certain cognitive capacities in conjunction with the exposure to new modes of social experience.

Based on research on Piaget's theory, researchers concluded that the children at all ages and all levels of egocentricity took into account both intentions and consequences when making moral judgments. The child would become subjective rather than objective. (Boehm, 1962; Hoffman, 1977). In some studies, it is found that children at all ages use intention cues, but the weightage given to intentions is less than the weightage given to consequences, (Nelson, 1980).

8. *Kohlberg's Theory of Morality:* Another important researcher who investigated morality through cognitive developmental approach was Lawrence Kohlberg (1968). While accepting the basic cognitive developmental approach of Piaget, Kohlberg is critical of much of the substance of Piaget's theory and has developed his own scheme of stages through analysis. Instead of using story pain as Piaget did for thinking about moral problems, Kohlberg presented more complicated dilemmas to subjects. Kohlberg's aim was to retain the best of the Piaget's scheme and fit it into a more refined, comprehensive and logically consistent framework.

   Kohlberg's system of morality consists of six developmental stages. The six stages were ordered into three levels of moral orientations. In each of the six moral stages, there are four kinds of decisional strategies or moral orientations, each focusing on one of the universal elements such as welfare, liberty, equality reciprocity, rules and social order in any social situation. The four decisional strategies are summarized below.

   1. Normative order: Orientation to prescribed rules and roles of social or moral Order.
   2. Utility consequence: Orientation to the good and bad welfare consequence of action in the situation for others and the self.
   3. Justice or fairness: Orientation to liberty, equality, reciprocity and contract between persons.
   4. Ideal-self: orientation to an image of actor as a 'good self' or as someone with conscience, and to his motives or virtues.

Kohlberg proposed three levels in moral development, each of which was further divided into two stages. So, there were six stages, out of the three levels. They are briefly given below as:

Level I: Pre-Conventional Level

Stage 1: Punishment and Obedience Orientation

Stage 2: The Instrumental Relativist Orientation

Level II: Conventional Level

Stage 3: Good Boy/ Girl Morality Orientation

Stage 4: society and authority maintenance orientation

Level III: Post- Conventional Level

Stage 5: Contrast and Legalistic Orientation

Stage 6: Principled Orientation

Kohlberg claims that the above sequence is universal and the cultural factors may only speed up, slow down, or arrest the development, but not change its sequence. These moral stages are primarily the products of child's interactions with others, rather than direct unfolding of biological or neurological structures. He says that both role-taking opportunity and cognitive development are necessary, but not sufficient conditions for moral development. It means that all morally advanced children are bright, but not all bright children are morally advanced. His findings suggest that intellectual development, social participation and role-taking opportunities in family, peer-group, and secondary institutions have positive impact on the development of morality.

Based on research on Kohlberg's theory, Turiel (1966) conducted a well-defined study by using six stories of Kohlberg's moral judgment interview technique. He concluded that experience of cognitive conflict might be an important factor in moral development. Keasey's (1973) study also confirmed that opinion agreement/disagreement has exerted greater influence on moral development.

Holstein (1976) also conducted a longitudinal study on 13-year-old adolescent males and females with 3 year interval gap. He administered five Kohlberg's stories to the subjects and found that there was sequentiality of development level-wise but not stage-wise as proposed by Kohlberg. Sullivan (1977) believed that Kohlberg had failed to integrate into his theory an account of moral sensitivity.

Kohlberg's claim of sequentially of moral stages was further confirmed by page's (1981) longitudinal study. These researches acknowledged that Kohlberg's theory of justice is necessary but not sufficient for defining the full domain of what is meant by moral development.

Need of the Morality

Morality studies the elements of moral consciousness, viz., the ideas of rightness and wrongness, of moral obligation and responsibility, of merit and demerit and of virtue and vice, together with the sentiments or emotions arising in the mind from these. It also an investigation of the rational precepts of conduct and deals with moral reasoning as well as moral judgment. John Dewey (1959) stated that every aspect of the learning process was pregnant with moral possibility as they more future teachers from self-centeredness to social intelligence, social power and social interest.

Researches found positive correlation between morality and intelligence. They revealed that all students who were morally advanced, were bright in various aspects. Bull (1969) and Benniga (1977) conducted that intellectual abilities were more closely associated with development of morality. Keasey (1973) indicated that morality was positively correlated with role-taking abilities which were needed for interaction between the self and the other. These abilities can make specific inferences about another's capabilities, attributes, expectations, feeling and potential reactions.

Kautner (1976) and goldsmith (1929) found that morality had influenced the personality characteristics of an individual. Kohlberg and Bull reported that morality was an important factor in social participation and socialization. Zavadowsky indicated that mature principled morality required high autonomy and high empathy.

Gururaja (1978) investigated the relation between self-concept and morality in boys at school level. It was found that the boys who made relatively advanced in morality tended to be self-assured and confident in the areas of social relationships. Furthermore, these boys regarded themselves as adaptable, assertive, and decisive individuals capable of coping with new situations as they arose. Gewirth and Singh found that morality had influenced self-concept of students. Rorty and Wong identified that morality was positively connected with internal locus of control, creativity and field-dependence and field-independence.

Based on the reviews related to morality, it is clean that morality is very much needed for individuals to manifest their behaviour, thoughts, attributes, motives, feelings, dispositions of the agent. Morality gives standards, principles, ideals of action that are thought to be fitting for human beings to live happily in physical and socio-cultural world. It also influences intelligence, creativity, locus of control, self-control, personality characteristics, role-taking abilities, socialization, field-dependence and field-independence.

It seems that Sinha and Verma (1972) are the first persons who studied morality. They conducted a cross sectional study to assess the moral values of children of 6-11 years. Most of the researchers have been done on Kohlberg's theory of morality, Piaget's theory of morality, moral judgment, moral reasoning, moral education and moral status relevant to children studying at school level. But, a few researchers were done on morality of teachers and prospective teachers. Not much of work has been undertaken regarding morality of prospective teachers. Keeping in view the importance of morality of prospective teacher in teacher education institutions, morality as one of the important dependent variables is selected in this study.

Sources and Factors related to Morality

Lord Sri Satya Sai Baba has mentioned that Satya (truthfulness), Dharma (righteousness), Shanti (peace), Prema (love) and Ahimsa (non-violence) are the main moral virtues of Sanatana Dharma. Without imbibing these moral values, acquisition of education, performance of all acts of charity and undertaking of all spiritual practices is of little worth, what else is to be conveyed to this assembly of noble souls. Yagnavalka in his *Smriti* speaks of nine moral values – 1) Non-Injury, 2) Sincerity, 3) Honesty, 4) Cleanliness, 5) Control of Senses, 6) Charity, 7) Self-Restraint, 8) Love and 9) Forbearance (Rao, 2004).

In addition to above said moral values, morality includes dutifulness, wisdom, humility, humanity, faithfulness, thankfulness, kindness, respectability, responsibility, sincerity, punctuality, discipline, service-mindedness, self-respect, self-control, regularity, industriousness, deligence, courage, egalitarianism (welfare for all), equality, protection of environment, justice, sympathy, team-spirit, tolerance, brotherhood, courtesy, forgiveness etc are also termed as moral virtues which are interrelated and interdependent.

In this study, the important sources are: 1) Truthfulness, 2) Dutifulness, 3) Good Conduct, 4) Helping Nature, 5) Honesty and 6) Self-Control. Truth is a moral value by itself. Being truthful is being reliable. It is basic quality of human life. It makes man capable of thinking rationally and meaning of mental life. It develops self-awareness among individuals. It serves to eliminate evil-social activity. So, it is essential quality for teachers and prospective teachers. Dutifulness is essential quality to reach goal. Dignity of human life relates to duty. Success depends upon dutifulness. As a prospective teacher, s/he should have dedication, devotion and discipline in her/his duty and that will make him/her to think constructively and independently after s/he becomes a real teacher.

Good conduct improves self-discipline and purity. It fosters simplicity and systematic nature. Good conduct makes prospective teachers to be capable and responsible for himself/ herself and for her/his choices in teaching-learning process. Helping nature is an important moral virtue of teachers and prospective teachers. When prospective teachers become real teachers, they have to provide guidance and counseling for progressive out look of students. They have to develop team-spirit within the students through democracy, secularism and socialism. They have to act as an agent between authorities and students.

Honesty is the starting stage of ethical behaviour. It is a social obligation. Every individual should be honest to his/ her family, friends, teachers, colleagues and state. The beam of sincerity comes out from the light of honesty. It helps prospective teacher to modify her/his behaviour and shape the behaviour in a desirable way. Self- control gives moral and spiritual strength. A balanced and peaceful mind is possible only through self-control. Will-power will be attained through self-control. As a prospective teacher, s/he should have control on evil thoughts and should have ideals. He/ she should avoid taking of narcotics.

Keeping in view the sources of morality, morality attitude scale for prospective teachers due to lack of tool in assessing the morality of prospective teachers is prepared. Final form is made of the morality attitude scale including six subtests (dimensions). They are: 1) Truthfulness, 2) Dutifulness, 3) Good Conduct, 4) Helping Nature, 5) Honesty and 6) Self-Control. Each dimension consists of 7 items with 5 alternatives, namely Strongly Agree (SA), Agree (A), Undecided (UN), Disagree (D) and Strongly Disagree (SD).

Relationship among Teaching Aptitude, Intellectual Level and Morality

Classroom behaviour patterns of teachers are strongly connected to teacher's aptitude towards teaching profession. The teaching aptitude of teachers is important in teaching profession.

Researches reveal that intelligence influences the personality factors of the individuals and intelligence is a significant factor in influencing the achievement. Brubacher (1966) expressed that intellectual teacher could produce quality education to students in a democratic setup.

Morality can reflect the character and personality of teachers (Hogan, 1975). The morality is the feeling of accountability and responsibility (Wolman, 1982). Personality characteristics are influenced by morality.

Adaval (1952) revealed that there was high correlation between teaching aptitude and intellectual level of prospective teachers. Prasad (1970) identified that teacher's professional efficiency was depended upon her/his intellectual ability. Singh stressed that performance of teaching skill was strongly associated with teacher's intellectual level. Mann (1980) indicated that successful teachers were significantly more efficient in abstract thinking and had right aptitude towards teaching profession. Sherry and Vyas rightly pointed out that the success in teaching was internally connected to teacher's aptitude and intellectual level. Bondarkar (1980) emphasized that if teachers had aptitude in teaching and were intelligent, they would have been able to provide suitable environmental setup for students and give guidelines for children's psychological safety. These studies revealed the positive correlation between teaching aptitude and intellectual level of teacher.

Intelligence is an essential element in development of moral reasoning and moral judgment. Nayar (1996) indicated that teaching profession should have a sound philosophical and psychological base that emphasizes teacher's aptitude towards teaching, intellectual level and morality. Singh (1996) expressed that enhancement of professionalism among teachers was regarded as major step in educational scenario. In teaching field, teacher must be intelligent and should have teaching aptitude with moralistic elements. These three factors are essential for developing their professionalism. Uberoi (1996) elicited that teacher needed teaching aptitude, intellectual skills and moral virtues which had been helpful to act as decision maker, planner, implementor, evaluator, counsellor and socializer. The professional status of teacher is also depended upon her/his aptitude in teaching, intellectual ability and moral development.

Thus, there is significant positive relationship among teaching aptitude, intellectual level and morality. These three components are very much needed for teachers and prospective teachers in teaching-learning process. Without these three qualities, teacher cannot become as an effective teacher and prospective teacher cannot become as an efficient teacher after becoming real teacher in teaching-learning process.

Need of the Study

Teaching is an honoured profession. Teaching is an intellectual and moral duty. It is a pious obligation of teacher. Teaching profession is a sense of public service and a lifetime commitment to career. It is a defined body of knowledge, intellectual skills and code of ethics with specialized training. It requires professional interest, professional responsibility, professional accountability, professional knowledge, professional skills and professional ethics. These can be attained by the teacher if and only if s/he has aptitude towards teaching profession, sufficient intellectual abilities and moral virtues. Thus, the important ingredients in the teaching profession are teaching aptitude, intelligence and morality of the teacher (Kundu, 1996).

There are two factors which are most essential for any profession. First one is the pursuit of excellence and second one is the code of ethics. Pursuit of excellence is an intellectual target. The individuals must be intelligent to achieve excellence in any profession. The code of ethics is a moral target. The individuals should have moral virtues to bring standards of performance in reaching higher stage in any profession. But, in teaching profession, these two factors are internally connected to another factor i.e., right aptitude towards profession. A wise and moral teacher with right aptitude in teaching profession can produce quality education to the students. (Saraf, 1996; Singh, 1996).

National Commission of Teachers II (1983) has given higher importance to pursuit of excellence and professional ethics in teaching profession. It stressed that creation of new generation of dedicated teachers and enhancement of their professional status are possible through teachers' aptitude in teaching profession, their intellectual abilities and their moral qualities. Standards of Education in India, depends upon quality of teachers and nothing can be achieved if the teachers do not possess the necessary intellectual abilities, professional ethics and interest towards teaching work (Chaurasia, 1996).

UNESCO's Inter-Governmental Conference on the status of teacher, held in (1966) declared that the status of teacher was related with their professional intellectuality, professional ethics and professional commitment. National Council of Teacher Education (NCTE), All India Federation of Education (AIFEA) and ILO also point out the importance of teacher's aptitude, intellectual ability and morality (Chaurasia, 1996). World Conference on Education For All (EFA), at Jomtien, Thailand in 1990, provided new impetus for universalizing education. It has identified that the advancement in education depends largely upon the teachers' qualifications, intellectual ability, morality and teaching staff. Ernest Green Wood (1984) expressed three basic attributes for teaching profession. They were: 1) Cognitive Component, 2) Ethical Component and 3) Aptitude for Cultural Development. These three components make the teacher effective in teaching-learning process.

Success in teaching is entirely related to teacher's aptitude towards teaching (Sherry, 1964). Teaching aptitude is a sound predictor of teacher effectiveness. Mann (1980) revealed that teachers with good teaching aptitude were significantly more expressive, co-operative, attentive, generous, bright and alert, fast in learning, efficient in abstract thinking, realistic about life, effective in adjustment, preserving, responsible and dominated by sense of duty, spontaneous and abundant in emotional responses.

Professional efficiency of teacher is associated with teacher's teaching aptitude. Debnath (1971) stressed that knowledge of subject matter, sincerity in teaching, mastery of methods of teaching, sympathetic attitude towards children, democratic behaviour etc., were positively related to teaching aptitude of teacher. Mehta and Singh found the positive correlation between personality characteristics and teaching aptitude of teachers.

Vijendra and Jain observed that classroom behaviour patterns of teachers were strongly connected to teacher's aptitude towards teaching profession.

Intelligence has a direct connection to the quality of life and more effective teachers are characterized by higher level of intellectual capacity and intellectual functioning (Bedi, 1982). Good performance depends on intellectual level of teacher in teaching-learning process. Kumar (1980) reported that intellectual persons could possess independence, alertness in supervision, impartiality, boldness, honesty and communicative skills. revealed that Intelligence is the base for social interaction and self-concept (Dlima, 1979).

Brubacher expressed that intellectual teacher could produce quality education to students in a democratic setup. Guilford said that teacher's intellectual ability reflected the teaching work. From these reviews, it is evident that intelligence is a prominent agent in influencing the personality, learning, creativity, performance, achievement, adjustment, self-concept, social interaction, emotional behaviour and leadership styles.

Morality could reflect the character and personality of teachers (Hogan, 1975). Wolman (1982) indicated that the morality was the feeling of accountability and responsibility. Researches found that personality characteristics were influenced by morality and self-concept was positively related with morality. So, morality is also an important factor in influencing self-concept, role-taking abilities, personality characteristics, accountability and professional responsibility.

There is high correlation between teaching aptitude and intellectual level of prospective teachers. identified that teacher's professional efficiency is depended upon her/his intellectual ability (Prasad, 1970). Performance of teaching skill is strongly associated with teacher's intellectual level (Singh, 1970). Mann (1980) indicated that successful teachers were significantly more efficient in abstract thinking and had right aptitude towards teaching profession. Sherry and Vyas rightly pointed out that success in teaching was internally connected to teacher's aptitude in teaching and his /her intellectual level. Dorothy (1984) emphasized that if teachers had aptitude in teaching and were intelligent, they would be able to provide suitable environmental setup for students and give guidelines for children's psychological safety. These studies revealed the positive correlation between teaching aptitude and intellectual level of teacher.

Researches find positive correlation between morality and intelligence and they identified that intellectual development was a necessary condition for the development of morality, and concluded that intelligence was an essential element in the development of moral reasoning and moral judgment.

Thus, there is significant positive relationship among teaching aptitude, intellectual level and morality. These components are very much needed for teachers in teaching-learning process. In other words, these three components are three vertices of triangle or three sides of triangle. Unless teacher has teaching aptitude, intellectual level and morality, teacher cannot become as an effective teacher.

Teacher Education Institution needs such intellectual trainees, who has right aptitude towards teaching and follow moral virtues. These three components make the trainees to become as models after they become real teachers in teaching field. Such trainees can be well-adjusted and well-informed with trends, techniques, skills, strategies in teaching-learning process.

If prospective teachers have right aptitude in teaching, intelligence and are moral agents, certainly, they can train and educate the children in developing their personality and character. They can mould the students to think intellectually, to act morally and to adjust and maintain things effectively. And they can frame the suitable and desirable social, emotional and rational behaviour in children. And also, they can help children in attaining the goals of education.

In view of the significance for requirement of teaching aptitude, intellectual level and morality among prospective teachers, this study has been undertaken assessing the level of teaching aptitude, intellectual level and morality among prospective teachers, who are undergoing training at B.Ed. level in a Andhra Pradesh district.

Objectives of the Study

1) To develop a tool to assess the level of morality among prospective teachers studying in Colleges of Education at B.Ed level.
2) To find out the number and percentage of prospective teachers having teaching aptitude as per the classification of Excellent, Good, Average, Low and Poor given in Teaching Aptitude Test (TAT).
3) To find out the number and percentage of prospective teachers having intellectual level as per the classification of Gifted, Above Average, Below Average and Poor given in the Test of General Intelligence (TGI).
4) To find out the number and percentage of prospective teachers having morality as per the classification of Excellent, Good, Average, Low and Poor given in the Morality Attitude Scale (MAS).
5) To find out the significant differences if any, in the teaching aptitude of prospective teachers due to variation in their gender, age, type of locality, type of management, educational qualification, type of group, methods of teaching-I, methods of teaching-II, community, parental income, parental education and marital status.
6) To find out the significant differences if any, in the Intellectual level of prospective teachers due to variation in their gender, age, type of locality type of management, educational qualification, type of group, methods of teaching-I, methods of teaching-II, community, parental income, parental education and marital status.
7) To find out the significant differences if any, in the morality of prospective teachers due to variation in their gender, age, type of locality, type of management, educational qualification, type of group, methods of teaching-I, methods of teaching-II, community, parental income, parental education and marital status.

8) To find out the relationship between
   a) teaching aptitude and its dimensions such as professional knowledge, attitude towards children, school related information, social aspects, educational aspects and communicative aspects.
   b) teaching aptitude and dimensions of intellectual level such as word meaning, analogy, classification, number series, code transformation and syllogism.
   c) teaching aptitude and dimensions of morality such as truthfulness, dutifulness, good conduct, helping nature, self-control and honesty.
9) To find out the relationship between
   a) intellectual level and its dimensions such as word meaning, analogy, classification, number series, code transformation and syllogism.
   b) intellectual level and dimensions of teaching aptitude such as professional knowledge, attitude towards children, school related information, social aspects, educational aspects and communicative aspects.
   c) intellectual level and dimensions of morality such as truthfulness, dutifulness, good conduct, helping nature, self-control and honesty.
10) To find out the relationship between
   a) morality and its dimensions such as truthfulness, dutifulness, good conduct, helping nature, self-control and honesty.
   b) morality and dimensions of teaching aptitude such as professional knowledge, attitude towards children, school related information, social aspects, educational aspects and communicative aspects.
   c) morality and dimensions of intellectual level such as word meaning, analogy, classification, number series, code transformation and syllogism.
11) To find out the relationship between
   a) teaching aptitude and intellectual level of prospective teachers studying in colleges of education at B.Ed level.
   b) intellectual level and morality of prospective teachers studying in colleges of education at B.Ed level.
   c) intellectual level and teaching aptitude of prospective teachers studying in colleges of education at B.Ed level.
12) To predict how far and to what extent the independent variables (gender, age, type of locality, type of management, educational qualification, type of group, methods of teaching-I, methods of teaching-II, community, parental income, parental education and marital status) influence the dependent variables (teaching aptitude, intellectual level and morality) of prospective teachers studying in Colleges of Education at B.Ed level.

Hypotheses

On the basis of objectives, hypotheses were formulated. The hypotheses were set up in a null form as this form of hypotheses is a akin to the legal principle that a man/woman is innocent until he/she is proved guilty (Guilford 1978; Garret and Wood worth, 1966).

1. There exists no significant difference in teaching aptitude of prospective teachers due to variation in their gender, age, type of locality, type of management, educational qualification, type of group, methods of teaching- I, methods of teaching-II, community, parental income, parental education and marital status.
2. There exists no significant difference in intellectual level of prospective teachers due to variation in their gender, age, type of locality, type of management, educational qualification, type of group, methods of teaching- I, methods of teaching-II, community, parental income, parental education and marital status.
3. There exists no significant difference in morality of prospective teachers due to variation in their gender, age, type of locality, type of management, educational qualification, type of group, methods of teaching-I, methods of teaching-II, community, parental income, parental education and marital status.
4. There exists no significant relationship between teaching aptitude and its dimensions such as professional knowledge, attitude towards children, school related information, social aspects, educational aspects and communicative aspects.
5. There exists no significant relationship between teaching aptitude and dimensions of intellectual level such as word meaning, classification, series, analogy, code transformation and syllogism.
6. There exists no significant relationship between teaching aptitude and dimensions of morality such as truthfulness, dutifulness, good conduct, helping nature, self-control and honesty.
7. There exists no significant relationship between intellectual level and its dimensions such as word meaning, classification, series, analogy, code transformation and syllogism.
8. There exists no significant relationship between intellectual level and dimensions of teaching aptitude such as professional knowledge, attitude towards children, school related information, social aspects, educational aspects and communicative aspects.
9. There exists no significant relationship between intellectual level and dimensions of morality such as truthfulness, dutifulness, good conduct, helping nature, self-control and honesty.
10. There exists no significant relationship between morality and its dimensions such as truthfulness, dutifulness, good conduct, helping nature, self-control and honesty.
11. There exists no significant relationship between morality and dimensions of teaching aptitude such as professional knowledge, attitude towards

children, school related information, social aspects, educational aspects and communicative aspects.

12. There exists no significant relationship between morality and dimensions of intellectual level such as word meaning, classification, series, analogy, code transformation and syllogism.
13. There exists no significant relationship between teaching aptitude and intellectual level of prospective teachers.
14. There exists no significant relationship between intellectual level and morality of prospective teachers.
15. There exists no significant relationship between morality and teaching aptitude of prospective teachers.

Scope of the Study

Teaching is a dynamic interplay between the teacher and the pupils and is an interactive process involving classroom talk, certain definable activities that are designed and performed to produce change in behaviour potential of other individuals. It is system of actions that intended to produce learning. It is an arrangement and manipulation of situation. Teaching profession is the noblest one that calls for a sense of personal and corporate responsibility of education. The teacher is stimulator of inquiry, dispenser of knowledge and moral educator. He is the central pillar for the personality development of child and progress of the nation.

Prospective teachers are to be functional with multiple roles in Pre-Service Programme and they have to gain capacity for the purpose of guiding and directing the learning experiences intellectually and morally in a public or private educational institutions. He/she needs basically aptitude towards teaching. He/she must be intelligent in planning, organizing and evaluating the teaching-learning process and he/she must be moral educator in upholding good habits, manners, cultures and values.

Research studies pertaining to teaching aptitude, intellectual level and morality of prospective teachers, help in identifying whether they have real aptitude in teaching or not, whether they are intellectual agents or not and whether they are moral educators or not. Also, these studies indicate hard spots of the educational system. This kind of research facilitates for providing better recommendations for prospective teachers to become effective and model teachers in their real teaching- learning situations.

Hence, the present investigation primarily aims at developing a tool to assess the morality of prospective teachers. Secondly, the study focuses its attention in finding out the significant differences if any, in the teaching aptitude, intellectual level and morality of prospective teachers due to variations in their gender, age, type of locality, type of management, educational qualification, type of group, methods of teaching-I, methods of teaching-II, community, parental income, parental education and marital status.

Thirdly, the study attempts to study the relationship among teaching aptitude, intellectual level, morality and dimensions involved among these three dependent variables. Finally, the present study pays its attention on how far and to what extent the independent variables (gender, age, type of locality, type of management, educational qualification, type of group, methods of teaching-I, methods of teaching- II, community, parental income, parental education and marital status are contributing to the dependent variables (teaching aptitude, intellectual level and morality) of prospective teachers.

2

Studies on Teaching Aptitudes, Intelligence and Morality

Introduction

An attempt has been made to include all available studies in this study. The main purposes for gathering related literature are:

1. To show whether the evidence already available solves the problem adequately without further investigation, and thus to avoid the risk of duplication.
2. To provide ideas, theories, explanations or hypotheses valuable in formulating the problem.
3. To suggest methods of research appropriate to the problem.
4. To locate comparative data useful in the interpretation of results.
5. To contribute to the general scholarship of the investigator.

In this study, studies related to teaching aptitude, intelligence and morality are collected, and divided these reviews into three categories for better understanding of the present study. They are: 1. Studies on Teaching Aptitude, 2. Studies on Intelligence and 3. Studies on Morality

Studies on Teaching Aptitude

Adaval (1952) conducted an experimental investigation on aptitude for teaching. He examined the nature of aptitude and interest through aptitude test of teaching ability (prepared by Knight and others). This instrument was administered to 429 student-teachers in 10 teacher training institutions in U.P. and Delhi. The poor response to the test was attributed by the author to either the carelessness of the student-teachers or to the lack of aptitude for teaching profession in them.

Aggarwal (1969) studied on measurement and competence of teachers of primary schools. The major objectives of the study were: 1) To develop and validate a tool to measure the competence of teachers on process criteria and measure their teaching competence.2) To measure intelligence, teaching abilities and subject knowledge of teachers as presage criteria. The study revealed that more than 53 per cent teachers were not intelligent enough to be teachers and intelligence was significantly and positively related to subject knowledge. In the classroom teaching, about 52 per cent of teachers were below average where as 47.35 per cent of teachers were weak in the competence of organizing and co-organizing the co-curricular activities, school programmes and other activities of the school.

Aggarwal (1980) conducted a study on motivation factors in the choice of teaching as profession and its relationship with some other variables. The major objective of the study was to identify the motivational factors in B.Ed. trainees' choice of teaching as a profession. The major findings of the study were: 1) Teaching had been consistently a very popular aspiration from high school to college education. 2) A large majority of the B. Ed trainees wanted to take up teaching, but very few wanted to start their own schools. There was no significant difference in aptitude towards the teaching of high, middle and low socio-economic status groups.

Ahmed and Salma (2010) investigated on teaching aptitude of prospective teachers in relation to their academic background. The main objectives of the study were: 1) To examine the differences between high academic background and low academic background prospective teachers in relation to their teaching aptitude. 2) To explore differences between male and female prospective teachers in regard to their teaching aptitude. The investigators have adopted the questionnaire survey method to find out the level of teaching aptitude of prospective teachers in relation to their academic background. This study was conducted in 10 colleges of Purvanchal University. The sample consisted of 496 prospective teachers of whom 312 are male and 184 female. Tools of the study were: 1) Teaching Aptitude Test Battery (TATB) by R.P. Singh and Dr. S.N. Sharma; 2) The percentages secured by the prospective teachers in the High School, Intermediate, Graduation and Post-Graduation. The main findings of the study were: 1) There is significant difference between male and female prospective teachers on measure of teaching aptitude. 2) There is significant difference between high academic background and low academic background prospective teachers on measure of teaching aptitude.

Anand (1961) investigated on teachers' qualities through projective tests. The main purpose of his investigation was of determining the usefulness of certain psychological tests of the projective type in the assessment of qualities relevant to success in teaching. For this, he developed projective tests for the assessment of teachers' characteristics; there were three approaches to estimate the teachers' qualities as follows: rankings by class students, colleagues and heads of the institutions. Analysis of variance suggested that teachers of Mathematics and English were ranked higher than the teachers of Drawing. Pupils' ranks also agreed more for qualities like expression, sympathy, loveliness and beauty. The correlation coefficient between pupils' and principals' ratings was 44 which was significant.

Banerji (1956) studied specific ability and attainment in the teaching profession in junior high and higher secondary schools at GCPI in Allahabad. The aims of the study were – (i) To investigate into the interrelationship of the two aspects of training, viz., practice teaching and theoretical studies, and (ii) To ascertain to what extent these two aspects were related to general intelligence and teaching aptitude as measured by objective tests. The results of the study were: 1) Intelligence and thinking are the basic qualities for becoming a good and efficient teacher; 2) Aptitude towards successful teaching needs qualities like quick thinking, ready wit, easy adaptability and humour which make a teacher bright and smart in the class.

Bhattacharya and Shah (1967) have studied teacher efficiency inventory. This investigation has endeavoured to develop an instrument for the selection of primary and secondary school teachers with a view to covering the important aspects viz., teachers' attitude and teachers' resourcefulness. Certain items were constructed for the inventory. Item analysis was carried out and the results were compared with the experts' estimation. Based on item analysis and the opinions of the experts, fifty and thirty items were selected. The final test was administered to 1000 primary and secondary school teachers. The reliability coefficient established by split-half method was 0.75. The face validity was determined by obtaining the opinions of three expert judges. The predictive validity, by correlating percentile ranks corresponding to the raw scores was also calculated.

Bhoom Reddy (1991) studied on teaching aptitude of secondary school teachers in Andhra Pradesh, using the existing tools on aptitudes and attitudes, which have to be further streamlined and standardized. The test used in this study consisted of 50 items covering; the dimensions of the study were: 1) The aims and objectives of teaching, 2) Curricular and co-curricular activities, 3) Classroom teaching-learning situations and 4) Discipline in the classroom. The sample consisted of 332 teacher trainees of collages of education under Kakatiya University. 80 teachers with a service of more than 10 years, and 20 teachers who were given special awards as best teacher awards at the national, state and district levels were selected. The study revealed that there was a significant relationship between teaching aptitude and attitude of secondary school teachers.

Channa (1952) has made an investigation into the reasons that influences men to take up the teaching profession. Survey method was employed. The sample of the subjects consisted of 500 teachers and student-teachers in the high schools and training colleges in Punjab. Twenty reasons for choice of the teaching profession were traced and they were ranked in the questionnaire.

Based on results of the study, the investigator suggested that teachers generally did not want their sons to take up teaching profession nor did the sons' like to join the profession of their father. The rich and the people of high social status did not seem to patronize teaching profession. Regarding satisfaction over choice of the profession, 41 per cent of teachers expressed satisfaction, 26 per cent of teachers expressed partial satisfaction and 33 per cent of teachers expressed dissatisfaction. The reasons advanced for dissatisfaction was low salary.

Dosajh (1956) reported that imagination and maturity were indicators of success in the teaching profession. Contingency coefficients of correlation between levels of imagination and maturity in teaching were calculated and were found to be 0.71 and 0.80. He remarked that the imaginative power of the teacher would reflect the effectiveness of teaching also. Among the five predictors of success of teaching, namely, intelligence, social adjustment, personality adjustment, socio-economic status and academic adjustment; intelligence was found to be the most important predictor. Confidence was an important trait of a teacher of high teaching ability. The favourable aptitude towards teaching was likely to be proved helpful to teachers in maintaining harmonious relations with their pupils, characterized by mutual affection and sympathetic understanding. It was found that effective teachers had real love and strong liking towards teaching profession which made them to get satisfied with their job (Budhisagar & Sansanwal, 1991; Chakrabarti Mohit, 2005).

Jain (1982) studied classroom behaviour patterns of teachers in relation to their attitude towards profession, morale and values. The sample of the study consisted of 100 trained graduate teachers (50 male and 50 female), teaching Mathematics in class VIII of Government higher secondary schools of Delhi. The findings of the study were: (i) Male teachers devoted more time in asking questions than female teachers. (ii) Teachers with positive attitude towards teaching profession, classroom teaching, child-centered practices and educational process reacted to ideas and feelings of pupils and frequently created an emotional climate in the classroom.

Kulanclaivel and Rao (1990) attempted a study for knowing qualities of a good teacher and a good student. The study was undertaken to analyze the qualities of a good teacher and a good student. The major findings of the study are: 1) Good teacher inspires good qualities in the students. 2) He/she treats them alike without showing caste prejudices. 3) He/she reprimands students for their follies then and there and tries to modify students' personality. 4) He/she is conscientious and acts as a guide to the students.

Lakshmikuttamma (1978) reported that the some of the major roles expected from the teachers were: 1) They should try to eliminate illiteracy. 2) They should be thorough in the subject matter. 3) They should co-operate with the headmaster and the staff in maintaining discipline. 4) They should treat the pupils kindly. 5) They should not be political workers. 6) They should be social agents. 7) They should mould the character of the pupils, they should work for the communal harmony and they should keep close contact with the parents.

Mann (1980) investigated on some correlates of success in teaching of secondary school teachers. The major objectives of the study were: 1) To find out the concept of teacher of success in teaching. 2) To assess the success in teaching of secondary school teachers teaching Science, Mathematics and Social Sciences. 3) To identify successful and unsuccessful teachers. The major findings were: 1) The successful teachers were significantly more expressive, ready to cooperate, attentive to people, generous in personal relations, bright and alert, fast in learning, efficient in abstract thinking, emotionally mature, realistic about life, effective in adjustment, dependable conscientious, persevering, responsible and dominated by sense of duty, socially aware, spontaneous and abundant in emotional responses. 2) The relationship between attitude of teachers towards the teaching profession and success in teaching was significant. 3) Teaching experience was not related to success in teaching. 4) There was significant difference in personality characteristics and attitude towards the teaching profession.

Mathew (1980) carried out a study on identification of desirable teaching competencies of IX class Physics teacher in the context of certain input, process and product variables. He identified 13 factors. They were: 1) General teaching competency, 2) Competency of the teacher's concern for students, 3) Competency of using audio-visual aids, 4) Competency of professional perception, 5) Competency of giving assignment, 6) Competency of illustrating with examples, 7) Competency of pacing while introducing logical exposition, 8) Classroom management, 9) Use of questions, 10) Initiating pupil participation, 11) Use of blackboard, 12) Recognizing attending behaviour and 13) Competency of achieving closure. These were the competencies identified through factor analysis. They were expected by the students from the teachers also.

Meera and Jayalakshmi (1990) studied the relationship between teacher behaviour and teaching aptitude of teacher trainees on random selection of 60 student-teachers undergoing B.Ed course in the Avinashlingam institute of Home science and Higher Education (Deemed University), Coimbatore in Tamil Nadu state. There were 12 student-teachers from each of the five disciplines, i.e., English, History, Biological Science, Physical Science and Mathematics. They used Flander's (1970) ten category system of interaction analysis to study classroom vertical bahaviour of the student teachers and teaching aptitude test was constructed by Tilakam (1986) to measure teaching aptitude. The results of the study were: (1) Teaching aptitude and teacher behaviour had been found to be related. 2) Aptitude for teaching was an important criterion that determined classroom teacher behaviour. (3) Teaching aptitude significantly influenced the amount of teacher talk. (4) Mental ability was an important component of teaching aptitude.

Mehta (1972) stated that the contribution of personality variables for teaching success was more in female student-teacher than male student-teachers. In both men and women student-teachers, the cognitive abilities contributed more than the personality variables for teaching success. It was also found that men student-teachers were more outgoing, assertive, venturesome, and radical than the women student-teachers. Women student-teachers, on the other hand, were more tender.

Mohinder Singh (1965) carried out a study in finding out the factors which were highly correlated to teaching skills. A sample of 48 students was chosen at random, out of 200 B.T. students of a government training college. He stated that previous teaching experience and age were positively correlated with scores in teaching skills.

Narasimhamurthy (2007) emphasized that there was no relationship among teaching competency, total burnout and teacher attitude. Male and female teacher educators in D.Ed colleges differed in their emotional exhaustation, depersonalization, personal accomplishment and total burn out. Teacher-educators in the D.Ed. colleges belonging to Hindu and Muslim communities differed significantly in their depersonalization. personal accomplishment, emotional exhaustation and total burn out.

NCERT (1971) conducted a study which sought to determine the extent of the teacher's acceptance of the role in which they find themselves. The objectives of the survey were: (i) To know how teachers were getting various issues related to their professional life and efficiency, (ii) To study how the reactions were related to the factors like management, area, sex, age, experience, academic and professional qualifications, marital status etc. Major findings of the survey were: (a) The attitude of teachers differed significantly under different managements; (b) The tenure of service did not have any effect on the attitude of teachers; (c) The attitude of male and female teachers differed significantly; (d) The marital status did not influence the attitude of teachers; (e) Teachers showed more positive attitude towards the profession than elder teachers; (f) Teachers with lower educational qualifications had more positive attitude than those with higher qualifications; (g) Experience and positive attitude were inversely proportionate; (h) The attitude of trained and untrained teachers did not differ much on negative items; (i) Training appeared to be a contributing factor in the development of apparent positive attitude.

Pandey (1980) made a study on construction and standardization of a teaching aptitude test. The study aimed at developing a standardized tool for use as a teaching aptitude test in the selection of trainee in the institutions of teacher education. The test included the following eight subtests: 1) Professional Knowledge, 2) Vocabulary, 3) Inferential Reasoning, 4) Number Series, 5) Numerical Reasoning, 6) Logical Selection, 7) General Formation and 8) Reading Comprehension. Item analysis was made after the first tryout. The final draft was administered to a representative sample of 1190 (650 males and 540 females) trainees of the normal schools of Uttar Pradesh. The draft took seventy five minutes for completion. Sex wise and qualification wise distributions of scores were also carried out. The percentile and T- score norms were calculated for the total sample. Using the Thurstone's Centroid Method, the data were analyzed which yielded the four factors, viz., General Educational Factor, Reasoning Factor, Numerical Skill Factor and Reading Comprehension Factor.

Patel (1980) studied on construction and standardization of an aptitude test for primary school teachers in Gujarat State. The test was administered in Gujarat and covered eight teacher traits, viz., 1) Interest in the Profession, 2) Attitude towards Community, 3) Mental Ability, 4) Professional Information, 5) Attitude towards Children, 6) Skill in Teaching Ability to maintain Discipline, 7) Health and 8) Interest in Reading. These traits were grouped. The test was standardized on the sample of 1700 trainees with 125 test items.

Prasad (1970) investigated on evaluation of professional efficiency (abilities) of primary school teachers. The main purpose of the study was to evaluate the professional efficiency of primary school teachers. Professional efficiency has been studied from three angles, namely, efficiency in classroom teaching, efficiency in organizing curricular activities and efficiency in maintaining relationships. In this study, intelligence of teachers was measured, teachers' aptitude towards teaching profession was also measured. Teacher efficiency observation schedule was developed and validated. He stated that intelligence and teachers' aptitude had taken important role in evaluating the professional efficiency of the primary school teachers. Prasad (1970) developed the teacher efficiency observation schedule. It was a standardized research tool for measuring teacher efficiency. The teacher attitude scale developed by Samanatory (1971), was used to measure the overall attitude of high school teachers.

Shah (1962) investigated on construction and standardization of an aptitude test for secondary school teachers. The objective of the study was to develop a tool to measure teaching aptitude. Construction of the test started with the job analysis, besides personal experience, the sources tapped were: (i) training college teachers, (ii) education department personnel, (iii) secondary school principals (v) successful and unsuccessful teachers. The battery of tests was formed with five subtests, viz., mental ability, attitude towards children, adaptability, professional information and interest in the profession. A preliminary form was prepared with 183 items classified into five subtests. Most of the items were of multiple choice type. The try-out of the test was done with the group of 153 graduates. A pilot testing was done on a sample of 371 student-teachers from five training institutions from Pune, Bombay and Baroda. The scores were tested for normal distribution by three techniques, viz., diversion measures, chi-square test and superimposition of an ideal curve. Reliability of the tests was studied by various methods. Validity was tested against the part I and part II examination marks of the subjects. Factor analysis was carried out by using Thurstone's Technique. Norms were calculated in the form of standard scores and T-scores. The study revealed that the reliability co-efficient of the tests ranged from 0.802 to 0.878; the multiple 'R' of the final test battery was 0.533; the predictive efficiency of the test was sixteen per cent.

Shah (1965) prepared aptitude test for secondary school teachers. He took a sample of 530 trainee teachers of Arts and Science graduates from Maharastra and Gujarat states. The test contains 120 items distributed among the five sub-tests. The major findings of the study were: (1) The five factors selected in the beginning initiatively were really contributing to the success in teaching. (2) The forecasting ability of the test battery was 16 per cent. This was satisfactory at some extent. The final test battery included all the five sub-tests. But, the sub-test III was to be given zero weightage, while using "prediction equation".

Sharma (1969) prepared a teaching aptitude test for elementary school teachers. The main objective of the study was to develop a test in Hindi for measuring teaching aptitude of elementary school teachers. The investigator identified twenty one factors contributing to success, in teaching on the basis of job analysis. This number was finally reduced to six on the basis of the ratings of 275 judges, consisting of training college principals and teachers, headmasters, inspectors and experienced teachers of elementary schools. Finally, five subtests were included in the battery, viz., Mental Ability, Attitude towards Children, Adaptability, Professional Information and Interest in the Profession. After item analysis, 120 items were retained for the final form of the test. The test was standardized on a sample of 380 male and 120 female trainees selected at random from different training schools. The reliability coefficients of the test, calculated by split-half method, test-retest method and K.R. formula-20, were 0.98, 0.97 and 0.89 respectively. Predictive validity coefficients with internal assessment and with ratings by a board of instructors were 0.36 and 0.42. respectively. The factorial validity of the test was established by applying Thurstone's Centroid Method. Content validity of the test was also established.

Sharma (1984) studied on teaching aptitude, intellectual level and morality of prospective teaching. The objectives of the study were: (i) To find out aptitude, intellectual level and morality of prospective teachers, (ii) To compare these factors between male and female teachers. The sample of the study included 412 student-, teachers who were studying in ten teachers' colleges. The tools were: Teaching Aptitude Test (TAT), Group Mental Ability Test (GMAT) and Self-made Morality Test. The findings were: i) About 75 per cent of student teachers were below average in aptitude and intellectual ability. ii) An insignificant difference was found in teaching aptitude ability in sex-wise and discipline-wise comparison. iii) A positive correlation was found between teaching aptitude, intellectual level and morality of prospective teachers.

Sherry (1964) made a battery of psychological tests for prediction of success in teaching. This study aimed at testing the following hypotheses: 1) Success in teaching is determined by a teacher's interest in the subject, in children and in teaching: 2) Success in teaching is related to teacher's attitude towards teaching. The study was confined to pupil teachers of department of education and the training colleges affiliated to the Agra University. Reliability of the tests was calculated by the test-retest method and split-half method. Validity coefficients of the tests were found for each college as well as for the whole group by correlating the scores with the criteria. The battery of prediction of teaching efficiency included self-prepared tools i.e. intelligence test, interest inventory, personality inventory and attitude scale. The validity coefficients ranged between 0.47 and 0.71. The study revealed that supervisors' ratings could be predicted to a satisfactory extent by all the four tests. Classroom teaching duties were considered more essential than non-teaching duties by a large number of experts in the field of education. Intelligence was found to be most important factor and attitude occupied a more important place than interest.

Singh (1978) investigated the teaching behaviour of 100 trained graduate science teachers in higher secondary schools of Delhi. The findings were: (i) There was no significant relationship between the verbal creativity in teachers and their attitude towards teaching; (ii) There was no significant relationship between the indirect/direct (I/D and i/d) teaching behaviour of teachers and their attitude towards teaching. Singh (1979) reported that stimulated social skill training (SSST) technique in teacher training programme was more effective than the traditional method in developing favourable attitude among student-teachers towards the teaching profession.

Thilakam and Visveswaran (1986) constructed a teaching aptitude test. They took a sample of thousand graduate and post-graduate teacher trainees of both sexes from different Colleges of Education in Tamil Nadu, teacher-trainees were drawn from rural and urban areas of private and government colleges of education, with varied families of socio-economic, educational and occupational groups. The findings of the study were: (1) The attitude and aptitude of the trainees were highly related with each other and the positive correlation coefficients indicated that those who had high aptitude in teaching also had high positive attitude towards teaching profession; (2) Eleven traits selected for the five sub-tests were really contributing to success in teaching.

Studies on Intelligence

Abrol (1977) studied achievement motivation in relation to intelligence, vocational interests, achievement, sex and socio-economic status. The hypotheses were: Achievement motivation and intelligence were positively correlated; Achievement motivation and scholastic achievement were correlated positively. The variables studied were: achievement, motivation, achievement value, intelligence, sex, scholastic achievement, vocational interest, maturity and three components of socio-economic status, viz., educational level of fathers and mothers, income level of parents and occupational level of fathers and schools. The tools used were: Achievement Motivation Test (Mehta), Sentence Completion Test (Mukherjee) for achievement value, Vocational Interest Record (Singh) and Standard Progressive Matrices. Scholastic achievement scores were obtained from the school records. The major statistical techniques used were: product moment correlation analysis of variance, t-test and regression analysis with intelligence as the independent variable and scholastic achievement as the dependent variable.

A significant and positive correlation of moderate value was found between achievement motivation and intelligence. The socio-economic status of students affected correlation coefficients between these two variables. A significant and positive correlation of low value was found between intelligence and n-ach. On the other hand, intelligence was negatively correlated to value achievement again with a low value.

Ajwani (1979) studied problem-solving behaviour in relation to personality, intelligence and age. The objectives of the study were: 1) To find out the effect of personality, intelligence, age, sex and their interactions of the problem-solving behaviour of students and (2) To investigate the directions intended to assist the individual to bring about any improvement in the problem-solving ability.

The sample of the first phase consisted of 2,400 subjects, representing three age groups, i.e., 10-11 years, 14-16 years and 19-23years. The subjects with high intelligence proved to be better problem-solvers than those with low intelligence. The problem-solving ability of the subjects increased with an increment in age. The interaction between personality factors, intelligence, age and sex had no effect on the problem-solving ability of subjects.

Bhagavathy (1977) carried out an analytical study of the personality, intelligence, values and problems of adolescent girls. The aim of the investigation was to study the personality patterns and adjustment problems of adolescent girls in relating to intelligence. The major findings of the study were: (i) Significant differences were seen in the personality variables and intelligence (both verbal and non-verbal) between the four deviant and one normal group studied; (ii) The five groups could be differentiated on the number and nature of problems in the areas of health, family, personality and intelligence.

Bhullar (1976) investigated on the attitude of university students towards physical activity in relation to academic performance, intelligence, socio-economic status and personality characteristics. The major hypotheses of the study were: (i) Intelligence and socio-economic status did not correlate significantly in respect of each sub-domain and all the sub-domains cumulatively. (ii) In multivariate analysis, the personality traits, intelligence, academic performance and socio-economic status jointly contributed to significant variance in respect of attitude towards physical activity. Multiple regression analysis results showed that high intelligence, high academic performance, and the variables of PF 15 and PF 16 tended to be associated with better perception of the impact of physical activity, leading to favourable attitude towards it.

Chakrabarti (1988) carried out a critical study of intelligence, socio-economic background of the family, educational environment in the family, and quality of schools in children of standard V in and around Pune. The major objective of the study was to study the effect of mental ability of students on their academic achievement. The major findings of the study were: 1) Students from urban areas were found better than students from rural areas in their intelligence. 2) Marathi-medium schools scored in intelligence test better than those of English medium schools.

Chatterji (1998) made a comparative study of personality, intelligence and achievement motivation of students in different academic groups. The objectives of the study were: (i) To compare the personality, intelligence and achievement-motivation of students. (ii) To find out the academic-group differences among high scores in each of these three variables. Jalota's Group Test of General Mental Ability was used to measure intelligence. The findings were: (1) There was a positive correlation between intelligence and personality. (2) There was no correlation between intelligence and SES.

Chaudhary (1971) used the Raven's Standard Progressive Matrices for Intelligence, the Kuppuswamy's socio-economic status scale and a self-developed vocational information questionnaire for knowing the relation of intelligence with n-achievement. The important findings were: The correlation coefficients between n-Achievement and intelligence scores for the combined samples, and for boys were not significant, whereas the same was significant at 0.01 level for girls; partial correlation (first and second order), multiple correlation, analysis of variance and regression equations indicated absence of correlation between these two variables.

Ganguly (1965) had done an experimental study of the intellectual factors in the students of the pre-school leaving class under different systems of secondary education. This study was aimed at verifying the claims that the quality of schooling, the mental flexibility and the capacity to form new concepts. The study was conducted on a sample of 180 boys, aged around thirteen to fifteen, of classes IX and X. The tool of research was the Raven's Progressive Matrices Test. He reported that the public school system offered the best quality of schooling for stimulating the growth of intellectual factors, even considering that the boys of these schools came from brighter and better socio-economic and intellectual home background.

Gupta (1980) carried out a factorial study of verbal and non-creativity, intelligence and socio- economic status. The objectives of the study were: (i) To analyze the scores on different dimensions of creativity (both verbal and non-verbal), intelligence and socio-economic status; (ii) To find out whether the constructs of creativity, intelligence and socio-economic status had any common underlying factors. The tools used were the verbal and non-verbal batteries of MIER Tests of Creativity, Group Test of General Mental Ability (Jalota, Hindi). There was no evidence of common factors among intelligence, socio-economic status and creativity, which were independent domains.

Jain (1983) rightly pointed out that PSM verbal intelligence test was found to be a good predictor of nature, form and kind of concept formation ability. High intelligent students scored significantly higher on this ability. He revealed that the high intelligence-high achievement motivation group was significantly better in concept formation ability than low intelligence and low achievement motivation group. Intelligence was found to be a better predictor of concept formation ability than achievement motivation. Verbal intelligence was found to had greater significant interactional effect on concept formation.

Kauser (1982) made a study on children's curiosity and its relationship to intelligence, creativity and personality. The study was an exploratory attempt to investigate the relationship of curiosity to intelligence, creativity, extraversion and neuroticism in elementary school children of 7 to 10 years of age. The major findings of the study were: (1) There was no significant relationship between curiosity and intelligence on overall basis except for girls of 10 years of age. (2) The two sexes did not differ significantly in terms of anxiety, health, social and emotional adjustment, intelligence, sociability, ascendancy and emotional stability. (3) The main effect of sex was significant only in the case of sociability and responsibility. (4) The correlation was high between risk-taking and adjustment (r = -0.384).

Kumar (1981) did a psychological study of intelligence and intellectual stimulation received by the students studying in different types of junior high students of Tarai area of Uttar Pradesh. The main hypothesis of the study was that the difference in intellectual or mental factors with reference to cognitive aspects among students of different educational systems might be accounted for the difference in quality of schooling, the intellectual abilities of convent students (CS) were more than the higher secondary school (HSS) students and municipal school (MS) students. A sample of 387 X class students was equally chosen from both the sexes. The results were: i) The intellectual abilities of convent students (CS) were more developed than those of higher secondary school (HSS) students and municipal school (MS) students; ii) The students belonging to different socio-economic status (SES), but studying in similar schools did not differ significantly from each other. No difference was observed in verbal and spatial abilities of students of the two sexes.

Kumari Sudha (1982) conducted a study of intelligence, achievement, adjustment and socio-economic patterns of different socio-metric groups of adolescents. The objectives of the study were: (i) To compare the intelligence of populars, neglectees, isolates and rejectees; (ii) To find out if any relationship exists in intelligence, achievement, adjustment and socio-economic status of different socio-metric groups. The findings of the study were: (i) The group combinations of populars and neglectees, populars and isolates, populars and rejectees differed significantly on intelligence; (ii) There was positive relationship between intelligence and achievement.

Mathew (1965) studied the relationship between the social attitudes and intelligence of the child delinquents among waifs and strays. The study aimed at testing the following hypotheses: (i) The delinquents among waifs and strays suffer from greater ego deficiency manifesting itself in defective functioning in major areas of its activity namely, maturity, reality testing, anxiety and guilt feeling. (ii) Waifs and strays are less intelligent than the delinquents and normals. The sample consisted of three groups selected by the random sampling method, composed of 15 delinquents, 15 waifs and strays and 15 normal boys. This study had been done by descriptive, exploratory and clinical methods. The theoretical orientation was mainly psycho-analytical. Reality testing was an important function of the ego. With respect to the second hypothesis, the study revealed that while the delinquents had a mean intelligence quotient of 124.5 and the normals 127.5 the waifs and strays obtained a mean score of only 107.8. The differences were not statistically significant.

Menon (1982) attempted a study on performance of students at polytechnics in relation to their academic achievement intelligence, adjustment and aspiration level. The major objectives of the study were: (i) To find out whether general mental ability (intelligence) had any effect on the performance of students in polytechnics; (ii) To find out the cumulative effect of all the variables on students' performance through the technique of multiple regression analysis. The tools used for data collection were: General Mental Ability Test of Tandon and Jalota and Adjustment Inventory developed by Patel (1967) and others. The major findings of the study were: (i) Eight facts were differentiated between high and low performance. Some of theses factors were: general mental ability, space gauge usage (spelling), language usage (grammar) and academic achievement. (ii) In the co-relational study, only seven variables were significantly related to the students' performance. They were: numerical ability, general mental ability, abstract reasoning, mechanical reasoning, academic achievement, language usage and space relations.

Mishra (1969) attempted a study on variations of intelligence with occupational training courses, age, sex, and locality. The first sample was for the study of the variation of intelligence with reference to age, sex and locality and the second sample was for the variations of intelligence and attainment with reference to the occupational training courses. The data were collected with the help of the following: (i) Vernon's Nonverbal Intelligence Test; (ii) Raven's Progressive Matrices. The study revealed that (i) Boys did significantly better than girls in intellectual level. (ii) Urban high scores did significantly better than the rural high scores in intellectual level.

Muddu (1980) studied some personality correlates of intelligence and creative abilities among high school students in Andhra Pradesh. The study was designed as a quantitative empirical field study. The tools adapted and used in the study were: (i) Passi Test of Creativity and (ii) Group Test of General Mental Ability. The findings of the study were: (i) The high creative group was found to be negatively correlated with intelligence; (ii) Relationships between intelligence and fluency ($r = 0.124$), flexibility ($r = 0.114$) and originality ($r = 0.125$) were positive and significant; (iii) The high as well as the low creative groups did not show any significant correlation with intelligence; (iv) There was no significant relationship between the high intelligent group and the low creative group and between the high creative group and the intelligent group.

Prahallada (1982) reported that there was a positive relationship between intelligence and moral judgment. There was significant difference between Science and Arts students, Science and Commerce students and Arts and Commerce students in intelligence and moral judgement.

Sen Gupta (1979) investigated on intellective and non-intellective factors associated with engineering creativity. The main objectives were: (i) To investigate, systematically, differences in mechanical reasoning between high and low creative groups; (ii) To find out differences between high and low creative groups in their perception of cognitive simplicity and complexity. The formulated hypotheses were: (i) There was no significant difference between high and low creative subjects on the mechanical reasoning ability which could be regarded as one aspect of intelligence. (ii) There was no significant difference between high and low creative individuals in their perception of cognitive simplicity and complexity. The study used Purdue Creativity Test, Culture Fair Intelligence Test and Mechanical Reasoning Test. Intelligence, mechanical reasoning, economic value, religious value and perceptual simplicity-complexity were significantly correlated with total creativity. The single best predictor of creativity was intelligence.

Sharma (1978) did comparative study of self-concept of high and low achievement and intelligent groups of students of class tenth in urban schools of Bareilly. The main objectives of the study were: (i) To find out the relationship between any two of the four main variables, namely, intelligence, socio-economic status (SES), academic achievement and self-concept; (ii) To find out the relationship among academic achievement, intelligence, SES and self-concept respectively and (iii) To predict self-concept on the basis of intelligence, SES and achievement. The findings of the study were: (i) Intelligence showed strongest relationship with achievement, but the relationship between intelligence groups. (ii) SES showed weak positive relationship with intelligence. (iii) Students having high intelligence also had high self-concept. (iv) Intelligence showed strong relationship with six areas under self-concept and achievement; intelligence made high positive and significant contribution. In the low intelligence group it was negatively correlated. (vi) Achievement showed highest relationship with intelligence. (vii) Self-concept showed high positive and significant relationship with achievement and intelligence.

Singh (1988) investigated on some personality factors of high and low intelligent boys and girls of Bhagalpur. The main purposes of the study were: (i) To determine the difference and association between intelligence of boys and girls in general; (ii) To find out the relationship between intelligence and personality. The major conclusions were: (i) Intelligence seemed to be influenced by certain factors such as sex, faculty, cultural condition. (ii) Boys were superior in intelligence to girls. (iii) Personality traits were more or less independent of intelligence. (iv) High intelligence boys and girls were scholastic, suspicious-skeptical and controlled. (v) The low intelligent group was outgoing, happy-go-lucky and apprehensive. (vi) High intelligent girls were scholastic, controlled and shrewd. (vii) Low intelligent boys were outgoing, emotionally immature, happy-go-lucky and imaginative. Viii) Low intelligent girls were outgoing, less scholastic and apprehensive.

Verma (2001) carried out the study of teaching aptitude in relation to general teaching competency, professional training and academic achievement of B.Ed pupil teachers. The main objectives of the study were: 1) To study the relationship among teaching aptitude, general teaching competency, professional training and academic achievement of B.Ed pupil teachers. 2) To study the effect of sex, discipline, general teaching competency and their interaction on teaching aptitude. 3) To study the effect of sex, discipline, professional training and their interaction on teaching aptitude. 4) To study the effect of sex, discipline, academic achievement and their interaction on teaching aptitude. The important findings were: 1) Discipline and sex of the pupil teacher did not contribute towards teaching aptitude of male and female pupil teachers. 2) It was found that teaching aptitude of pupil teachers was significantly correlated with general teaching competency and professional training.

Studies on Morality

Avanija (1987) studied moral adjustment and personality adjustment of teacher trainees. The conclusion was that most of the trainees possessed a low level of moral adjustment. Positive linear relationship was not found between moral judgement and home, moral adjustment and health, moral adjustment and emotionality. Sex and faculty did not effect on moral adjustment. The age groups of 18-19 and 19-26 scored significantly and the others did to differ.

Debruin and Van-Lange (1999) examined how behavioural information about the morality or intelligence of another person influences impressions, exceptions of co-operative behavior, and own co-operation in a mixed motive interdependence situation. Results (for 125 undergraduate Ss) revealed morality and intelligence had more impact (for 164 Ss) on impressions and interactions than positive information.

Desouza (1973) conducted on sociological study to know the factors which were influencing the moral development. He observed many public schools in India and revealed that house system, games and extra curricular activities were most important factors in influencing the social and moral development of the students. He also observed seven values- Dutifulness, Sincerity, Co-operation, Conformity to School Rules, Honesty, Loyalty and Respect to Seniors were very important components in moral development.

Durkheim (1925) found at that a child's intelligence was correlated with the level of his/her moral judgment. He adds that the problem of inculcating the ability among children to judge morally is infested with many problems. If an individual is intelligent, he may help for the development of moral judgment and ethics. An immoral person is not intelligent, but intelligence is being used for other dubious purposes.

Gourishankar (1999) conducted a study on Sri Satya Sai Baba on Education– Theory and Practice. He has clearly highlighted that the Educational Philosophy of Sri Sathya Sai Baba could improves the morality among the youth people at present age. He stressed that morality was an important factor in all fields and very essential for teachers also.

Grinder (1962) dealt with the relation between resistance to temptation and certain aspects of maturity of moral judgments. He used an apparatus to assess resistance to temptation. To measure children's ideas regarding morality, Grinder used familiar story situations and also tested children for the presence of the idea of immanent justice by means of an uncompleted story. Children were ranged from 7 to 12 years. The results showed that there was a sharp drift from age 7-8 to 11-12 in children's cognitive moral maturity. It shows the process of maturation and learning that underlies changes in children's understanding of moral concepts as they grow older.

Gupta (1963) stated that India's cultural heritage, cultural habits, traditions and conventions were remarkable in the inheritance of values and moral values had been emphasized in identifying the character, behaviour of individuals. Gururaja (1978) reported that the influence of the moral instructions seemed to be significantly affecting the knowledge of the moral values.

Hilton (1978) conducted a study to examine the relationship between the criterion variable of moral judgment and three independent variables of interpersonal trust socio-economic status and intelligence. There was also a correlation between moral judgment and socio-economic status. A combination of IQ and socio-economic status proved to be the best predictor of level of moral judgment and were significant at 0.01 level. In the view of Francis (1978), the relationship between cognitive, role-taking and moral judgment abilities of adolescent was examined. Results of this study indicated no difference between the two samples for mental and chronological ages or for intellectual abilities. A significant difference was found between the role-taking abilities of each sample and only a slight difference noted between the moral judgment skills of both groups with the emotionally disturbed adolescents being the weaker in each category.

Kumar (1980) reported that good nature, boldness and independence, alertness in supervision, impartibility, honesty, capability of meeting and talking with people without hesitation, capability of exerting influence, capability of persuading the peers and bringing them round to were very important. Honesty had the first rank in all the areas except captainship, good nature emerged as highly valued general trait. Boldness and independence, alertness in supervision and impartiality were not so uniformly higher on the ordinal ladder. However, all the ten general traits were adjudged essential for successful leadership. The validation of the traits like honesty, impartiality, patriotism, smartness, liberalism and task competencies are essential to all.

Lagerspez (1998) administered a Moral Approval of Aggression (MAA) Inventory and the Ben sex-role Inventory to 48 military officer trainers (OTs), 35 conscientious objects (COs) to armed service and 32 women of comparable age. Aggression was mostly approved among the OTs and least among the COs, with the women scoring in the middle somewhat closer to OTs. Women chose feminine and androgynous roles with equal frequency. MAA could not be explained on the basis of sex role identification.

Mischel and Mischel (1962) surveyed a variety of studies showing a clear relation between the cognitive competence and general adequacy of social functioning. Maturity on piagetian moral judgment is positively correlated with IQ and dishonest behaviour have been found to be negatively related, on the basis of such data. Aronfreed (1968) and Mischel and Mischel (1962) reveals that cognitive power is the operation of conscience. And general cognitive capacity shows significant variation in principles of conscience. Burtion's (1963) review of studies adds that the relation between IQ and honesty declines or disappears when the context is non-academic or when the risk of getting caught is low. He says that cognitive powers may be needed for principled moral thought, but it is not enough. History is full of examples of how human intelligence can be turned to great evil, the understanding of which stands the next critical challenges to a science of morality. Thus, a commonly accepted finding in moral conduct studies is intelligence and academic ability is positively correlated with honesty.

Muthamma (1982) investigated into the moral judgment of upper primary school children in the selected schools of the city of Mysore. The main objective of the study was to investigate the moral judgment of upper primary school children in the selected schools of the city of Mysore. The findings of the study were: (1) There was significant difference in moral judgment of boys and girls. (2) Occupational background of the parents influenced significantly the moral judgment and (3) The economic background of the students influenced their moral judgment.

Patil (1984) did a differential study of intelligence, interest and attitude of the B.Ed. college students as contributory factors towards their achievements in the compulsory subjects. The objectives of the study were: (i) To find out the effect of sex and academic qualification on intelligence. (ii) To find out the relationship between sex and academic qualification and experience and intelligence, interest and attitude of B.Ed. pupil-teachers. The tools used were the PSM Verbal Intelligence Test by Dani and Teacher Attitude Inventory (TAI) by Ahluwalia. The major findings were: i) There was a significant difference between the scores of male and female and inexperienced and experienced pupil-teachers in respect of intelligence but no significant difference in intelligence was found between graduate and postgraduate teachers. ii) Male and experienced pupil-teachers appeared more intelligent than female and experienced pupil-teachers.

Patric (1979) studied the relationship between moral development and personality and found most enduring and powerful relationship between P-score (preference for principled level) and California Personality Inventory measures of dependability, rational maturity and independent use of intelligence in Roman Catholic High School. Contrary to the above findings, Sawyer's (1977) study indicated that there was no significant correlation between subjects' scores on personality measures – absolutism, freedom from negativism, dependency, social anxiety, self-absorption, active interdependence and moral reasoning in 34 female subjects of 17-27 years of age.

Pradhan and Pande (1996) were studied the independent and interactive effects of tribal and non-tribal difference and sex on moral judgment of secondary school children. The study revealed that: (i) Tribal and non-tribal difference and sex has significant effect on moral judgment of secondary children independently, but interaction of sex and tribal non-tribal difference has no significant effect; (ii) Tribal and non-tribal and sex have neither independent nor interactive effect on attainment of autonomous level of moral judgment of secondary school children.

Rani (1968) studied on moral development in children. The main objective of the investigation was to study the pattern of morality among children. The findings were: (i) Age was found to be an important variable influencing the knowledge of moral values. (ii) Knowledge of different moral values seemed to increase with an increase in age. (iii) Children who did not get any moral instruction in school were in no way inferior in such knowledge to those receiving such instruction in school. (iv) A very similar pattern of moral values was found in the children of all the three age groups. (v) Respect was the most frequent moral value practiced by most children in their everyday behaviour. (vi) Betrayal of faith, greed, anger and falsehood were some of the negative values which were quite frequent in their behaviour. (vii) Truth, purity, punya and respect were some of the positive moral values which received approval by most of the children. (viii) Greed was considered to be a shameful behaviour by them. (ix) Parent's influence in the acquisition and development of moral values in children was of vital significance and other important sources for knowledge of morality were teachers and books.

Rani (1968) found that increase in age corresponded with an increase in the knowledge of moral values. A very similar pattern of moral values was found in the children of all the three age groups (6-7, 8-9, 10-11 years of age). As the children matured, their mental ability influenced their knowledge of moral value. Respect, forgiveness and Punya were the most frequently practiced moral values in everyday behaviour. The religion of the family did not contribute to the knowledge of moral values in children.

Schoffner (1997) examined decision making in the area of moral reasoning and its relationship with identity development, emotional super sensitivity and gender role flexibility. Results indicated that no statistically significant effects by age for any of the dependent variables. There were several main effects by gender, with gifted adolescent females tending to score higher on measures of super sensitivity, expressiveness, and ideological identity formation than gifted adolescent males. No gender differences were found in the focus partially sensitivity score. However, females and males seemed to focus partially on different issues while interpreting the situation.

Schruner (1976) investigated moral reasoning on 50 female and 50 male college undergraduates in education, between the age 19 and 25 years and also examined in the interaction of various personality characteristics with attained level of moral reasoning across and between sexes. The reasoning of young women were more pragmatic, stereotyped to immature. The reasoning of men was more vigorous, autonomous and independent.

Srivastava (1981) measured the moral ideals and values of PUC, BA and MA class students. The findings were: (1) For every increase in the educational ladder, there is a corresponding decrease in moral values. (2) After high school education, a decrease in the magnitude of moral values is observed corresponding with the increase in age.

Sugarman (1967) discovered that their moral judgment was positively correlated with socio-economic status. The higher the social class of the family, the higher the teacher rated the content of the mind. Studies by Kohn (1959), Kohlberg (1968) and Bull (1969) suggest that children from families of higher social status show greater maturity in moral judgments than those from lower social class background.

Sullivan (1977) thinks that the theory of moral development must be more than structuralist account of the ontogenesis of justice reasoning. He believes that Kohlberg has failed to integrate his theory into an account of moral sensitivity. According to Hogan (1975), there are two sets of physical ideals frequently employed to justify moral judgment and decisions: 1. Ethics of social responsibility or moral positivism, and 2. Ethics of personal conscience or moral intuitionism. The law is seen as a practical instrument of social reform and laws are justified in terms of the degree to which they promote the common good. Hogan (1975) suggests that the moral decisions reflect the person's moral character, which can be described along person logical dimensions. Thus personality structure may have an effect on moral decisions. Although both Kohlberg (1968) and Hogan (1975) are concerned with moral development, their theoretical orientations differ greatly. Kohlberg stresses the importance of moral reasoning and describes sequential process of moral development as cognitive transformations resulting from interaction with the environment. Hogan's theory is more concerned with the development of moral character, which is the result of interplay of socialization, autonomy, empathy, moral knowledge, and ethical orientation.

An Overview of the Studies Reviewed

Teaching is an intricate, complex and conscious activity. It is the stimulation, guidance, direction and encouragement of learning. It aims at achieving the objective of education to the optimum. It also aims at helping the learner to change his/her behaviour in a relatively permanent manner. Teaching aptitude helps to feel well in their job. Teaching aptitude focuses on high sense of duty and integrity. Teaching aptitude of teacher can influence teachers' behaviour, teacher performance, teacher competencies and teacher effectiveness. Sherry (1964) reveals that the success in teaching is related to teacher's aptitude towards teaching profession. Sharma (1969) reports that teaching aptitude is to be sound predictor of teacher effectiveness. Gupta (1976) finds that teaching aptitude is an important measure for teacher behaviour and teacher effectiveness. Hood (1976) identifies that teaching aptitude and teaching efficiency are found to be positively related. Thakur (1976) views that teaching aptitude reflects the teacher's behaviour in treating the children with kind and pleasing manners. Anderson (1974),

Anderson and Browne (1974), Anderson and lee (1975) revealed that the student's achievement was influenced by the teacher's styles of teaching.

Kulanclaivel and Rao (1968) attempts a study for knowing qualities of good teacher and good student. Meera and Jayalakshmi (1990) studied the relationship between teacher behaviour and teaching aptitude of teacher trainees. Sharma (1984) found out that there was significant positive correlation between teaching aptitude and intellectual level. Vyas (1982) reported that teaching aptitude had significant relationship with the promotion of proficiency in teaching. Mann (1980) revealed that teachers of right aptitude towards teaching were significantly more expressive, attentive, realistic and responsible.

Callis (1953), Chappel and Callis (1954), Wallen and Travers (1963), Munro (1964) and Morman (1965) elicited that personality characteristics could influence the teacher's aptitude towards teaching profession. Sundarajan, Sakthivel and Ponnalogoppan (1988), Jain (1982), Hood (1976) and Vijendra (1972), also identified that teacher behaviour and teaching efficiency were linked with teaching aptitude. Jayamma (1970) and Prasad (1970) said that professional efficiency of teacher was connected with teacher's aptitude towards teaching.

Shah (1962) constructed and standardized an aptitude test for secondary school teachers. This test included five subtests viz., mental ability, professional information, interest in the profession, attitude towards children and adaptability. Jai Prakash and Srivastava (1965) constructed teaching aptitude test and analyzed its functional phenomena. This test included ten personality traits. Pandey (1968) constructed and standardized a teaching aptitude test for selection purposes in teacher training institutions at primary level. This test also included eight subtests viz., professional knowledge, vocabulary, inferential reasoning, number series, numerical reasoning. Logical selection, general information and reading comprehension. Sharma (1969) prepared a teaching aptitude test included five subtests for elementary school teachers. Patel (1980) also constructed and standardized an aptitude test for primary school teachers in Gujarat state. From the above said researches, it is clear that teaching aptitude is a very important variable which influences the teachers' behaviour in all aspects in teaching-learning process.

Intelligent teacher is viewed as efficient, versatile, adaptive, acute, keen, Sharp, astute, bright and brilliant in teaching-learning process. Intelligent teacher has the ability to undertake activities that are characterized by 1) difficulty, 2) complexity, 3) abstraction, 4) economy, 5) adaptiveness to a goal, 6) social value and 7) the emergence of originals, and to maintain such activities under conditions that demand a concentration of energy and a resistance to emotional forces (Paul Kline, 1991; Stoddard, 1943; Anderson, 1992; Deese, 1993; Searle, 1980; James, 1983). Hence, intelligence of teacher takes a vital part in teaching-learning process.

Morality is essential for teachers to develop positive and healthy attitude towards life, to develop high degree of intellectual maturity and to learn adjustment with changing environmental conditions. Morality linked with basic virtues like sincerity, simplicity, humility, self-reliance, self-control, truthfulness, dutifulness, good conduct, non-violence, endurance, courtesy, values, habits, manners etc. (Prahallada, 2000; Rama Rao, 1994; Taneja 1990; Frankel 1988; Crittenden, 1972). Agarwal (1985), Aldeen (1991), Aleixo and Norris (2000), Anand Bhushan (1977), Avanija (1987), Ayesha Noor (2001), Tiwari (1975), Srivastava (1981), Sarangi (1994), Sugarman (1967), Thomas (1979), Saraswathi, Sundareshan and Saxena (1980), Sridhar (1995), Varma (1972) and Varma (1976) studied morality in relation to certain variables such as intelligence, personality, self-concept, social maturity, adjustment, socio-economic status, age, educational environment, reasoning, sex etc. These studies indicate that morality is very much needed for children and teachers. Johnson (1962), Boehm (1962), Keasey (1973) and Kohlberg (1981) found positive correlation between morality and intelligence. Bull (1969) and Kohlberg (1968) found that morality was a significant factor in social participation.

Aldeen (1991), Boehm (1962), Benning (1977), Bull (!969), Francis (1978), Hilton (1978), Johnson (1962), Keasey (1973), Kohlberg (1981), Sharma and Kaur (1992), Stuart (1965) and Tomliason (1975) found positive correlation between morality and intelligence. By observing and studying the reviews regarding teaching aptitude, intelligence and morality, it is evident that these three variables are treated as three vertices or three sides of a triangle. These three factors are very important for teacher in teaching-learning process. But, there are few researches on relationship among teaching aptitude, intelligence and morality of prospective teachers who are training in colleges of education. Hence, the investigator has selected these three variables as dependent variables in his study to identify the relationship between teaching aptitude, intellectual level and morality of prospective teachers.

3

Methodology
The Heart of Research

Introduction

Methodology is the heart of any research. It helps the investigator to proceed with proposed research in a systematic way. In this section, the research design is explained in detail. Methodology consists of "method" used in the study, various procedure followed in the preparation of tools for data gathering on different variables which are included in the study, reliability and validity of the tools, an accurate account of size and selection of sample, sampling technique, collecting of data, scoring procedure and statistical techniques used in the study.

Method Used

The research design in the present study is descriptive in nature. Hence, the investigator has used 'survey method' to obtain information. Survey involves describing, recording, analyzing and interpreting conditions or contrasts and attempts to discover relationships between existing non-manipulated variables (Best and Khan 1989). Survey method is concerned itself with the present phenomena in terms of conditions, practices, beliefs, processes, relationships or trends.

Semato (2001) noted, "Surveys have contributed significantly to the understanding of what happens and are instrumented in finding out the current status of operations". Green (2000) mentioned, "Surveys are the most widely used technique in Education and the Behavioural Science for the collection of data". Survey Studies can collect three types of information, i.e., 1) What exists? 2) What do we want? 3) How to get there? It provides information useful to the solution of local problems and its scope is vast.

Selection of the Tools

Research tools are the sole factors in determining sound data and in drawing accurate conclusions about the problem in hard. The conclusions ultimately help in providing suitable remedial measures to the problem concerned (Rathaiah, 1997). The selection and use of tools can be done in two ways. The first one is the construction and development of a tool independently by the researcher for his/her own study. The second one is the right selection of tools from already standardized ones available in the field of study. It involves a tedious job in locating the tools and identifying their usefulness to the study on hard. But this technique of selecting standard tools is very useful when a research work involves a good number of variables. The most logical process that can be followed is to choose the best instruments available for the purpose (Pearl, 1974).

The tools used in the study are:

1. Teaching Aptitude Test (TAT)
2. Test of General Intelligence (TGI)
3 Morality Attitude Scale (MAS)
4. Personal Data Sheet (PDS)

1) Description of Teaching Aptitude Test (TAT)

Surender S. Dahiya and L.C. Singh's (2004) Teaching Aptitude Test is adopted by the investigator to assess the aptitude of prospective teachers towards teaching profession. This test has been designed to measure the potentiality of a graduate person who intends to take up a teaching job at the secondary school stage. A candidate getting higher marks on this test is likely to do better in the teaching job after him/her getting professional training at B.Ed. level. And also, he/she is likely to perform well during the teacher training period. Hence, this test is named as a Teaching Aptitude Test (TAT).

The term "Aptitude" is used in several ways. First, it is used to denote a combination of traits and abilities, which result in a person's being qualified for some type of occupations or activities. Second, it is intended to convey the idea of a discrete unitary characteristic, which is important in varying degrees in a variety of occupations and activities.

Teaching aptitude is a condition or set of characteristics including knowledge, understanding and attitude regarded as symptomatic or indicative of individual's ability to acquire with training abilities for teaching work (Dahiya & Singh, 2004). Teaching aptitude is a person's potential for teaching, the sum total of all the traits and abilities which are needed for success in teaching (Srivastava, 1965; Pandey (1968) constructed and standardized a Teaching Aptitude Test (TAT) to be used for selection purposes in institutions of teacher education for primary level. It included eight subtests, namely, 1) Professional Knowledge, 2) Vocabulary, 3) Inferential Reasoning, 4) Number Series, 5) Numerical Reasoning, 6) Logical Selection, 7) General Information and 8) Reading Comprehension.

Patel (1980) constructed and standardized an aptitude test for primary school teachers in Gujarat state. It covered 10 teacher's traits, namely, 1) Interest in the Profession, 2) Attitude towards Community, 3) Mental Ability, 4) Professional Information, 5) Attitude towards Children, 6) Skill in Teaching, 7) Ability to maintain Things, 8) Discipline, 9) Health and 10) Interest in Reading. Shah (1962) constructed and standardized an aptitude test for secondary school teachers. It included five subtests, namely, 1) Mental Ability, 2) Attitude towards Children, 3) Adaptability, 4) Professional Information and 5) Interest in the Profession.

Sharma (1969) also prepared a Teaching Aptitude Test (TAT) for elementary school teachers. It included five sub-tests Namely, Mental Ability, Attitude towards Children, Professional Information, Adaptability, and Interest in the Profession. Jai Prakash and Srivastava (1965) conducted a study on teaching aptitude and its functional phenomena. It included 10 personality traits such as Co-operative Attitude, Kindliness, Patience, Wide-Interest, Fairness, Moral Character, Discipline, Optimum, Scholarly Taste and Enthusiasm. He selected this test for student-teachers under training.

Teaching aptitude test constructed and standardized by Dahiya and Singh (2004) being more reliable, valid and appropriate to measure the teaching aptitude of prospective teachers, is adopted here in the study. This test consists of 50 test items of multiple-choice type. Each item has four alternative answers -- A, B, C and D. There is no time limit for answering the entire test. However, usually a student-teacher can finish the test in 30 minutes approximately. For clear understanding and convenience, the investigator has divided this test into 6 dimensions in the light of previous studies without changing items and alternative answers and their order of arrangement. The dimensions of teaching aptitude test are: 1) Professional Knowledge 2) Attitude towards Children 3) School related Information 4) Social Aspects 5) Educational Aspects and 6) Communicative Aspects. There are 13 items in Professional Knowledge, 9 items in Attitude towards Children, 7 items in School related Information, 10 items in Social Aspects, 7 items in Educational Aspects and 4 items in Communicative Aspects.

A) Preparation of Items in TAT: Initially, Dahiya and Singh (2004) prepared the Teaching Aptitude Test (TAT) comprising 140 items related to teaching aptitude of prospective teachers. These items had been examined in light of concept, set of characteristics, abilities to acquire with training, theories, principles and related literature. These 140 items had been reviewed and adopted to the list for including in the tryout form.

i) Try out and Item Analysis: The try-out form of the TAT comprising 140 items was administered on a sample of 217 B.Ed. students of selected colleges of education located in the state of Haryana, during the session 2001-02. On the scores of the try-out, item analysis was done. Item analysis is a statistical procedure used to determine the quality of individual test items; usually, it includes analyses of item discriminability and item difficulty (Tyler, 1979; Weiner, 1984). Difficulty value and Discriminating index of each item were computed. Only those items were selected which have difficulty value ranging 41-93 and discrimination index between 25-82. Thus, only 50 items were finally included in the test.
ii) Administration: Before administrating the test, Examiners should go through the instructions for the users. They are: 1) The test administrator should explain briefly the purpose of this test. 2) It is an administrating verbal group test. The examiner should read the instructions given on the top page of the test and the testers should read them silently with the examiner. 3) There is no time limit for answering the entire test; usually, it takes less than fifty minutes. 4) The test administrator should emphasize

on the outset that the testers must attempt all the items in the test. The prospective teachers were enlightened about the need for giving the correct responses to the various items of the test. They were instructed that there were 50 multiple-choice items which had four alternative answers A, B, C and D to select the most appropriate and answer out of the four alternatives and indicate their answer by putting a tick mark (√) in the appropriate cell □ below that select response.

The final form of the test was administered on a sample of 820 B.Ed student-teachers. Twenty cases were rejected since they were not properly answered. The distribution of scores for the total test was tested for its normal distribution. The distribution was very near to normal.

B) Reliability of TAT: Reliability is one of the important characteristics of any test. It is the consistency of scores obtained from one set of measures to another. A test is reliable if its results are reproducible and consistent. The reliability refers to the extent to which a score or measure is free of measurement, test scores must be consistent both among items and across time".

The reliability of a test can be measured in different ways. The commonly used methods are: 1) Test-retest method 2) Alternative or Parallel forms 3) Split- half method 4) Rational equilence method or Kuder-Richardson Estimate (KR-20 formula). Out of these methods, split-half method is regarded as the best method. In this method, the data for calculating the reliability can be obtained in one single occasion, so that variations brought about by difference between the two testing situations are eliminated. (Garrett, E. Henry and Woodsworth, 1981).

In the split half method, the test is divided into two equivalent 'halves' and the correlation is found for these half-tests by using Karl Pearson's correlation coefficient formula

$$r = \frac{N\sum xy - \sum x \sum y}{\sqrt{[\sum x^2 - (x)^2][N\sum y^2 - (\sum y)^2]}}$$

Where,

r = correlation co-efficient

X = score obtained in one half of the test

Y = score obtained in another half of the test

$\sum x$ = sum of obtained x values

$\sum y$ = sum of obtained y values

$\sum x^2$ = sum of squared x values

$\sum y^2$ = sum of squared y values

$(\sum x)^2$ = squared value of the sum of obtained x values

$(\sum y)^2$ = squared value of the sum of obtained y values

N = number of cases

From the reliability of the half test, the self-correlation of the whole test is estimated by using Spearman Brown Prophecy formula.

$$rl1 = \frac{2rl/21/11}{1 + rl/21/11}$$

r 11 = reliability of coefficient of the whole test
r ½ = reliability of coefficient of the half test found experimentally

In this Teaching Aptitude Test (TAT), reliability of the test was calculated by split- half method on a sample of 800 students. The reliability coefficient r = 0.828.

C) Validity of TAT: The validity of a test is concerned with the question of what is measured. The validity refers to the extent to which an instrument really measures the intended variable. The validity of a test is established by obtaining evidence that the test indeed measures what it is supposed to measure. The establishment of the validity of a test is a complex endeavour, involving many different procedures. Test developers will often conduct studies to demonstrate a test's construct validity, criterion related validity, content validity, factorial validity etc.

In this Teaching Aptitude Test (TAT), the factorial validity was calculated. Inter correlations matrix (50X50) was factor analyzed using Principal Component Analysis Extraction Method and Quartimax with Kaiser Normalization Rotation Method. Five major factors were extracted accounting for 69.45% of the total variance. The results of the factors analysis are given in table 3.1.

D) Norms of TAT: Norms are the statistical summaries of the performance of a group of individuals upon which a test is standardized. According to Thorndike (1930), norms are defined as the average performance on a particular test made by a standardized sample. The term 'norm' refers to the present performance while the term 'standard' refers to expected future performance. The exact comparison between individuals of different groups is possible only with the help of well-prepared norms. Here, standard score norms and percentile norms were established. By converting raw scores into Z-scores and standard scores, it is possible to compare characteristics between given goups. Table 3.2 gives Z–scores, standard score norms, table 3.3 gives the percentile norms and table 3.4 shows scoring key.

Table 3.1: Shows Factor wise Test Items of TAT

Factor	*Per Cent Variance*	*N*	*Test Items*
I	34-66	24	06, 10, 15, 17, 21, 23, 24, 26, 27, 31, 33, 35, 36, 37, 39, 40, 41, 42, 43, 44, 45, 46, 49, 50
II	12-42	07	14, 25, 28, 32, 34, 47, 48
II	12-42	07	14, 25, 28, 32, 34, 47, 48
III	8-24	06	02, 07, 18, 20, 30, 38
IV	7-16	07	01, 04, 05, 08, 09, 11, 12
V	6-99	06	03, 13, 16, 19, 22, 29

Table 3.2: Shows Z Score and Standard Score Norms of TAT

Raw Score	*Z-score*	*Standard Score M=50, u=10*	*Raw Score*	*Z-score*	*Standard Score M=50, u =10*
1	–4.08	9.23	26	–1.13	38.68
2	–3.96	1041	27	–1.01	39.86
3	–3.84	11.59	28	–0.90	41.04
4	–3.72	12.77	29	–0.78	42.21
5	–3.61	13.95	30	*0.66	43.39
6	–3.49	15.12	31	–0.54	44.57
7	–3.37	16.30	32	–0.43	45.75
8	–3.25	17.48	33	–0.31	46.93
9	–3.13	18.66	34	–0.19	48.10
10	–3.02	19.84	35	–0.07	89.28
11	–2.90	21.01	36	0.05	50.46
12	–2.78	22.19	37	0.16	51.64
13	–2.66	23.37	38	0.28	52.82
14	–2.55	24.55	39	0.40	53.99
15	–2.43	25.72	40	0.52	55.17
16	–2.31	26.90	41	0.63	56.35
17	–2.19	22.08	42	0.75	57.53
18	–2.07	29.26	43	0.87	58.70
19	–1.96	30.44	44	0.99	59.88
20	–1.84	31.61	45	1.11	61.06
21	–1.72	32.79	46	1.22	62.24
22	–1.60	39.97	47	1.34	63.42
23	–1.49	35.15	48	1.46	64.59
24	–1.37	36.33	49	1.58	65.77
25	–1.25	36.50	50	1.69	66.95

Table 3.3: Shows Percentile Norms of TAT

Percentile	*Score*	*Percentile*	*Score*	*Percentile*	*Score*	*Percentile*	*Score*
P1	9.36	P26	31.00	P51	38.00	P76	41.00
P2	12.36	P27	32.00	P52	38.00	P77	41.00
P3	16.08	P28	33.00	P53	38.00	P78	42.00
P4	17.00	P29	33.00	P54	38.00	P79	42.00
P5	17.00	P30	33.40	P55	38.00	P80	42.00
P6	20.00	P31	34.00	P56	38.00	P81	42.58
P7	20.00	P32	34.00	P57	39.00	P82	43.00
P8	20.00	P33	34.00	P58	39.00	P83	43.00
P9	21.00	P34	35.00	P59	39.00	P84	43.00
P10	22.80	P35	35.00	P60	39.00	P85	44.00
P11	22.98	P36	35.00	P61	39.00	P86	44.00
P12	25.00	P37	36.00	P62	39.00	P87	44.00
P13	25.34	P38	36.00	P63	39.00	P88	44.00
P14	26.00	P39	36.00	P64	40.00	P89	45.00
P15	27.00	P40	36.00	P65	40.00	P90	45.00
P16	27.00	P41	37.00	P66	40.00	P91	45.00

(Table 3.3 Continued)

(Table 3.3 Continued)

Percentile	*Score*	*Percentile*	*Score*	*Percentile*	*Score*	*Percentile*	*Score*
P17	28.00	P42	37.00	P67	40.00	P92	45.00
P18	28.00	P43	37.00	P68	40.00	P93	46.00
P19	28.00	P44	37.00	P69	40.00	P94	46.00
P20	29.00	P45	37.00	P70	40.00	P95	47.00
P21	29.78	P46	37.00	P71	41.00	P96	47.00
P22	30.00	P47	37.00	P72	41.00	P97	47.46
P23	30.00	P48	38.00	P73	41.00	P98	48.00
P24	31.00	P49	38.00	P74	41.00	P99	49.00
P25	31.00	P50	38.00	P75	41.00	–	–

Table 3.4: Shows Scoring Key of TAT

Sr. No.	*Correct Answer*	*Sr. No.*	*Correct Answer*	*Sr. No.*	*Correct Answer*	*Sr. No.*	*Correct Answer*	*Sr. No.*	*Correct Answer*
1.	D	11.	D	21.	D	31.	B	41.	C
2.	B	12.	D	22.	A	32.	B	42.	C
3.	B	13.	B	23.	D	33.	B	43.	C
4.	C	14.	C	24.	A	34.	B	44.	D
5.	D	15.	D	25.	C	35.	B	45.	C
6.	A	16.	A	26.	C	36.	A	46.	B
7.	A	17.	A	27.	A	37.	B	47.	D
8.	D	18.	A	28.	D	38.	A	48.	C
9.	D	19.	C	29.	D	39.	A	49.	C
10.	A	20.	A	30.	C	40.	A	50.	C

Table 3.5: Shows Percentile/Standard Score Ranges and the corresponding Rating on the TAT

Percentile Range	*Standard Score Range*	*Interpretation*
P90 – Above	Above 61.06	Excellent
P90 – P70	61.06 – 5.17	Good
P70 – P30	55.17 – 47.40	Average
P30 – P10	47.40 – 33.73	Low
Below P10	Below 33.73	Poor

In order to get the rating on the Teaching Aptitude Test of student teacher, corresponding percentile range/ standard score range in which the student stands may be seen from the table 3.5.

2) Description of Test of General Intelligence (TGI)

Intelligence has played prominent role in the history of humankind. Intelligence is a behaviour determining attribute. It is an inference drawn from the behaviour. Different scholars have defined intelligence in different ways. Terman (1916) says that an individual is intelligent in proportion to his ability to carry on abstract thinking. According to Thorndike (1930), intelligence consists in the capacity for mere association or connection. Kline (1991) says that intelligence is the person's ability to learn, understand and deal with novel situations. According to Thurstone (1938), intelligence is the capacity to make impulses focal at their early unfinished stage of formation. Binet (1905) holds that intelligence involves the tendency to take and maintain a definite direction, the capacity to make adaptations for the purpose of attaining a desired end and the power of self criticism. Wechsler (1901) said, intelligence is the global capacity to act purposefully, to think rationally and to deal effectively with the environment.

Intelligence tests are useful to measure the general learning abilities. With the help of intelligence tests, it is possible to categorize a particular class into several convenient groups and to plan instructional strategies. They useful for testing general or specific skills such as verbal, spatial, performance, memory, educational, vocational and personal guidance. It is essential to note that intelligence test administration and interpretation is a skilled affair. Verbal group tests are useful to test large samples in a relatively short time in the same conditions. Non-verbal group tests provide additional evidence of mental competence where verbal opportunities in our culture have not been satisfactory. Individual tests are one more useful as diagnostic tools (Vernon, 1960; Wiseman, 1967).

Intelligence is not unitary, but it comprises abilities. Several efforts have been made to construct verbal tests for measuring intelligence. Bhatt and desai (1969) constructed group test of intelligence in Gujarathi for VII to XI grades. The test battery included six subjects, namely, 1) Following Directions, 2) Opposites, 3) Disarranged Sentences, 4) Differentiation, 5) Arithmetical Reasoning and 6) Verbal Reasoning. The final version of the test comprised 100 items.

Bhatt (1962) constructed and standardised group test of intelligence for Gujarati pupils of standards V, VI & VII. It included Matching Legs of Tables (non-verbal) and Pictorial Absurdities (non-verbal). Bora (1969) constructed and standardized verbal group test of intelligence for VII to X class students. It included twenty items in each of the subtests-Opposites, Analogy, Number Series, Classification and ten items in each of the subtests – Arithmetical Reasoning and Verbal Reasoning. Desai (1954) constructed and standardised a battery of group test of intelligence for age-group 12-18 studying in standards VII to XI. The subtests included in the test were: 1) Following Directions, 2) Opposites, 3) Disarranged Sentences, 4) Proverbs, 5) Reasoning, 6) Number Sequence 7) Analogies, 8) Similarities, 9) Narrative Completion, 10) Memory And Suggestibility, 11) Synonyms and Autonyms, 12) Classification, 13) Arithmetical Problems, 14) Geometrical Problems, 15) Family Tree, 16) Arranging in Alphabetical Order-Imagery Tests, 17) Code Language, 18) Mirror Images and 19) General Information.

Jobbi's (1961) test has items of seven types – Synonym, Autonym, Numerical Ability, Classification, Best Answer, Reasoning and Analogy. It was for students of VIII to XII classes. Mehta's (1958) test had 60 items of ten types, namely, Logical Selection, Number Series, Classification, Analogy, Best Answer, Information, Disarranged Sentences, Absurdities, Inference and Arithmetical Reasoning. It was meant for 12-14 year old students. Patel's (1970) test for 14-16 year old students had items related to Series, Analogy, Synthesis and Classification.

Bajpaye (1970) conducted a study of socio-economic status and its relations to intelligence and interest. In this study, intelligence was measured by group test of general mental ability by Joshi (1961). Bedi (1982) studied on aspirations of adolescences as related to socio-economic status, intelligence and sex. In this study, the tool for measuring intelligence was group test of general mental ability by Jalota. Bhagavathy (1977) did analytical study of personality, intelligence, values and problems of adolescent girls. He used Mathew's Test of Mental Ability (Verbal and Numerical) for measuring intelligence of adolescent girls. Desai (1971) conducted study about effects on intelligence of birth order and sex. He administered Desai–Bhatt verbal intelligence test on 383 subjects. Ojha (1962) conducted study on intelligence and intellectual stimulation during adolescence. In this study, he used verbal intelligence test (Ray–Chowdhury–Ojha). Makhija (1973) studied interactions among values, interests and intelligence and its impact on scholastic achievement. Jalota's Group test of General Mental Ability is used in this study.

By studying the above tests on intelligence, it is found that there is no suitable standard tool to measure intelligence of students studying in degree and post-graduate classes. So, authors Pal and Mishra (2004) experienced the need for a suitable test for measuring the intelligence of students studying in graduate and post graduate classes. They constructed and standardized a test to measure intelligence of graduate and post graduate students. This test is known as Pal and Mishra's Test of General Intelligence (PMTGI). In the present study, the investigator has adopted this tool to measure intelligence of prospective teachers studying in colleges of education at B.Ed level.

A) Preparation of Items in TGI: To begin with, several items were prepared and subjected to initial screening by the authors. Consequently, 25 items in Vocabulary (Word Meaning), 27 items in Analogy, 30 items in Classification, 25 items in Number Series, 19 items in Syllogistic Reasoning and 25 items in Code Transformation were retained for inclusion in the tryout form. Tryout and item analysis were done as given below.

i) Tryout and Item Analysis: The tryout form of the Test of General Intelligence (TGI) was administered to 36 B.A., 30 B.Ed., 28 B.Sc. and 16 M.A. students studying in two degree colleges, two colleges of education and two university departments at Allahabad. Item analysis was done by calculating difficulty value and discrimination index for every item belonging to a particular subset. Item analysis is often used to determine objectively in which items should be selected for the final version of the test. Item difficulty is defined by the percentage of subjects who answer an item correctly; test developers usually select items with a range of difficulty. Item discriminability index measures the extent to which each potential item is related to performance on the whole test. Test developers often select only test items in which individuals of highest ability consistently answer correctly and in which individuals of least ability consistently answer incorrectly (Aiken, 1991, Weiner, 1984). For item analysis, 30 students were selected from either ends of the answer-sheet arranged in descending order of scores on a particular subtest. 10 items were selected for inclusion in each subtest of TGI. The difficulty value of these items ranged from 20 to 73 while the discrimination index ranged from 0.20 to 0.85. The selected items were arranged in an increasing order of difficulty. Thus, items were selected. The difficulty value and discrimination index for the selected items have been given in Table 3.6.

Table 3.6: Shows Difficult Value and Discrimination Value of Each item in the Test

Item No.	*Sub-Test*	*Diff. Value*	*Disc. Value*
1.	WM	69	.37
2.	WM	64	.40
3.	WM	62	.23
4.	WM	60	.47
5.	WM	57	.40
6.	WM	52	.77
7.	WM	52	.57
8.	WM	52	.50
9.	WM	48	.37
10.	WM	32	.43
11.	AN	73	.53
12.	AN	70	.60
13.	AN	65	.57
14.	AN	65	.50
15.	AN	65	.57
16.	AN	62	.57
17.	AN	62	.63
18.	AN	50	.67
19.	AN	33	.20
20.	AN	25	.30
21.(a)	CL	73	.50
(b)	CL	62	.50
22.(a)	CL	73	.40
(b)	CL	55	.60
23.(a)	CL	68	.57
(b)	CL	48	.37
24.(a)	CL	68	.30
(b)	CL	45	.57
25.(a)	CL	62	.30
(b)	CL	47	.20
26.(a)	CL	63	.30
(b)	CL	33	.30
27.(a)	CL	63	.20
(b)	CL	37	.27

(Table 3.6 Continued)

(Table 3.6 Continued)

Item No.	*Sub-Test*	*Diff. Value*	*Disc. Value*
28.(a)	CL	62	.57
(b)	CL	35	.37
29.(a)	CL	43	.27
(b)	CL	28	.37
30.(a)	CL	40	.37
(b)	CL		
31.	NS	50	.60
32.	NS	48	.37
33.	NS	48	.50
34.	NS	48	.63
35.	NS	47	.40
36.	NS	45	.50
37.	NS	42	.63
38.	NS	42	.57
39.	NS	40	.60
40.	NS	30	.33
41.	CT	70	.27
42.	CT	69	.31
43.	CT	58	.69
44.	CT	42	.85
45.	CT	38	.62
46.	CT	38	.77
47.	CT	35	.23
48.	CT	35	.37
49.	CT	25	.37
50.	CT	25	.30
51.	SY	57	.73
52.	SY	55	.57
53.	SY	53	.30
54.	SY	50	.40
55.	SY	42	.43
56.	SY	38	.44
57.	SY	32	.37
58.	SY	27	.27
59.	SY	27	.33
60.	SY	20	.20

ii) Administration: Before administrating the test, examiners should go through the instructions printed on the test booklet. He should read the instructions loudly and ask the examinees to read the instructions themselves. In the beginning of this test, examinees will be made to understand the method of solving and writing the answers of 6 subtests with examples. They will be given a time of 24 minutes for understanding these instructions. After every 4 minutes they will be asked to solve the questions of the next subtest. Unless they are told, the questions of the next test are not be read. If they complete the answers of all questions of any subtest before 4 minutes, then, they can check their answers in the remaining time. Examiner should move around in the room when examinees are responding to various items and s/ he has to check whether examinees are doing their work sincerely or not.

B) Reliability of TGI: The reliability of any set of measurements is logically defined as the proportion of their variance, that is, true variance. In educational, psychological and other behavioral and social measurements, reliability depends upon population measured as well as upon the measuring instrument. According to Henry E Garrett (1966), "A test score is called reliable when we have reasons for believing the score to be stable and trustworthy". The correlation of the test with itself computed in several ways is called the reliability coefficient of the test.

Guilford (1959) says that there have been three standard procedures to the estimation of reliability, know loosely as the 'split-half', 'alternative forms' and 'retest' methods. However, in the Test of General Intelligence (TGI), two methods were applied in determining the reliability of the test namely, 1) Split-half method 2) Test–retest method. In order to find out split-half reliability, the coefficient of correlation was computed between sets of scores of the two halves comprising even and odd numbered items, and then reliability of the whole test was calculated by using Spearman Brown Prophecy Formula. Test- retest reliability is a common way of determining consistency, by administering the same test twice to the same persons (Walsh and Nancy & others). Split-half as well as test-retest reliability of the test scores have been calculated for 148 students in degree and post-graduate classes. Their values have been given in table 3.7.

Table 3.7: Shows Split-half reliability and Test - retest reliability of each subtest of Test of General Intelligence (TGI)

S.No.	*Test*	*Split-half Reliability*	*Test-Retest Reliability*
1	Word Meaning	.58	.68
2	Analogy	.80	.74
3	Classification	.72	.71
4	Number Series	.84	.76
5	Code Transformation	.93	.82
6	Syllogism	.51	.50
7	Total test	.95	.81

Table 3.8: Shows Coefficient of Correlations between various Subtests

S.No.	*Sub-test*	*1*	*2*	*3*	*4*	*5*	*6*
1	Word Meaning	-	.34	.59	.40	.38	.45
2	Analogy	-	-	.69	.67	.33	.26
3	Classification	-	-	-	.34	.67	.38
4	Number Series	-	-	-	-	.70	.32
5	Code Transformation	-	-	-	-	-	.35
6	Syllogism	-	-	-	-	-	-

C) Validity of TGI: Validity is the correlation of the test with some criterion. Validity refers to the degree to which evidence and theory support the interpretation of test scores entailed by proposed uses of tests (Joint Committee on Standards for Educational and Psychological Testing, 1999, p-9). Validity has to do with both the attributes of the test and the uses to which it is put. The validity of the test is established by obtaining evidence that the test indeed measures what it is supposed to measure. There are different types of validity, namely, content validity, face validity, criterion validity, construct validity etc. Criterion validity is linked with how well the test relates to present performance or predict future performance.

In the present Test of General Intelligence (TGI), criterion related validity was calculated by finding out Product Moment Coefficient of Correlation between scores on TGI and scores on Cattell's Culture Fair Test of Intelligence, scale 3 form A. The value of correlation was .68 (for N =36). Correlations between various subtests of TGI were also calculated. They are as follows.

Observation of the above table shows that scores on the six sub-tests are significantly and positively related to one another. These subtests' scores can also be used as indices of six distinct abilities. Word meaning test measures 'verbal facility ability', Analogy test measures 'Analytical thinking ability. Third subtest 'Classification' measures classification ability. Number Series test measures numerical reasoning ability. Code Transformation test measures symbolic transformation ability and the last i.e., sixth test measures syllogistic reasoning ability.

D) Norms of TGI: Norms of the psychological test represent the test performance of the standard group or sample selected from a specified population norms are empirically established by determining what a representative group of persons actually performs on the test. According to Freeman (1965), "A norm is the average or standard scores on a test made by a specified population". Norms are a statistical procedure to minimize the interpretive error of a test scores. Here, raw scores are transformed into percentile ranks or standard scores. With the help of norms, the position of a particular person (score) is determined.

In the Test of General Intelligence (TGI), the percentile norms for the scores on TGI are shown in table 3.9. They are based on a sample of 384 students studying in BA, B.Sc., B.Com, M.A. M.Sc. L.T/B.Ed. and M.Ed. classes.

Table 3.9: Shows the Percentile Norms for the scores on TGI

Percentile	*Score*	*Percentile*	*Score*	*Percentile*	*Score*	*Percentile*	*Score*
1	11	30	26	60	34	90	44.5
5	15	35	27.5	65	35.5	95	48
10	18	40	29	70	37	99	55.5
15	21	45	30	75	38.5	–	–
20	23	50	31.5	80	40	–	–
25	25	55	33	85	42	–	–

Table 3.10: Shows Conversion of Raw Scores into Normalized Standard Scores

Score	*IQ*	*Score*	*IQ*	*Score*	*IQ*	*Score*	*IQ*
11	63	22	83	33	103	44	123
12	65	23	85	34	105	45	125
13	67	24	87	35	107	46	128
14	69	25	88	36	108	47	130
15	71	26	90	37	110	48	132
16	72	27	92	38	112	49	132
17	74	28	94	39	114	50	134
18	76	29	96	40	116	51	135
19	78	30	97	41	117	52	137
20	79	31	99	42	119	53	139
21	81	32	101	43	121	54	141

Table 3.11: Shows scoring key of TGI

Subtest-1		*Subtest-2*		*Subtest-3*		*Subtest-4*		*Subtest-5*		*Subtest-6*	
S.No	*Ans.*	*S.No*	*Ans.*	*S.No*	*Ans.*	*S.No*	*Ans.*	*S.No*	*Ans.*	*S.No*	*Ans.*
1	D	11	C	21	D, E	31	20	41	CATCH	51	√
2	B	12	C	22	A, C	32	28	42	20,18,1,14,19,6,5,18	52	X
3	A	13	B	23	A, D	33	33	43	OPPAINT	53	√
4	A	14	D	24	A, D	34	6	44	DYRDM	54	X
5	B	15	B	25	A, D	35	19	45	KIDNAP	55	X
6	D	16	A	26	B, C	36	120	46	MBVHI	56	X
7	A	17	B	27	C, E	37	32	47	LARTUEN	57	X
8	A	18	D	28	B, E	38	49	48	GNISUNOC	58	X
9	C	19	A	29	A, C	39	72	49	ALESVE	59	X
10	B	20	D	30	E, C	40	2/1, 6/4	50	CONTED	60	X

Table 3.10 can be used to convert raw score into a normalized standard score IQ with a mean of 100 and a standard deviation of 16. IQ gives the relationship between the individual's performance and their age (Aiken, 1991).

3) Description of Morality Attitude Scale (MAS)

Morality is constructed to solve some of the problems that arise from the complexity of our nature and the diversity of our central connections to the world (Rorty, 1992). It is designed to produce certain types of persons, with specific virtues, manners, cultures, mentalities, habits and skills directed to affect the world in a certain way. Morality is directed to activity, however internal or spiritual, however self-perfection it may be (Rorty and Wong, 1990). Morality means the conformity to the moral code of the social group (Chambers 20th Century Dictionary, 1983). Different faculties have viewed morality from different points of view. According to Rigveda, the best basic moral principles were equality, mutuality and freedom (Sathaye, 1970). The most prominent sociologist, Durkheim (1925) viewed moral development as a process of socialization.

According to Freudian theory (1933), moral standards are largely unconscious products of powerful irrational motives and are based on the need to keep anti- social impulses from conscious awareness. For the Freudians, what is moral is that which is socially sanctioned. Piaget (1932) said that the core of morality was two-fold process. i.e., 1) Respect for the rules of the social order and 2) A sense of justice. Kohlberg (1976) believes that the essential structure of morality is the 'principle of justice' and that the core of justice is the distribution of rights and duties regulated by the concepts of equality and reciprocity.

The test of morality is useful to assist the young people to live more meaningfully and with qualities like, truthfulness, non-violence, good conduct, self- control, honesty, fortitude, fairness courtesy, tolerance against the vicious grip of dishonesty, intemperance, backsliding, prejudice and spite. (Rorty, 1991; Rorty and Wong, 1990; Sharma and Kaur, 1992; Sharma, 1984).

There are a few research studies on morality in India when compared with abroad. Kumari (1981) conducted study on personality needs, moral judgement and value patterns of secondary school teachers. She concluded that morality was a dominant factor in personality of teachers. Kapur (1986) studied on moral education of primary school children. He collected data with the help of observation, piagetian interviews on the acquisition of moral judgment by children. Sharma (1984) used self-made tool to measure the morality of prospective teachers. He said that test of morality for prospective teacher is essential because they are 'would be teachers' and most responsible in moulding behaviour and personality of children and themselves.

By observing and studying above studies, it is clear that, there are standard tools for measuring moral values of children but not for teachers or adults. Hence, in the present study, the investigator constructed and developed an attitude scale to measure morality of prospective teachers studying in colleges of education at B.Ed. level. Before going to describe the construction and development of an attitude scale for assessing morality of prospective teachers, it is needed to discuss the nature and meaning of attitude scale.

A) The meaning and measures of attitude: Attitude is familiar word and is used freely to express one's way of thinking, feeling or behaving. It is complex one relating to human mental process. Attitude is a readiness for attention or action of a definite sort. Allport (1929) refers to attitude as a mental and neutral state of readiness, organized through experience, exerting a directive or dynamic influence upon the individual response to all the objects and situations with which it is related. According to Freeman (1968), attitude is a dispositional readiness to respond to certain situations, or objects in a constant manner which has been learned and has become one's typical mode of response.

Guilford (1959) defined attitude as a personal disposition common to individuals but possessed in different degrees which impels to react to object situations or positions in ways that can be called favourable or unfavourable. According to Morgan (1934), attitudes are literally mental postures, guides, for conduct before a response is made. Warren (1934) defined attitude as specific mental disposition towards an incoming (or arising) experience, where by that experience is modified or a condition of readiness for certain type of activities. Good (1959) defined attitude as a state of mental and emotional readiness to react to situations, persons or things in a manner in harmony with these stimuli. Though attitude and opinion are related terms, they are not synonymous. Attitude is the inner feeling or belief of a person towards a psychological phenomenon, where as opinion is a verbal expression of attitude.

Attitude can be measured by direct observation of overt behaviour of the individual. This has all the defects of observation in addition to the difficulty of experimentally creating a real situation, where in behavior can be observed. Projective techniques can also be used to assess an individual's attitudes. The basis for the use of projective techniques to measure attitude is that attitudes can be inferred by one's unconscious responses to certain stimuli like photographs, cartoons etc. This method has all the disadvantages in administration, scoring, low inter-scorer reliability etc.

The most common method of estimating a person's attitude is through a questionnaire, where the individual is asked to express his/her opinion on several controversial statements about some psychological object. The logic behind the use of opinion to measure attitude is that there is positive correlations between what people say about a subject and what they will do about it. A person's particular action cannot be predicted with a high degree of accuracy, yet, one's position on an attitude scale can be assessed. This method of assessing attitude from expressed opinion is also, subject to some limitations like taking of response by the individual where he/she tends to give socially acceptable responses thereby concealing his/her real attitude. But, this could be overcome in several ways, like making the questionnaire anonymous.

The two more well known methods of measuring attitude are: 1) Thurstone's (1929) method of equal appearing intervals, 2. Likert's (1932) method of summated ratings. Likerts method is considered as an improvement over Thurston's method. The first step in Likert method is collection of a number of items. They must express definite favourableness or unfavourableness to a particular view point and their number should be approximately equal. A trial test would be administered to a number of subjects and only those items that correlate with the total test should be retained. Five alternative responses, namely, Strongly Agree (SA), Agree (A), Undecided (UN), Disagree (D) and Strongly Disagree (SD) are given and a scaled value is given to each of the five responses. For positive items, it is from 5 to 1 and for negative items, it is from 1 to 5. The total of these scores on all items measures a respondent's favourableness or unfavourableness towards the subject in question.

In the present study, Likert's method of summated rating is used, because it yields scores very similar to those obtained by Thurstone's method, and at the same time, it is less laborious than the latter. The coefficient of correlation between measure of attitude obtained by the two methods was as high as 0.92 (Edwards and Kenney, 1946).

For assessing morality of prospective teachers, an attitude scale is constructed based on previous related literature. De's (1974) study on seven moral values – Dutifulness, Sincerity, Co-operation, Conformity to School Rules, Honesty, Loyalty and Respect to Seniors concluded that there was no significant relation in moral values among teachers, students and parents. Anand (1977) studied the impact of denomination and secular schools on 18 instrumental values of adolescents. Some of important findings were: 1) Students gave top rank to obedience, honesty and self-control, 2) Students of denominational schools prefer being helpful, loving and clean while students of secular schools prefer being polite, courageous and independent. Sharma (1984) studied on 10 moral values. He concluded that the level of morality of male student-teachers was less than the level of morality of female student-teachers. Srivastava (1981) measured the moral ideals of P.U.C., B.A and M.A class students. The findings were: 1) For every increase in the educational ladder, is a corresponding decrease in moral values, 2) A decrease in magnitude of moral values is observed corresponding with increase in age. But, Rani (1968) found that increase in age corresponded with an increase in knowledge of morality. Morality scale is developed keeping in mind all precautions.

B) Construction of the Preliminary Form of MAS: Since there is no suitable standardized tool to measure the attitude of prospective teachers towards morality, the investigator has decided to develop an attitude scale to suit his purpose. Bearing the important areas of morality in mind, a number of items related to morality are collected from a number of sources as follows. Secondary school teachers, Head masters, teacher-educators of colleges of education, principals of colleges of education, university teachers were requested to write the different favourable and unfavourable statements keeping attention in the light of concept, nature and dimensions of morality and some of the statements were prepared by investigator after going through the related literature on morality.

The statements thus obtained have been scrutinized and adopted to the list. All the statements have been reviewed and rewritten in order to avoid ambiguity and overlapping. This list of statements was supplemented by a careful study of related literature and informal interviews with teachers, teacher educators, principals and university teachers. The pool of items or universe of items as Gutman (1947) calls it, thus collected was refined by observing the following criteria laid down by different authors. Their suggestions are summarized as given below.

1) The statements must be clear, precise and straight forward.
2) Each statement should contain only one complete thought.
3) Statement should be short and to the point of view.
4) Avoid statements that are irrelevant to the psychological object.
5) Avoid statements that may be interpreted in more than one way.
6) Avoid statements that refer to the past rather than to the present.
7) Both favourable and unfavourable statements must be included.
8) The negative and positive statements must be arranged randomly through out the attitude scale so that the space error may be avoided.

Then, the item pool, thus prepared consisting of 150 statements that represent both positive and negative statements regarding attitude of prospective teachers towards morality. And presented to a panel of 2 experts.

According to the suggestions given by experts, finally 120 items were prepared for the pilot form of which 60 statements were negative and remaining were positive statements. Each of the items was arranged on a unipolar five point scale with the following alternatives – Strongly Agree (SA), Agree (A), Undecided (UD), Disagree (D) and Strongly Disagree (SD).

C) Pilot Study and Item Analysis: The aim of piloting is to ensure that the instruments to be used are appropriate. It involves asking a small sample to work through the test in the presence of the researcher and then give feed back to the researcher. Piloting can help not only with the working of questions but also with the ordering of question sequences and the reduction of non-response rates. It gives an insight into the acceptability of the test items to all the subjects it concerned. (Munard Drever, 1990).

The Pilot study was conducted on 30 prospective teachers studying B.Ed course at Dravidian University, Kuppam. The sample consisting of 15 male and 15 female prospective teachers. The Pilot form of the attitude scale thus formulated has been administered in order to examine whether the statements are easily understood by them or not and to know whether they possess clarity or not. Even though the scale is self administering, as a matter of motivating the prospective teachers, they were explained the purpose of the research and the way they had to answer the items.

They were also assured that the data would be used only for research work and would be kept confidential. For the purpose of scoring, numerical values were assigned as shown below, to each of five categories of responses, namely, Strongly Agree (SA), Agree (A), Undecided (UN), Disagree (D) and Strongly Disagree (SD). Numerical weights given to the five alternative responses are shown as below.

	Response				
Type of statement	*Strongly Agree*	*Agree*	*Undecided*	*Disagree*	*Strongly disagree*
Positive	5	4	3	2	1
Negative	1	2	3	4	5

This method of weighing responses is simple and is highly satisfactory. Likert (1932) found that scores based upon this relatively simple assignment of integral weights correlated 0.99 with complicated and time consuming normal deviate system of weighing.

Item analysis is often used to determine objectively which item should be selected for the final version of the test. Usually, it includes analysis of item discriminability and item difficulty. After scoring the responses of the prospective teachers as described above, item analysis was carried out by the method of criterion of internal consistency suggested by Likert (1932). The results obtained by this method of criterion of internal consistency agree very well with the result of the traditional method of item analysis. This method consists of rank ordering the subjects with respect to their total scores and taking a high group and a low group on the basis of the total score and calculating the internal consistency of each statement by finding the difference between high and low groups on the statement.

In the present item analysis the top 27% and bottom 27% of subjects have been identified on the basis of total score. They are identified as criterion groups and the mean scores obtained by these two groups on each item have been calculated. The difference between the mean scores is discrimination value or item validity (Edward 1969). The detailed discrimination index table is presented below.

Table 3.12: The Total Attitude Scores of Top and Bottom Groups of Prospective Teachers on Each Item and Discrimination Values of all Items in the Pilot Form

Items	*Total score of the top group on each item*	*Mean (Mt)*	*Total score of the bottom group on each item*	*Mean (Mb)*	*Discrimination index= Mt–Mb*
1	180	3.60	170	3.40	0.02
2	163	3.26	177	3.54	-0.28
3	127	2.54	121	2.42	0.12
4	160	3.20	159	3.18	0.02
5	115	2.30	106	2.12	0.18
6	210	4.20	177	3.54	0.66*
7	106	2.12	96	1.92	0.20
8	143	2.86	204	4.08	-1.22
9	172	3.44	115	2.30	1.14*
10	88	1.76	135	2.70	-0.94
11	70	1.40	81	1.62	-0.22
12	217	4.34	158	3.16	1.18*
13	235	4.70	189	3.78	0.92*
14	241	4.82	193	3.86	0.96*
15	222	4.44	168	3.36	1.08*
16	216	4.32	217	4.34	-0.02
17	159	3.18	145	2.90	0.28
18	160	3.20	159	3.18	0.02
19	224	4.48	147	2.94	1.54*
20	227	4.54	216	4.32	0.22
21	208	4.16	163	3.26	0.90*
22	244	4.88	224	4.48	0.40*
23	236	4.72	228	4.56	0.16
24	145	2.90	132	2.64	0.26
25	68	1.36	61	1.22	0.14
26	216	4.32	217	4.34	-0.02

(Table 3.12 Continued)

(Table 3.12 Continued)

Items	*Total score of the top group on each item*	*Mean (Mt)*	*Total score of the bottom group on each item*	*Mean (Mb)*	*Discrimination index= Mt–Mb*
27	240	4.80	203	4.06	0.74*
28	62	1.24	83	1.66	-0.42
29	249	4.98	199	3.98	1.00*
30	68	1.36	61	1.22	0.14
31	160	3.20	159	3.18	0.02
32	217	4.34	158	3.16	1.18*
33	221	4.42	180	3.60	0.82*
34	238	4.76	188	3.76	1.00*
35	216	4.32	217	4.34	-0.02
36	106	2.12	96	1.92	0.20
37	143	2.86	204	4.08	-1.22
38	88	1.76	135	2.70	-0.94
39	159	3.18	145	2.90	0.28
40	115	2.30	106	2.12	0.18
41	228	4.56	130	2.60	1.96*
42	194	3.88	81	1.62	2.26*
43	160	3.20	159	3.18	0.02
44	222	4.44	145	2.90	1.54*
45	99	1.98	119	2.38	-0.40
46	115	2.30	106	2.12	0.18
47	166	3.20	159	3.18	0.02
48	106	2.12	96	1.92	0.20
49	159	3.18	145	2.90	0.28
50	191	3.82	106	2.12	1.70*
51	216	4.32	207	4.14	0.18
52	247	4.94	236	4.72	0.22
53	192	3.84	86	1.72	2.12*
54	239	4.78	225	4.50	0.28
55	123	2.46	129	2.58	-0.12
56	164	3.28	157	3.14	0.24
57	194	3.88	81	1.62	2.26*
58	225	4.50	176	3.52	0.98*
59	227	4.54	216	4.32	0.22
60	163	3.26	171	3.54	-0.28
61	216	4.32	130	2.60	1.72*
62	160	3.20	159	3.18	0.02
63	159	3.18	145	2.90	0.28
64	106	2.12	96	1.92	0.20
65	186	3.72	101	2.02	1.70*
66	159	3.18	145	2.90	0.28
67	227	4.54	216	4.32	0.22
68	236	4.72	228	4.56	0.16
69	145	2.90	132	2.64	0.26

Items	*Total score of the top group on each item*	*Mean (Mt)*	*Total score of the bottom group on each item*	*Mean (Mb)*	*Discrimination index= Mt–Mb*
70	231	4.62	126	2.52	2.10*
71	237	4.74	205	4.10	0.64*
72	68	1.36	61	1.22	0.14
73	62	1.24	83	1.66	-0.42
74	237	4.74	168	3.36	1.38*
75	80	1.60	104	2.08	-0.48
76	239	4.78	225	4.50	0.28
77	123	2.46	129	2.58	-0.12
78	190	3.80	129	2.58	1.22*
79	164	3.28	157	3.14	0.14
80	216	4.32	207	4.14	0.18
81	279	4.58	192	3.84	0.74*
82	247	4.94	236	4.72	0.22
83	191	3.88	115	2.30	1.58*
84	180	3.60	170	3.40	0.20
85	163	3.26	177	3.54	-0.28
86	99	3.96	119	2.38	-0.48
87	127	2.54	121	2.42	0.12
88	160	3.20	159	3.18	0.02
89	115	2.30	106	2.12	0.18
90	106	2.12	96	1.92	0.20
91	143	2.86	204	4.08	-1.22
92	226	4.52	146	2.92	1.60*
93	216	4.32	217	4.34	-0.02
94	227	4.50	216	4.32	0.22
95	211	4.22	181	3.62	0.60
96	236	4.72	228	4.56	0.16
97	145	2.90	132	2.64	0.26
98	227	4.54	148	2.96	1.58*
99	241	4.82	161	3.22	1.60*
100	197	3.94	137	2.74	1.20*
101	247	4.94	236	4.12	0.22
102	245	4.90	162	3.24	1.66*
103	216	4.32	207	4.14	0.18
104	237	4.74	202	4.04	0.70*
105	239	4.78	225	4.50	0.28
106	123	2.46	129	2.58	-0.12
107	164	3.28	157	3.14	0.14
108	216	4.32	207	4.14	0.18
109	247	4.94	236	4.72	0.22
110	249	4.98	230	4.60	0.38*
111	180	3.60	170	3.40	0.20
112	127	2.54	121	2.42	0.12

(Table 3.12 Continued)

(Table 3.12 Continued)

Items	*Total score of the top group on each item*	*Mean (Mt)*	*Total score of the bottom group on each item*	*Mean (Mb)*	*Discrimination index= Mt–Mb*
113	224	4.48	147	2.97	1.54*
114	193	3.86	85	1.70	2.16*
115	160	3.20	159	3.18	0.02
116	115	2.30	106	2.12	0.18
117	159	3.18	145	2.90	0.28
118	216	4.32	207	4.14	0.18
119	212	4.24	114	2.28	1.96*
120	219	4.38	193	3.86	0.52*

Note: The items with * are retained in final form as discrimination is more than 0.3.

D) Preparation of Final Form: Out of 120 items, 42 items have been selected for inclusion in the final form of attitude scale of prospective teachers on morality. There were 21 positive and 21 negative statements. These statements were divided into six dimensions namely, Truthfulness, Dutifulness, Helping Nature, Good Conduct, Honesty and Self-Control. Each dimension consists of 7 items including positive and negative items. The English version of the final form of the attitude scale is presented in Appendix A3.

E) Reliability of MAS: Reliability is one of the important characteristics of any test. Statistically, reliability is also defined as the self-correlation of the test. It is the consistency of scores obtained from one set of measures to another.

According to Best and Khan (2006), "A test is reliable to the extent that it measures whatever it is measuring consistently". Best and Khan (2006) say that there are a number of types of reliability: 1) Stability over time (test-retest), 2) Stability over item samples (Parallel forms) 3) Stability of items (split halves and K.R. formula 20 for measuring internal consistency) and 4) Stability over scores (Inter-scorer).

Of four methods of establishing the reliability of a test, the split-half method is regarded by many as the best of the methods for measuring the reliability (Garret & Woodsworth, 1981). This method is used by many investigators because the data for calculating reliability are obtained from one occasion so that variations brought about by differences between the two testing situations are eliminated.

In split-half method, the scale with 42 items was split into two halves by pooling the odd numbered and even numbered item scores. The correlation between these two sets of test scores have been established by using Karl Pearson's Formula. The reliability of half test was 0.83. This was correlated for full length of the test by using Spearman-Brown Prophecy Formula. The reliability of full test was 0.905.

F) Validity of MAS: Validity is another criterion considered to estimate the appropriateness of any tool developed to examine a particular aspect. According to John Best (1989), "Validity is the quality of a data gathering instrument or procedure that enables it to measure what it is supposed to measure". The index of reliability is some times taken as a measure of validity (Garrett and Woodworth, 1981). The following types of validity were established for the present tool.

i) Content Validity*:* Content validity indicates how adequate is the content of a test about which inferences are to be made. It refers to the establishment and evaluation of the significance of the test items individually and as a whole. Every item should be a sampling of that aspect which the test purports to measure. Selection of item should be based on careful analysis, field experts, and review of related literature, empirical findings and actual subject matter.

   In the present study, the items in the attitude scale are based on the review of related literature and consultation with related field experts. Their suggestions have been taken into account to enhance the contents and quality of items. Thus, it can be reasonably assumed that the attitude scale developed possesses satisfactory content validity.

ii) Item Validity: There are numerous indices and procedures for determining item validity. One of which stresses the number of discriminations of the desired sort that the item is capable of making. It emphasizes the content to which the item predicts segregation examinees into those with high versus those with low criterion scores. The discriminative power of each of the items was established before including them in the final form. Thus, the items chosen for the scale have been found to be satisfactorily valid.

iii) Intrinsic Validity: According to Guilford (1959), "Intrinsic validity indicates the degree to which the test measures what it purports to measure". In other words, it can be stated in terms of how well the obtained scores measure the test's true score component. This validity is obtained by calculating the square root of its reliability. Hence, intrinsic validity of the attitude scale of morality is 0.92.

iv) Criterion Validity: Criterion validity is connected with a question of how well the test relates to present performance or predict future performance. The total sample of prospective teachers was classified into two groups on the basis of their answers to an overall item, given at the end of the scale. The two groups were, those who gave responses of strongly agree and agree were merged into one (satisfied group) and those who gave responses of strongly disagree and disagree were merged into one (dissatisfied group). The mean scores and SD's of these two groups were calculated and critical ratio has been employed. The obtained critical ratio is 3.13 which is greater than table value at 0.01 level (at 88 df.). In other words, the mean of satisfied group is significantly greater than the mean of dissatisfied group. Thus, the instrument to measure the attitude of prospective teachers on morality is said have criterion validity.

v) Face Validity: Face validity refers to the way the test appears to those it is measured to experts and educationists or if the common thread of an attitude runs through all the scale items, the resultant scale has "face validity" for that attitude. The investigator here assured that, by the opinion of the experts, who are familiar with test development, morality attitude scale and questionnaire used in this study have face validity.

4) Personal Data Sheet (PDS)

The information with regard to sex, age, educational qualification, type of locality, type of management, type of group, methods of teaching-I, methods of teaching-II, community, parental income, parental education and marital status of prospective teachers was obtained from carefully worded personal data sheet. This sheet could be seen in Appendix A4.

Locale of the Study

The area of the study is the Chittoor district of Andhra Pradesh. Chittoor district belongs to Rayalaseema region of Andhra Pradesh. It consists of 66 mandals. Under this district, there are mainly five Universities, namely, Dravidian University, Kuppam; Sri Venkateswara University, Tirupati; Sri Padmavati Mahila Viswavidyalayam, Tirupati; Sanskrit Vidyapeetam, Tirupati, Sri Venkateshwara Veternary University, Tirupati. There are three University Colleges of Education for studying B.Ed. course and there are about eight Private Colleges of Education in and around the Chittoor district.

Selection of the Sample

For the study, three university colleges of education namely, Sri Venkateswara University, Tirupati, Sri Padmavathi Mahila Viswavidyalayam, Tirupathi and Dravidian University, Kuppam were selected. And also, researcher again selected randomly one private college of education located in Tirupati out of eight private colleges of education in and around the Chittoor district. A sample of 300 prospective teachers studying at three university colleges of education and one private college of education were selected by stratified random sampling techniques. The characteristics of the selected sample are as follows:

Table 3.13: Shows Characteristics of Selected Sample

S. No	*Name of the Variable*	*Name of the sub-variable*	*No. of Prospective Teachers*
1	Gender	Male	147
		Female	153
2	Age	21-26years	204
		26-30years	49
		30 above	47
3	Type of Locality	Rural	204
		Urban	96

(Table 3.13 Continued)

(Table 3.13 Continued)

S. No	Name of the Variable	Name of the sub-variable	No. of Prospective Teachers
4	Type of Management	Government	181
		Private	119
5	Educational Qualification	Graduate	203
		Post graduate	97
6	Type of Group	Science	146
		Arts	154
7	Methods of Teaching-I	Physical Science	40
		Mathematics	52
		Biological Science	60
		Social Studies	148
8	Methods of Teaching-II	English	139
		Telugu	161
9	Community	OC	64
		BC	115
		SC and ST	121
10	Parental Income	₹0-15,000	165
		₹15,000-30,000	115
		₹30,000 above	20
11	Parental Education	Literate	134
		Illiterate	166
12	Marital Status	Married	96
		Unmarried	204

Data Collection

After selecting sample, three university colleges of education and one private college of education were visited. A good rapport has been developed with the Heads of institutions. They have given permission to administer the tools on prospective teachers studying in colleges of education at B.Ed. level. These prospective teachers have been instructed to sit in a separate room where no teacher educator would observe what they do. Teaching Aptitude Test (TAT) in the form of multiple choices, which measures aptitude of prospective teachers towards teaching profession; Test of General Intelligence (TGI), which is a questionnaire for measuring intellectual level of prospective teachers and attitude scale to assess the morality of prospective teachers with five-point pattern i.e., Strongly Agree (SA), Agree (A), Undecided (UN). Disagree (D) and Strongly Disagree (SD) along with personal data sheet were given to the prospective teachers (B.Ed trainees).

The prospective teachers were explained about the purpose of the study and what they should do. It was emphasized that the data would be kept confidential and were directed to respond to all the items in the given three tools. For collecting information about personal and demographic variables, various items have been given and the subjects have been instructed to fill those items properly. Before administering each test, the prospective teachers were given the needed instructions to attempt the tests correctly. Time limit is fixed flexibly to respond to the Teaching Aptitude Test (TAT), Test of General Intelligence (TGI) and attitude scale for measuring morality of prospective teachers. Apart from this, the investigator has studied different aspects of colleges of education and noted down the important points while interacting with Heads, faculty members and others during the period of his stay in each college of education. Thus, the investigator collected the data from the prospective teachers studying in colleges of education at B.Ed. level.

Scoring Procedure

For the purpose of statistical analysis and interpretation, the collected data should be quantified. In order to find out quantification, the following scoring procedure was adopted.

First, Teaching Aptitude Test (TAT) is supplied to the prospective teachers personally and they are requested to give responses to all items in the test. There are 50 multiple choice items. Each item is followed by four alternative items, the testee is to select the most appropriate answer out of the four alternatives. Each correct answer as per the "Answer key" is given one point score. There is no negative marking for scoring the test. The maximum possible score, one can obtain on this test is 50. Scoring can be done with the help of scoring key.

Secondly, Test of General Intelligence (TGI) is handed over to the prospective teachers and they are directed to respond to all items on answer sheet only, but not expect that they would answer all the questions correctly. Correct answers should be marked by putting the "√" mark. Number of tick marks for every sub-test of questionnaire should be counted and then these sub scores should be added together to get a composite score.

Thirdly, Morality Attitude Scale (MAS) is given to prospective teachers studying in colleges of education at B.Ed level and instructed to give responses to all items freely and frankly. This Likert type of attitude scale has been scored on a five point scale by giving weights 5,4,3,2 and 1 in the case of positive items and 1,2,3,4 and 5 in the case of negative items respectively. The grand total to each individual on the entire test has been obtained by adding the weights on all the statements. The information provided by the respondents in the personal data sheets is also numerically coded to suit the computer analysis.

Statistical Techniques

The obtained data is analyzed by using appropriate statistical techniques such as mean, standard deviation, percentages, t-test, F-test, correlation and step-wise multiple regression analysis. To find out the teaching aptitude of prospective teachers, mean and standard deviations have been computed. The number and percentage of prospective teachers have been calculated based on classification given in the test. To find out intellectual level of prospective teachers, mean and standard deviations have been computed. The number and percentage of prospective teachers have been calculated based on classification given in the test. To find out morality of prospective teachers, mean and standard deviations have been computed. The number and percentage of prospective teachers have been calculated based on classification given in the test.

To study the effects of gender, age, type of locality, type of management, educational qualification, type of group, methods of teaching-I, methods of teaching-II, community, parental income, parental education and marital status of prospective teachers on teaching aptitude, intellectual level and morality of prospective teachers mean, SD, t-test and F-test have been worked out. Whenever two groups are involved in a variable, t-test has been used to know significant differences between these groups, when more than two groups are involved in a variable, F-test has been worked out to know the significant differences among these groups.

To find out relationship among teaching aptitude, intellectual level and morality of prospective teachers, Correlations have been worked out. To find out how far and to what extent the independent variables influence the dependent variables, Stepwise Multiple Regression Analysis has been carried out. With the help of statistical techniques, the results and discussion are presented in the next chapter.

4

Inter-relationship between Teaching Aptitude, Intellectual Level and Morality

Results and Discussion

Introduction

This chapter contains three parts. In part-I, Frequency Distribution, Descriptive Statistics such as, Measures of Central Tendencies, Measures of Dispersion, Measures of Skewness and Kurtosis were presented. By using Standard Score Range and Percentile Range, the number and percentage of prospective teachers having the level of teaching aptitude as per the classification, TAT were found out. By using Normalized Standard Scores (IQs), the number and percentage of prospective teachers having the intellectual level as per the classification TGI were found. By using Score Range, the number and percentage of prospective teachers having level of morality as per the classification given in MAS prepared were found out.

In Part – II, differential studies were presented. One of the major objectives of the study is to find out the significant differences if any, in the teaching aptitude, intellectual level and morality of prospective teachers due to variations in their gender, age, type of locality, type of management, educational qualification, type of group, methods of teaching-I, methods of teaching-II, community, parental income, parental education and marital status. To realize this objective, mean and standard deviation of each group in a variable with respect to teaching aptitude, intellectual level and morality were calculated. Based on mean and SD, t-test/ F-test was worked out to know the significant difference between/among the groups. Whenever two groups are involved in a variable, t-test was applied and in case of more than two groups, F-test was used to know the significant difference among the groups. Here, the influence of independent variables (gender, age, type of locality, type of management, educational qualification, type of group, methods of teaching-I, methods of teaching-II, community, parental income, parental education and marital status) on dependent variables (teaching aptitude, intellectual level and morality) was statistically analyzed with help of mean, standard deviation, t-test and F-test.

In Part – III, correlation studies were presented. Correlation studies were made to find out the relationship between i) teaching aptitude and intellectual level, ii) teaching aptitude and morality and iii) intellectual level and morality of prospective teachers. For this, Karl Pearson Correlation was used. To predict the contribution of independent variables on the dependent variables, Stepwise Multiple Regression Analysis was carried out. This analysis facilitates to realize the objective that how far and to what extent the independent variables influence the dependent variables

Part I: Descriptive Analysis

Descriptive Analysis of Teaching Aptitude, Intellectual Level and Morality of Prospective Teachers

The study assumes that the prospective teachers with teaching aptitude, intellectual level and morality are normally distributed in the population. The raw score distribution of prospective teachers (B.Ed trainees) for teaching aptitude, intellectual level and morality is presented here. To see whether the distribution of scores follow the normality or not, the general descriptive statistics such as – Measures of Central Tendency, Measures of Dispersion, Skewness and Kurtosis are calculated.

By using Standard Score Range and Percentile Range, the number and percentage of prospective teachers having the level of teaching aptitude as per the classification, namely, (1) Excellent, (2) Good, (3) Average, (4) Low and (5) Poor given in Teaching Aptitude Test (TAT) are found out.

By using Normalized Standard Scores (IQs), the number and percentage of prospective teachers having the intellectual level as per the classification, namely, (1) Gifted, (2) Above Average, (3) Average, (4) Below Average and (5) Poor given in the Test of General Intelligence (TGI) are found out.

By using Score Range, the number and percentage of prospective teachers having level of morality as per the classification, namely, (1) Excellent, (2) Good, (3) Average, (4) Low and (5) Poor given in Morality Attitude Scale (MAS) prepared by the present investigator, are found out.

From the table 4.1, it is clear that the teaching aptitude scores obtained through the administration of the TAT to the prospective teachers, have been arranged in a systematic manner by grouping them into classes and tabulating

Table 4.1: Frequency Distribution of Scores of Teaching Aptitude of Prospective Teachers

S.No.	*Class Interval (CI)*	*Mid Point (MP)*	*Frequency (F)*	*Cumulative Frequency (CF)*	*Cumulative Frequency Percentage (CFP)*
1	1-10	5	4	4	1.33
2	11-20	15	67	71	23.67
3	21-30	25	158	229	76.33
4	31-40	35	64	293	97.67
5	41-50	45	7	300	100.00

N = 300 Standard Deviation = 7.061
Mean = 25.873 Range = 42.00
Median = 26.000 Skewness = 0.201
Mode = 28.000 Kurtosis = -0.002

them into frequency distribution. The analysis is carried out to know the kind of average (mean), range and scatteredness.

The teaching aptitude scores obtained by 300 prospective teachers are tabulated into frequency distribution and various descriptive statistics such as mean, median, mode, range, standard deviation, skewness and kurtosis are calculated to understand the nature of distribution. The frequency distribution and values of descriptive statistics are presented in table 4.1.

The mean teaching aptitude scores of prospective teachers on six dimensions of TAT is 25.873. The values of median and mode are 26.000 and 28.000. The mean and median are almost equal and therefore, it may be concluded that the distribution is normal. The values indicate that the aptitude level of prospective teachers towards teaching profession is low. In other words, the prospective teachers have below average aptitude towards teaching profession.

The range of the scores obtained by the 300 prospective teachers is 42. The standard deviation of the teaching aptitude scores is 7.061. This shows that there is normal dispersion in the aptitude of prospective teachers towards teaching profession in all dimensions of TAT.

The value of skewness is 0.201. It states that the scores are more or less normally distributed. The kurtosis value is – 0.002. It indicates peakedness or flatness of a frequency distribution as compared with the normal distribution. Then, the teaching aptitude scores are analyzed by employing different parametric statistical methods to test the hypotheses.

From the table 4.2, it is noticed that the prospective teachers are classified into five types based on percentile range and standard score range. Initially, the raw scores obtained by prospective teachers in TAT are converted into standard scores and percentiles as per the instructions given in the manual of TAT.

According to instructions given in the manual of TAT, the prospective teachers who get standard scores more than 61.06 and percentile score more than P90, are referred as 'Excellent'. The prospective teachers who gain standard scores in between 61.06 and 55.17 and percentile in between P90 and P70, are referred as 'Good'. The prospective teachers who obtain standard scores in between 55.17 and 47.40 and percentile in between P70 and P30, are referred as

Table 4.2: Classification of Prospective Teachers on the basis of their Percentage Range and Standard Score Range; Number and Percentage of prospective Teachers as per the given Classification

S.No.	*Classification*	*Percentile Range*	*Standard Score Range*	*Number*	*Percentage*
1	Excellent	P90	61.06 above	15	5%
2	Good	P90 – P70	61.06 – 55.17	36	12%
3	Average	P70 – P30	55.17 – 47.40	105	35%
4	Low	P30 - P10	47.40 – 33.73	120	40%
5	Poor	Below P10	Below 33.73	24	08%

'Average'. The prospective teachers who get standard scores in between 47.40 and 33.73 and percentile in between P30 and P10, are referred as 'Low'. The prospective teachers who get standard scores below 33.73 and percentile below P10, are referred as 'Poor'.

Table 4.2 shows that there are 15 prospective teachers, come under the classification of 'Excellent' out of the sample of 300 prospective teachers. It means, there are 5% of prospective teachers, come under the classification of 'Excellent'. There are 36 prospective teachers, come under the classification of 'Good' out of the sample of 300 prospective teachers. It means, there are 12% of prospective teachers, come under the classification of 'Good'. There are 105 prospective teachers, come under classification of 'Average' out of sample of 300 prospective teachers. It means, there are 35% of prospective teachers, come under classification of 'Average'.

There are 120 prospective teachers, come under classification of 'Low' out of the sample of 300 prospective teachers. It means, there are 40% of prospective teachers, come under classification of 'Low'. Finally, there are 24 prospective teachers, come under category of 'Poor' out of the sample of 300 prospective teachers. It means, there are 8% of prospective teachers, come under domain of 'Poor'. By observing the table, it is clear that, there are more prospective teachers come under the category of low (40%) and there are less prospective teachers come under the category of excellent (5%).

From the table 4.3, it is clear that the intellectual level scores obtained through the administration of the TGI to the prospective teachers, have been arranged in a systematic manner by grouping them into classes and tabulating them into frequency distribution. It is clear that the TGI includes six dimensions relating to Word Meaning, Analogy, Classification, Number Series, Code Transformation and Syllogism.

The analysis is carried out to know the kind of mean, range and variability. The intellectual level scores obtained by 300 prospective teachers are tabulated

Table 4.3: Frequency Distribution of Scores of Intellectual Level of Prospective Teachers

S.No.	*Class Interval (CI)*	*Mid Point (MP)*	*Frequency (F)*	*Cumulative Frequency (CF)*	*Cumulative Frequency Percentage (CFP)*
1	1-10	5	0	0	0
2	11-20	15	55	55	18.33
3	21-30	25	147	202	67.33
4	31-40	35	89	291	97.00
5	41-50	45	9	300	100.00
6	51-60	55	0	300	100.00

N	=	300 Range	=	36.000
Mean	=	27.410 Standard Deviation	=	6.811
Median	=	28.000 Skewness	=	0.067
Mode	=	20.000 Kurtosis	=	-0.227

into frequency distribution and various descriptive statistics such as mean, median, mode, range, standard deviation, skewness and kurtosis are calculated to understand the nature of distribution. The frequency distribution and values of descriptive statistics are presented in this table.

The mean of intellectual level scores of prospective teachers on different dimensions of TGI is 27.410. The values of median and mode are 28.000 and 20.000. The mean and median are almost equal and therefore, it may be concluded that the distribution is normal. The values of median and mode (28 and 20 respectively) have confirmed that the general intellectual level in the Test of General Intelligence (TGI) among the sample of the subjects is lower than $M+\frac{1}{2}\sigma$ and hence, it may be concluded that the prospective teachers have not sufficient favourable intellectual level which is required in the teaching-learning process. Here, the value of mean is less than median, median is greater than mode and median is the highest.

The range of the scores obtained by the 300 prospective teachers is 36. The standard deviation of intellectual level scores is 6.811. This shows that there is a normal dispersion in the intellectual level of prospective teachers in the dimensions of Word Meaning, Analogy, Classification, Number Series, Code Transformation and Syllogism. In the distribution, mean and median fall at different points. So, the distribution is said to skewed. The value of skewness is 0.067. Thus, the distribution is said to be positively skew. The value of kurtosis is – 0.227. This value is less than the value of 0.263. So, the distribution is Lepto Kurtic.

The intellectual level scores are analyzed by employing different parametric statistical methods to test the hypotheses.

From the table 4.4, it is noticed that the prospective teachers are classified into five types based on Score Range and IQ Score. Initially, the raw scores obtained by prospective teachers in the TGI are converted into IQs as per the instructions given in the manual of TGI.

According to instructions given in the manual of TGI, the prospective teachers who gain score more than 47 and IQ of 130 are referred as 'Gifted'. The prospective teachers who get score in between 37-47 and IQ in between 110-130, are referred as 'Above Average'. The prospective teachers who obtain score in between 27-37 and IQ in between 90-110 are referred as 'Average'. The prospective teachers who get score in between 17-27 and IQ in between

Table 4.4: Classification of Prospective Teachers on the basis of their IQ Scores and Score Range; Number and Percentage of Prospective Teachers on given Classification

S.No	*Classification*	*IQs*	*Score Range*	*N*	*Percentage*
1.	Gifted	130+above	47 above	3	1%
2.	Above average	110-130	37-47	30	10%
3.	Average	90-110	27-37	132	44%
4.	Below average	60-90	17-27	90	30%
5.	Poor	60 below	17 below	45	15%

60-90, are referred as 'Below Average'. Finally, the prospective teachers who gain score below 17 and IQ below 60 are referred as "Poor".

Table 4.4 shows that there are 3 prospective teachers, fall under the classification of 'Gifted' out of the sample of 300 prospective teachers. It means that there are 1% prospective teachers fall under the classification of 'Gifted'. There are 30 prospective teachers, fall under classification of 'Above Average' out of the sample of 300 prospective teachers. It means that there are 10% prospective teachers fall under the classification of 'Above Average'. There are 132 prospective teachers, fall under the classification of 'Average' out of the sample of 300 prospective teachers. It means that there are 44% prospective teachers fall under category of 'Average'. There are 90 prospective teachers, fall under the category of 'Below Average' out of the sample of 300 prospective teachers. It means that there are 30% prospective teachers fall under category of 'Below Average'. Finally, there are 45 prospective teachers, come under the category of 'Poor' out of the sample of 300 prospective teachers. It means that there are 15% prospective teachers come under the category of 'Poor'.

By observing the table, it is evident that there are more prospective teachers in the classification of Average (45%) and less prospective teachers in the classification of Gifted (1%).

From the table 4.5, it is clear that the morality scores obtained through administration of the MAS to the prospective teachers, have been arranged in a systematic manner by grouping them into classes and tabulating them into frequency distribution. It is clear that the MAS includes six dimensions relating to Truthfulness, Dutifulness, God conduct, Helping nature, Self-Control and Honesty.

The analysis is done to know the measures of central tendency, measures of dispersion, skewness and kurtosis. The morality scores obtained by 300 prospective teachers are tabulated into frequency distribution and various descriptive statistics such as mean, median, mode, range standard deviation,

Table 4.5: Frequency Distribution of Scores Morality of Prospective Teachers in Colleges of Education at B.Ed. Level

S.No.	*Class Interval (CI)*	*Mid-Point (MP)*	*Frequency (F)*	*Cumulative Frequency (CF)*	*Cumulative Frequency percentage (CFP)*
1	80-100	90	1	1	0.33
2	101-120	110	4	5	1.67
3	121-140	130	96	101	33.69
4	141-160	150	86	187	62.33
5	161-180	170	83	270	90.00
6	181-200	190	30	300	100.00

N = 300 Range = 153

Mean = 152.537 Standard Deviation = 20.882

Median = 150.000 Skewness = - 0.204

Mode = 135.000 Kurtosis = 1.150

skewness and kurtosis are calculated to understand the nature of distribution. The frequency distribution and values of descriptive statistics are presented in this table.

The mean morality scores of prospective teachers on different dimensions in MAS is 152.537. The values of median and mode are 150.500 and 135.00. The values of median and mode have confirmed that the morality in the MAS among the sample of subjects is lower than M + ½σ and hence, it may be concluded that the prospective teachers have sufficient favourable morality which is required in the teaching – learning process. As the measures of central tendency are in the descending order, the value of mean is greater than median, median is greater than mode and mean is the highest.

The range of the score obtained by the 300 prospective teachers studying in Colleges of Education at B.Ed. level is 153. The standard deviation of morality scores is has been calculated. The SD of morality scores is 20.882.

This shows that there is a normal dispersion in the morality of prospective teachers in the dimensions of Truthfulness, Dutifulness, Good conduct, Helping nature, Self-Control and Honesty.

In the distribution, mean and median fall at different points. So, distribution is said to be skewed. The value of skewness is – 0.204. This value is less than the value of 0.263. So, the distribution is Lepto Kurtic. Therefore, the morality scores are analyzed by employing different parametric statistical methods to test the hypotheses.

From the table 4.6, it is noticed that the Prospective teachers studying in Colleges of Education at B.Ed. level are classified into five types based on score range. Initially, the raw scores obtained by prospective teachers are collected and classified as follows: The prospective teachers who get score more than 190 are classified as 'Excellent'. The prospective teachers who gain score in between 160 and 190 are classified as 'Good' the prospective teachers who obtain score in between 130 and 160 are categorized as 'Average'. The prospective teachers who get score between 100 and 130 are classified as 'Low'. Finally, the prospective teachers who obtain score below the 100 are classified as 'Poor'.

Table shows that there are 24 prospective teachers come under domain of 'Excellent' out of the sample of 300 prospective teachers. It means that there are 8% of prospective teachers come under domain of 'Excellent'. There are 81

Table 4.6: Classification of Prospective Teachers on the basis of their Morality Scores; Number and Percentage of Prospective Teacher on given Classifications.

S.No.	*Classification*	*Score Range*	*Number*	*Percentage*
1	Excellent	190 above	24	8%
2	Good	160-190	81	27%
3	Average	130-160	90	30%
4	Low	100-130	99	33%
5	Poor	100 below	6	2%

prospective teachers come under classification of 'Good' out of the sample of 300 prospective teachers. It means that there are 27% of prospective teachers come under classification of 'Good'. There are 90 prospective teachers come under classification of 'Average' out of the sample of 300 prospective teachers. It means that there are 30% of prospective teachers come under classification of 'Average'.

There are 99 prospective teachers come under category of 'Low' out of the sample of 300 prospective teachers. It means that there are 33% of prospective teachers come under category of 'Low'. Finally, there are 6 prospective teachers come under classification of 'Poor' out of the sample of 300 prospective teachers. It means that there are 2% of prospective teachers come under classification of 'Poor'. By observing the table, it is clear that, there are more prospective teachers come under the category of 'Low' (33%) and there are less prospective teachers come under the category of Poor (2%).

PART II: DIFFERENTIAL ANALYSIS

Influence of Gender, Age, Type of Locality, Type of Management, Educational Qualification, Type of Group, Methods of Teaching-I, Methods of Teaching-II, Community, Parental Income, Parental Education and Marital Status on the Teaching Aptitude of Prospective teachers.

In order to study the significant difference between two or more than two groups of sample, differential studies are made. For this, the mean scores of the two or more number of groups in the sample are compared. In this part, as first step know the significant differences, if any, in the teaching aptitude, intellectual level and morality of prospective teachers due to variation in their gender (male/female), age (21-26 years/ 26-30 years and 30 years above), type of locality (rural/ urban), type of management (government/private), educational qualification (graduation/ post-graduation), type of group (science/arts), methods of teaching-I (Physical Science/ Maths/ Biology/ Social Studies), methods of teaching-II (English/ Telugu), community (OC/ BC/ SC & ST), parental income (₹0-15,000/ ₹15,000-30,000/ ₹30,000 above), parental education (Literate/ Illiterate) and marital status (married/ unmarried), mean and SD for each dimension of teaching aptitude, intellectual level and morality were calculated.

Based on means and SD, T-test is applied to identify the significant differences between the two groups in the variable, wherever more than two groups are involved in a variable, F-test is applied to know the significant difference among these groups. The t-test and F-test are useful in determining the significant difference which is of such magnitude that it cannot be attributed to chance factors or sampling variations. The obtained results are presented in the form of tables and discussed.

One of the major objectives of the study was to find out the significant differences if any, in the prospective teachers' teaching aptitude, intellectual level and morality due to variations in their independent variables. To know the significant differences if any, in the teaching aptitude of prospective teachers due to variations in gender, age, type of locality, type of management, educational qualification, type of group, methods of teaching-I, methods of teaching-II, community, parental income, parental education and marital status, mean and SD have been calculated for each dimension of teaching aptitude of each group in the variable.

Based on the mean and SD, t-values were worked out to know the significant differences between the two groups in the variable, F-values were worked out to know the significant difference among three or more than three groups in the variable. The same procedure was adopted for intellectual level and morality of prospective teachers studying in Colleges of Education at B.Ed. level The obtained values are presented in tables.

Table 4.7 shows that t-values with respect to professional knowledge (3.592), attitude towards children (2.824), and school related information (3.138), educational aspects (2.613) and teaching aptitude (3.859) are significant at 0.01 levels. It indicates that male and female prospective teachers studying in Colleges of Education are significantly differ with respect to professional knowledge, attitude towards children, school related information, educational aspects and teaching aptitude.

Contrary to this, the t-values with respect to social aspects (1.185) and communicative aspects (1.588) are not significant at 0.01 level indicating no variations in the social aspects and communicative aspects of male and female prospective teachers studying in Colleges of Education. Hence, based on teaching aptitude, the formulated hypothesis, "There exists no significant difference in teaching aptitude of prospective teachers due to variation in gender" is rejected. Further, the mean values of male and female prospective teachers reveal that female prospective teachers have more teaching aptitude (27.373) than male prospective teachers (24.313).

Table 4.7: Showing t- values of Teaching Aptitude Scores of Male and Female Prospective teachers:

	Gender				
	Male (N = 147)		*Female (N= 153)*		
Dimensions of Teaching Aptitude	*Mean*	*SD*	*Mean*	*SD*	*t-values*
1.Professional knowledge	5.850	2.445	6.837	2.305	3.592**
2.Attitude towards children	4.361	1.862	5.000	2.058	2.824**
3.School related information	3.946	1.446	4.458	1.377	3.138**
4.Social aspects	5.401	1.854	5.660	1.927	1.185@
5.Educational aspects	3.204	1.414	3.634	1.436	2.613**
6.Communicative aspect	1.551	1.038	1.784	1.477	1.588@
Teaching aptitude	24.313	6.470	27.373	7.254	3.859**

Note: ** = Significant at 0.01 level, * = Significant at 0.05 level & @ = Not significant.

Table 4.8: Showing F-test values of Teaching Aptitude Scores of Prospective Teachers from different Age Groups

Dimensions of Teaching Aptitude	*Age*						
	20-26 years (N = 204)		*26-30 years (N = 49)*		*30 years above (N =47)*		
	Mean	*SD*	*Mean*	*SD*	*Mean*	*SD*	*F-values*
1. Professional knowledge	6.10	2.39	6.51	2.29	7.30	2.42	4.90**
2. Attitude towards children	4.38	2.01	5.12	1.74	5.55	1.79	8.38**
3. School related information	4.08	1.43	4.24	1.28	4.70	1.45	3.62**
4. Social aspects	5.30	1.89	6.18	1.62	5.87	1.94	5.32**
5. Educational aspects	3.31	1.43	3.57	1.47	3.74	1.39	2.02@
6. Communicative aspects.	1.59	1.12	1.82	1.89	1.85	1.11	1.44@
Teaching aptitude.	24.77	6.97	27.45	6.38	29.02	6.75	8.82**

Note: ** = Significant at 0.01 level, * = Significant at 0.05 level & @ = Not Significant

From the above table, it can be concluded that 'gender' has significantly influenced the professional knowledge, attitude towards children, school related information, educational aspects and teaching aptitude of prospective teachers studying in Colleges of Education; where as, it has not significantly influenced the social aspects and communicative aspects of prospective teachers in Teaching Aptitude Test (TAT). Female prospective teachers have more teaching aptitude than male prospective teachers.

The F-values in the table 4.8 with respect to Professional Knowledge (4.906), attitude towards children (8.380), social aspects (5.323) and teaching aptitude (8.822) are significant at 0.01 level. F-value with respect to school related information (3.626) is significant at 0.05 levels. It means, the variations in age of prospective teachers has brought significant differences in their teaching aptitude with respect to professional knowledge, attitude towards children, social aspects and teaching aptitude.

Contrary to this, the F-values with respect to educational aspects (2.024) and communicative aspects (1.44) are not significant at 0.01 levels and 0.05 levels. It means, the variations in the age of prospective teachers have not brought any significant difference in their teaching aptitude with respect to communicative aspects and educational aspects. Hence, based on teaching aptitude, the formulated hypothesis, "There exists no significant difference in teaching aptitude of prospective teachers due to variations in age" is rejected. The mean values also reveal that the prospective teachers with age group of 30 years above have more teaching aptitude (29.02), followed by prospective teachers with age group between 26-30 years (27.45) and age group between 20-26 years (24.77).

From the table, it can be concluded that age has significantly influenced the professional knowledge, attitude towards children, school related information, social aspects and teaching aptitude of prospective teachers; whereas age has not influenced the educational aspects and communicative aspects of prospective teachers in Teaching Aptitude Test (TAT). Age group of 30 years above have more teaching aptitude than age group between 26-30 years and age group between 20-26 years.

From the collected data, it is revealed that the t-values for attitude towards children (3.665), school related information (4.664), social aspects (2.811) and teaching aptitude (3.731) are significant at 0.01 level and the obtained t-value for professional knowledge (2.094) is significant at 0.05 level. It means, the type of locality has significant impact on the attitude towards children, school related information, social aspects and teaching aptitude. It is interesting to note from the mean values that the prospective teachers from rural background have more teaching aptitude (26.905) than the prospective teachers from urban background (23.677). In rural areas, prospective teachers may be influenced by in-service teachers working in and around the villages. Contrary to these prospective teachers, the prospective teachers from urban are better exposed to the outer world through mass media. Also, these prospective teachers may have interest in IT field or Business field for earning more rather than teaching field. As a result, the urban prospective teachers have better chances to exercise their knowledge and skills to get opportunities in banking, public service, management and IT fields. These may be the reasons for having less teaching aptitude when compare with rural prospective teachers.

On the other hand, the obtained t- value for educational aspects (1.745) and communicative aspects (0.315) are not significant at 0.05 level and 0.01 level. It states that prospective teachers' educational aspects and communicative aspects are similar irrespective of their type of locality. Hence, based on the teaching aptitude, the stated hypothesis, "There exists no significant difference in teaching aptitude of prospective teachers due to variation in type of locality" is rejected with respect to professional knowledge, attitude towards children, school related information, social aspects and teaching aptitude.

From the above, it is concluded that type of locality has a significant influence on professional knowledge, attitude towards children, school related information, social aspects and teaching aptitude. And, type of locality has not caused significant difference in educational aspects and communicative aspects.

From the obtained data, it is revealed that the obtained t-values for professional knowledge (2.185), attitude towards children (2.171), social aspects (2.067) and teaching aptitude (2.418) are significant at 0.05 level. It means, the variations in government and private prospective teachers have brought significant differences in their teaching aptitude with respect to professional knowledge, attitude towards children, social aspects, and teaching aptitude. Further, the mean values also reveal that the prospective teachers from private management have more teaching aptitude (27.076) than the prospective teachers from government management (25.083).

Contrary to this, the t-values with respect to school related information (1.347), educational aspects (1.538) and communicative aspects (0.448) are not significant at both levels. It means, the variations in prospective teachers from government and private institutions have not brought any significant difference in their teaching aptitude with respect to school related information, educational aspects and communicative aspects. Hence, the formulated hypothesis, "These exists no significant difference in teaching aptitude of prospective teachers due to variation in type of management" is rejected with respect to professional knowledge, attitude towards children, social aspects and teaching aptitude.

From the above table, it can be concluded that type of management has significantly influenced the professional knowledge, attitude towards children, social aspects and teaching aptitude; whereas type of management has not significantly influenced the school related information, educational aspects and communicative aspects. Further, prospective teachers from private management have more teaching aptitude than the prospective teachers from government management.

The t-values of teaching aptitude of prospective teachers for professional knowledge (3.157), attitude towards children (2.608) are significant at 0.01 level and t-value for teaching aptitude (2.400) is significant at 0.05 level indicating the variations in the teaching aptitude of prospective teachers with varied educational qualification background. It means, the educational qualification of prospective teachers is significantly influencing their teaching aptitude. The mean values reveal that the prospective teachers with post graduation have more teaching aptitude (27.299) than their counter part (25.192).

On the other hand, the variations in the educational qualification have not brought any significant differences in teaching aptitude of prospective teachers with respect to school related information (t-value 0.046), social aspects (t-value 0.046), educational aspects (t-value 0.842) and communicative aspects (t-value 0.760). Hence, the formulated hypothesis, "There exists no significant difference in teaching aptitude due to variation in educational qualification" is rejected, only for professional knowledge, attitude towards children and teaching aptitude.

From the data, it is concluded that educational qualification has significant impact on professional knowledge, attitude towards children and teaching aptitude; whereas the variations in the educational qualification have not brought any significant differences in teaching aptitude of prospective teachers with respect to school related information, social aspects, educational aspects and communicative aspects. Based on mean values, prospective teachers with post-graduation have more teaching aptitude than prospective teachers with graduation.

It is revealed that the obtained t-values for professional knowledge (2.077), social aspects (2.079) and educational aspects (2.360) are significant at 0.05 level. And also, the obtained t-values for attitude towards children (2.806), communicative aspects (2.997) and teaching aptitude (3.439) are significant at 0.01 level. It means, the variations in prospective teachers from Science and Arts back ground have brought significant differences in their teaching aptitude with respect to professional knowledge, attitude towards children, social aspects, educational aspects, communicative aspects and teaching aptitude. The mean values also indicate that the prospective teachers from science group background have more teaching aptitude (27.295) than the prospective teachers from arts group background (24.526).

Contrary to this, the t-values with respect to school related information (1.599) is not significant at 0.05 and 0.01 levels. It means, the variations in prospective teachers from Science group background and Arts group background have not brought significant differences in teaching aptitude of prospective teachers with respect to school related information. Hence, the formulated hypothesis, "There exists no significant difference in teaching aptitude of prospective teachers due to variation in type of group" is rejected for professional knowledge, attitude towards children, social aspects, educational aspects, communicative aspects and teaching aptitude.

From data, it is concluded that the variations in the type of group have brought significant difference in teaching aptitude of prospective teachers with respect to professional knowledge, attitude towards children, social aspects, educational aspects, communicative aspects and teaching aptitude; where as the variations in the type of group have not brought significant difference in teaching aptitude of prospective teachers with respect to school related information.

Table 4.9 demonstrates that the mean and standard deviation scores of prospective teachers with respect to professional knowledge, attitude towards children, school related information, social aspects, educational aspects, communicative aspects and teaching aptitude, based on their methods of teaching I and calculated F- values.

From the table, it is revealed that the obtained F-values with respect to professional knowledge (0.095), attitude towards children (0.043), school related information (0.461), social aspects (0.960), educational aspects (0.947), communicative aspects (0.509) and teaching aptitude (0.188) are not significant at both levels. It means, the variations in prospective teachers with different methods of teaching I i.e., Physical Science, Mathematics, Biological Science and Social Studies have not brought any significant differences in their teaching aptitude with respect to professional knowledge, attitude towards children, school related information, social aspects, educational aspects, communicative aspects and teaching aptitude.

Further, the mean values also indicate that the prospective teachers with methods of teaching I i.e., Biological Science have more teaching aptitude (26.20), followed by the prospective teachers with different methods of teaching I i.e., Mathematics (25.16), Physical Science (25.38) and Social Studies (26.02). Hence, the formulated hypothesis, "There exists no significant difference in teaching aptitude of prospective teachers due to variation in methods of teaching

Table 4.9: Showing F-test values of Teaching Aptitude Scores of Prospective Teachers with different Methods of Teaching I

Dimension of Teaching Aptitude	*Methods of Teaching-I*								
	Physical science (N=40)		*Mathematics (N=60)*		*Biological science (N=60)*		*Social studies (N=148)*		
	Mean	*SD*	*Mean*	*SD*	*Mean*	*SD*	*Mean*	*SD*	*F-values*
1. Professional knowledge	6.47	2.520	6.21	2.663	6.38	2.259	6.36	2.374	0.095@
2. Attitude towards children	4.65	2.340	4.62	2.095	4.68	1.756	4.72	1.938	0.043@
3. School related information	4.28	1.360	4.15	1.486	4.03	1.560	4.28	1.375	0.461@
4. Social aspects	5.07	2.114	5.50	2.333	5.63	1.853	5.63	1.645	0.960@
5. Educational aspects	3.28	1.597	3.23	1.367	3.65	1.424	3.44	1.415	0.947@
6. Communicative aspects	1.63	1.111	1.75	1.072	1.82	1.812	1.59	1.126	0.509@
Teaching aptitude	25.38	8.036	25.46	7.836	26.20	7.307	26.02	6.313	0.188@

Note: ** = Significant at 0.01 level, * = Significant at 0.05 level & @ =Not Significant

I" is accepted for professional knowledge, attitude towards children, school related information, social aspects, educational aspects, communicative aspects and teaching aptitude.

From the table, it can be concluded that the variations in the methods of teaching I have not brought any significant difference in teaching aptitude of prospective teachers with respect to professional knowledge, Attitude towards children, school related information, social aspects, educational aspects, communications aspects and teaching aptitude. Based on mean values, the prospective teachers with methods of teaching I i.e., Biological Science have more teaching aptitude than the corresponding methods of teaching I i.e Mathematics, Physical Science and Social Studies chosen by prospective teachers.

Table 4.10 depicts the mean and standard deviation of teaching aptitude scores of prospective teachers with respect to professional knowledge, attitude towards children, school related information, social aspects, educational aspects, communicative aspects and teaching aptitude, based on their methods of teaching-II and calculated F- values. The mean difference in the teaching aptitude score of prospective teachers for professional knowledge, attitude towards children, school related information, social aspects, educational aspects, communicative aspects and teaching aptitude, have not significantly varied as the calculated t-values (0.946, 1.015, 1.145, 0.174, 0.549, 0.263 and 0.825 respectively) are less than the table value. It means, the teaching aptitude of prospective teachers has not influenced by the variation in the methods of teaching II chosen by prospective teachers.

Table 4.10: Showing t-test values of Teaching Aptitude Scores of Prospective Teachers with different Methods of Teaching II

Dimensions of Teaching Aptitude	*Methods of Teaching-II*				
	English (N=139)		*Telugu (N=161)*		
	Mean	*SD*	*Mean*	*SD*	*t-values*
1. Professional knowledge	6.496	2.514	6.230	2.339	0.946@
2. Attitude towards children	4.813	2.093	4.578	1.890	1.015@
3. School related information	4.309	1.517	4.118	1.353	1.145@
4. Social aspects	5.554	1.950	5.516	1.849	0.174@
5. Educational aspects	3.374	1.461	3.466	1.423	0.549@
6. Communicative aspects	1.691	1.092	1.652	1.433	0.263@
Teaching aptitude	26.237	7.480	25.559	6.639	0.825@

Note: ** = Significant at 0.01 level, * = Significant at 0.05 level & @ = Not Significant

Further, the mean values also indicate that the prospective teachers with methods of teaching-II i.e., English, have more teaching aptitude (26.237) than the prospective teachers with methods of teaching-II i.e., Telugu (25.559). Hence, the formulated hypothesis, "There exists no significant difference in teaching aptitude of prospective teachers due to variation in methods of teaching-II" is accepted for professional knowledge, attitude towards children, school related information, social aspects, educational aspects, communicative aspects and teaching aptitude.

From the table, it can be concluded that the variable, methods of teaching-II has not influenced the teaching aptitude of prospective teachers with respect to the said dimensions. Based on mean values, the prospective teachers with methods of teaching-II i.e., English have more teaching aptitude than the prospective teachers with methods of teaching-II i.e., Telugu.

It is revealed from data that the obtained F-values with respect to professional knowledge (0.401), attitude towards children (1.641), and school related information (0.980), social aspects (0.737), educational aspects (0.144), communicative aspects (0.292) and teaching aptitude (0.209) are not significant at both levels. It means, the variations in prospective teachers with community background have not brought any significant differences in their teaching aptitude with respect to professional knowledge, attitude towards children, school related information, social aspects, educational aspects, communicative aspects and teaching aptitude.

Hence, the formulated hypothesis, "There exists no significant difference in teaching aptitude of prospective teachers due to variation in community" is accepted for professional knowledge, attitude towards children, school related information, social aspects, educational aspects, communicative aspects and teaching aptitude.

The mean values also indicate that the prospective teachers with BC community background have more teaching aptitude (26.11), followed by prospective teachers with SC and ST community background (25.55). But, it is important to note that the teaching aptitude of prospective teachers with OC community background is approximately similar to the teaching aptitude of prospective teachers with BC community background.

From data collected, it is concluded that the variations in the community have not brought significant difference in teaching aptitude of prospective teachers. As per the mean values, the prospective teachers with OC and BC community backgrounds are approximately similar in their teaching aptitude. The prospective teachers with BC community background have more teaching aptitude than the prospective teachers with SC and ST community background.

F- values with respect to professional knowledge (0.122), attitude towards children (0.236), school related information (1.848), social aspects (0.578), educational aspects (0.845) and teaching aptitude (1.146) are not significant at both levels. It means, the variable, parental Income has not significant impact on the professional knowledge, attitude towards children, school related information, social aspects, educational aspects and teaching aptitude. It is interesting to note from the mean values that the prospective teachers with parental Income ₹30,000 above have more teaching aptitude (27.95), followed by prospective teachers with parental Income ₹15,000-30,000 (25.39) and prospective teachers with parental income ₹0-15,000 (25.96).

On the other hand, the obtained F-values for communicative aspects (4.878) is significant at 0.01 level. It states that parental Income has significantly influenced teaching aptitude of prospective teachers with respect to communicative aspects. Hence, the formulated hypothesis, "There exists no significant difference in teaching aptitude of prospective teachers due to variation in parental Income" is accepted for professional knowledge, attitude towards children, school related information, social aspects, educational aspects and teaching aptitude.

It is concluded that parental Income has not significantly influenced the professional knowledge, attitude towards children, school related information, social aspects, educational aspects and teaching aptitude; whereas parental Income has significantly influenced the communicative aspects of prospective teachers in TAT. Prospective teachers with parental income of ₹30,000 above/annum have more teaching aptitude than the prospective teachers with Parental income ₹15,000-30,000 and prospective teachers with parental income ₹0-15,000.

Based on Parental education of prospective teachers, mean and standard deviation scores in professional knowledge, attitude towards children, school related information, social aspects, educational aspects, communicative aspects and teaching aptitude are presented with calculated t-values in the table 4.11.

The stated hypothesis, "There exists no significant difference in teaching aptitude of prospective teachers due to variation in parental education" is rejected with respect to attitude towards children, social aspects, educational aspects and teaching aptitude, as the obtained t- values for attitude towards children (4.723), social aspects (5.088) and teaching aptitude (4.417) are significant at 0.01 level

Table 4.11: Showing t-test values of Teaching Aptitude Scores of Prospective Teachers with Parental Education Backgrounds

Dimensions of Teaching Aptitude	*Parental Education* Literate (N=134) *Mean*	*SD*	Illiterate (N=166) *Mean*	*SD*	*t-values*
1. Professional knowledge	6.657	2.551	6.108	2.289	1.937@
2. Attitude towards children	5.269	1.905	4.217	1.933	4.723**
3. School related information	4.373	1.553	4.072	1.315	1.784@
4. Social aspects	6.127	1.797	5.054	1.838	5.088**
5. Educational aspects	3.634	1.406	3.253	1.447	2.305*
6. Communicative aspects	1.769	1.496	1.590	1.081	1.157@
Teaching aptitude	27.828	7.141	24.295	6.562	4.417**

Note: ** = Significant at 0.01 level, * = Significant at 0.05 level and @ = Not Significant

and educational aspects (2.305) is significant at 0.05 level. It implies that parental education has significantly influenced the teaching aptitude with respect to attitude towards children, social aspects, educational aspects and teaching aptitude.

Contrary to this, the t-values for professional knowledge (1.937), school related information (1.784) and communicative aspects (1.157) are not significant at both levels. It means, prospective teachers have not differed in their professional knowledge, school related information and communicative aspects due to variation in their parental education. The mean value of prospective teachers with literate parents (27.878) is greater than mean value of the prospective teachers with illiterate parents (24.295). It implies that prospective teachers with literate parents have more teaching aptitude than the prospective teachers with illiterate parents.

It can be summed up that the prospective teachers' teaching aptitude with respect to attitude towards children, social aspects, educational aspects and teaching aptitude are significantly influenced by the parental education. On the other hand, the prospective teachers' teaching aptitude with respect to professional knowledge, school related information and communicative aspects are not significantly influenced by the parental education. Further, it also implies that prospective teachers with literate parents have more teaching aptitude than the prospective teachers with illiterate parents.

The t-values for professional knowledge (4.384), attitude towards children (3.975), social aspects (4.311) and teaching aptitude (4.694) are significant at 0.01 level and F-value for school related information (4.311) is significant at 0.05 level. It means, marital status has significant influence on professional knowledge, attitude towards children, social aspects and teaching aptitude.

On the contrary, the F-values for educational aspects (1.010) and communicative aspects (1.074) are not significant at both levels. It means, marital status has not significant influence on educational aspects and communicative aspects. Further, it is observed through the mean values that unmarried prospective teachers have more teaching aptitude (27.152) than the married prospective teachers (23.156). Thus, the stated hypothesis, "There exists no significant difference in prospective teachers' teaching aptitude due to variation in marital status" is rejected for professional knowledge, attitude towards children, school related information, social aspects and teaching aptitude.

From the above, it can be concluded that prospective teachers' professional knowledge, attitude towards children, school related information, social aspects and teaching aptitude have been significantly influenced by their marital status, where as, prospective teachers' educational aspects and communicative aspects have not been significantly influenced by their marital status. The unmarried prospective teachers have more teaching aptitude than the married prospective teachers.

Influence of Gender, Age, Type of Locality, Type of Management, Educational Qualification, Type of Group, Methods of Teaching-I, Methods of Teaching-II, Community, Parental Income, Parental Education and Marital Status on the intellectual level of Prospective teachers.

One of the major objectives of the study was to find out the significant differences if any, in the prospective teachers' intellectual level due to variations in their independent variables To know the significant differences if any, in intellectual level of prospective teachers due to variations in gender, age, type of locality, type of management, educational qualification, type of group, methods of teaching-I, methods of teaching-II, community, parental income, parental education and marital status, mean and SD have been calculated for each dimension of intellectual level of each group in the variable.

Based on the mean and SD, t-values were worked out to know the significant differences between the two groups in the variable, F-values were worked out to know the significant difference among three or more than three groups in the variable. The same procedure was adopted for teaching aptitude and morality of prospective teachers. The Influence of Gender, Age, Type of Locality, Type of Management, Educational Qualification, Type of Group, Methods of Teaching-I, Methods of Teaching-II, Community, Parental Income, Parental Education and Marital Status on the intellectual level of Prospective teachers has been tested and explained here below.

Table 4.12 shows that t- values with respect to analogy (3.442), syllogism (2.843) and overall intellectual level (3.047) are significant at 0.01 level and t-value with respect to number series (2.020) is significant at 0.05 level. It indicates that male and female prospective teachers studying in Colleges of Education are significantly differ with respect to analogy, syllogism, number series and overall intellectual level. Contrary to this, the t-values with respect to word meaning (0.581), classification (0.011), and code transformation (0.933) are not significant at 0.01 level and 0.05 level indicating no variations in word

Table 4.12: Showing t-test values of Intellectual Level Scores of Male and Female Prospective teachers

Dimensions of Intellectual Level	*Gender*				
	Male (N=147)		*Female (N=153)*		
	Mean	*SD*	*Mean*	*SD*	*t-values*
1. Word meaning	2.619	1.655	2.510	1.601	0.581@
2. Analogy	4.656	1.946	3.863	1.893	3.442**
3. Classification	4.769	1.987	4.771	1.901	0.011@
4. Number series	6.102	2.725	5.471	2.686	2.020*
5. Code transformation	5.619	2.776	5.333	2.515	0.933@
6. Syllogism	4.878	1.803	4.307	1.666	2.843**
Intellectual Level	28.612	6.750	26.255	6.645	3.047**

Note:** = Significant at 0.01 level, * = Significant at 0.05 level and @ = Not Significant

meaning, classification and code transformation. Hence, based intellectual level, the formulated hypothesis, "There exists no significant difference in intellectual level of prospective teachers due to variation in gender is rejected.

Further, the mean values of male and female prospective teachers reveal that male prospective teachers have more intellectual level (28.612) than female prospective teachers (26.255).From the above table, it can be concluded that gender has significantly influenced the ability of analogy, syllogism, number series and overall intellectual level of prospective teachers studying in colleges of education; where as, gender has not significantly influenced the ability of word meaning, classification and code transformation of prospective teachers TGI.

The F-values with respect to analogy (8.773), number series (9.928) and overall intellectual level (14.439) are significant at 0.01 level. F-value with respect to classification (3.394) and code transformation (3.638) are significant at 0.05 level. It means, the variations in age of prospective teachers has brought significant differences in their intellectual level with respect to analogy, number series, classification, code transformation and overall intellectual level.

Contrary to this, the F-values with respect to word meaning (1.340) and syllogism (0.862) are not significant at 0.01 level and 0.05 level. It means, the variations in the age of prospective teachers have not brought any significant difference in their intellectual level with respect to word meaning and syllogism. Hence, based on overall intellectual level, the formulated hypothesis, "There exists no significant difference in intellectual level of prospective teachers due to variation in age" is rejected. The mean values also reveal that the prospective teachers with 30 years above of age group have more intellectual level (32.04), followed by prospective teachers with 26-30 years age group (27.29) and 20-26 years age group (26.37).

From the above table, it can be concluded that age has significantly influenced the ability in analogy, number series, classification, code transformation and overall intellectual level of prospective teachers studying in Colleges of Education at B.Ed level; where as, age has not influenced the ability in word meaning and syllogism of prospective teachers in Test of General Intelligence (TGI). Age group of 30 years above has more intellectual level than age group between 26-30 years and age group between 20-26 years.

The obtained t-value for analogy (3.721) is significant at 0.01 level and t-value for overall intellectual level (2.079) is significant at 0.05 level. It means, the type of locality has significant impact on the ability of analogy and overall intellectual level. It is important to note from the mean values that the prospective teachers from the rural background have more intellectual level (27.980) than the prospective teachers from urban background (23.677). There may be certain hereditary factors that impact on rural prospective teachers' intelligence. As a result, the urban prospective teachers have lower intellectual level than rural prospective teachers.

On the other hand, the obtained t-values for the ability on word meaning (0.156) classification (0.056), number series (`0.866), code transformation (1.669) and syllogism (0.228) are not significant at 0.05 level and 0.01 level. It indicates that the prospective teachers' ability on word meaning, classification, number series, code transformation and syllogism are similar irrespective of their type of locality. Hence, based on the overall intellectual level, the stated hypothesis, "There exacts no significant difference in intellectual level of prospective teachers due to variation in type of locality" is rejected with respect to analogy and overall intellectual level.

From the above, it is concluded that type of locality has a significant influence on analogy and overall intellectual level. And, type of locality has not caused significant difference in word meaning, classification, number series, code transformation and syllogism. Further prospective teachers of rural background have more intellectual level than the prospective teachers of urban back ground.

The obtained t-values for analogy (2.319) and syllogism (2.197) are significant at 0.05 level and the obtained t-values for number series (3.212), code transformation and overall intellectual level (4.087) are significant at 0.01 level. It means, the variations in prospective teachers from government and private management have brought significant differences in their intellectual level with respect to analogy, number series, code transformation, syllogism and overall intellectual level. Further, the mean values also reveal that the prospective teachers from private management have more intellectual level (29.328) than the prospective teachers from government management (26.149).

Contrary to this, the t-values with respect to word meaning and classification are not significant at 0.05 level and 0.01 levels. It means, the variations in prospective teachers from government and private institutions have not brought any significant difference in their intellectual level with respect to word meaning and classifications. Hence, the formulated hypothesis, "There exists no significant difference in intellectual level of prospective teachers due to variation in type of management" is rejected with respect to analogy, number series, code transformation syllogism and intellectual level.

From the above table, it can be concluded that type of management has significantly influenced the analogy, number series, code transformation, syllogism and overall intellectual level; whereas type of management has not significantly influenced the word meaning and classification. Further, prospective teachers from private management have more intellectual level than the prospective teachers from government management.

The t-values of intellectual level of prospective teachers, for word meaning (2.844), number series (2.655) and overall intellectual level (3.274) are significant at 0.01 level. It indicates that variations in the educational qualification have brought significant differences in intellectual level of prospective teachers with respect to word meaning, number series and overall intellectual level. The mean values reveal that the prospective teachers with post graduation have more intellectual level (29.278) than their counterpart (26.517).

On the other hand, the variations in the educational qualification have not brought any significant differences in intellectual level of prospective teachers with respect to analogy (F-value: 1.763), classification (t-value: 1.838), code transformation (t-value 1.109) and syllogism (t-value: 0.283). Hence, the formulated hypothesis, "There exists no significant difference in intellectual level of prospective teachers due to variation in educational qualification" is rejected only for word meaning, number series and overall intellectual level.

From the data collected, it is concluded that the variations in the educational qualification have brought significant difference in intellectual level of prospective teachers for word meaning, number series and overall intellectual level; where as the variations in the educational qualification have not brought any significant difference in intellectual level of prospective teachers with respect to analogy, classification, code transformation and syllogism. Based on mean values, prospective teachers with post graduation have more intellectual level than the prospective teachers with graduation.

The obtained t-values for analogy (1.984), code transformation (2.198) and syllogism (2.164) are significant are 0.05 level. And also, the obtained t-values for number series (4.110) and intellectual level (2.983) are significant at 0.01 level. It indicates that the variations in prospective teachers from Science and Arts group background have brought significant differences in their intellectual level with respect to analogy, number series, code transformation, syllogism and intellectual level. The mean values also indicate that the prospective teachers from Science group background have more intellectual level (28.596) than the prospective teachers from Arts group background (26.286).

Contrary to this, the t-values with respect to word meaning (0.407) and classification (1.349) are not significant at both levels. It means, the variations in prospective teachers from Science and Arts background have not brought any significant difference in intellectual level of prospective teachers with respect

Table 4.13: Showing t-test values of Intellectual Level Scores of Prospective Teachers of Methods of Teaching-I

Dimension of intellectual level	*Methods of Teaching -I*								
	Physical Science (N=40)		*Mathematics (N=52)*		*Biological Science (N=60)*		*Social Studies (N=148)*		
	Mean	*SD*	*Mean*	*SD*	*Mean*	*SD*	*Mean*	*SD*	*F-values*
1. Word meaning	2.30	1.52	2.73	1.923	2.63	1.807	2.55	1.439	0.569@
2. Analogy	3.80	2.100	4.56	1.955	4.73	1.788	4.04	1.924	2.963*
3. Classification	5.18	2.072	4.71	2.142	4.92	1.801	4.62	1.869	0.993@
4. Number series	5.82	3.024	6.48	2.784	6.38	2.381	5.28	2.640	3.913**
5. Code transformation	5.38	2.790	5.52	2.538	6.52	2.255	5.06	2.682	4.454**
6. Syllogism	4.55	1.564	4.19	1.851	4.57	1.755	4.74	1.752	1.272@
Intellectual Level	27.02	6.732	28.19	7.338	29.75	6.485	26.29	6.462	4.088**

Note: ** = Significant at 0.01 level
* = Significant at 0.05 level
@ = Not Significant

to word meaning and classification. Hence, the formulated hypothesis, "There exists no significant difference in intellectual level of prospective teachers due to variation in type of group" is rejected for analogy, number series, code transformation, syllogism and intellectual level. From the table, it can be concluded that the variations in the type of group have brought significant difference in intellectual level of prospective teachers with respect to analogy, number series, code transformation, syllogism and intellectual level; whereas the variations in the type of group have not brought any significant difference in intellectual level of prospective teachers with respect to word meaning and classification.

Table 4.13 depicts the mean and standard deviation of intellectual level scores of prospective teachers with respect to word meaning, analogy, classification, number series, code transformation, syllogism and overall intellectual level based on their methods of teaching I and calculated F-values.

From the table, it is revealed that the obtained F-values with respect to number series (3.913), code transformation (4.454) and overall intellectual level (4.088) are significant at 0.01 level and F-values with respect to analogy (2.963) is significant at 0.05 level. It means, the variations in prospective teachers with different methods of teaching-I i.e., Physical Science, Mathematics, Biological Science and Social Studies have brought significant differences in their intellectual level with respect to analogy, classification, number series, code transformation, syllogism and overall intellectual level. Further, the mean values also indicate that the prospective teachers with methods of teaching-I i.e., Biological Science have more intellectual level (29.75), followed by the prospective teachers with different methods of teaching-I i.e., Mathematics (28.19), Physical Science (27.02) and Social Studies (26.29).

On the other hand, F-values with respect to word meaning (0.569), classification (0.993) and syllogism (1.272) are not significant at both levels. It means, the variations in prospective teachers with different methods of teaching I i.e., Physical Science, Mathematics, Biological Science and Social Studies have not brought any significant difference in their intellectual level with respect to word meaning, classification and syllogism. Hence, the formulated hypothesis, "There exists no significant difference in intellectual level of prospective teachers due to variation in methods of teaching I" is rejected for analogy, number series, code transformation and overall intellectual level.

From the table, it can be concluded that the variations in the methods of teaching I have brought significant difference in intellectual level of prospective teachers with respect to analogy, number series, code transformation and overall intellectual level; whereas the variations in the methods of teaching I have not brought any significant difference in intellectual level of prospective teachers with respect to word meaning, classification and syllogism. Based on mean values, the prospective teachers with methods of teaching I i.e., Biological science have more intellectual level than the corresponding methods of teaching I i.e., Mathematics, Physical Science and Social Studies chosen by prospective teachers.

Table 4.14 demonstrates the mean and SD of intellectual level scores of prospective teachers with regard to word meaning, analogy, classification, number series, code transformation, syllogism and overall intellectual level, based on methods of teaching II and calculated t- values.

The formulated hypothesis, "There exists no significant difference in intellectual level of prospective teachers due to variation in methods of teaching-II" is accepted with respect to word meaning, classification, code transformation and overall intellectual level, as the calculated 't' values for word meaning, classification, code transformation and overall intellectual level (0.958, 1.120, 1.457 and 1.763 respectively) based on their teaching aptitude scores are not significant at both levels.

Table 4.14: showing t-test values of Intellectual Level Scores of Prospective Teachers of Methods of Teaching-II

Dimensions of Intellectual level	*Methods of Teaching-II*				
	English (N=139)		*Telugu (N=161)*		
	Mean	*SD*	*Mean*	*SD*	*t-values*
1. Word meaning	2.468	1.485	2.646	1.739	0.958@
2. Analogy	4.669	2.074	3.863	1.764	3.592**
3. Classification	4.906	2.095	4.652	1.795	1.120@
4. Number series	6.115	2.636	5.491	2.764	2.000*
5. Code transformation	5.712	2.631	5.267	2.649	1.457@
6. Syllogism	4.281	1.803	4.851	1.673	2.825**
Intellectual Level	28.151	6.763	26.770	6.765	1.763@

Note: ** = Significant at 0.01 level,* = Significant at 0.05 level & @ = Not Significant

On the other hand, the formulated hypothesis is rejected with respect to analogy and syllogism, as their t-values (3.592, 2.825 respectively), based on their teaching aptitude scores are significant at 0.01 level and for number series (2.000), is significant at 0.05 level. It means, the intellectual level of prospective teachers differ due to variation in methods of teaching II. Further, the mean values also reveal that the prospective teachers with methods of teaching II i.e., English, have more intellectual level (28.151) than the prospective teachers with methods of teaching II i.e. Telugu (26.770).

From the table, it can be concluded that the methods of teaching II has influenced the intellectual level of prospective teachers with respect to analogy, number series and syllogism; whereas the methods of teaching II has not influenced the intellectual level of prospective teachers with regard to word meaning, classification, code transformation and overall intellectual level. As per the mean values, the prospective teachers with English as methods of teaching II, have more intellectual level than the prospective teachers with Telugu as methods of teaching-II.

The obtained F-values with respect to word meaning (0.833), analogy (1.143), classification (0.298), number series (2.789), code transformation (0.451), syllogism (2.295) and overall intellectual level (2.025) are not significant at both levels. It indicates that the variations in prospective teachers with community background have not brought any significant difference in their intellectual level with respect to word meaning, analogy classification, number series, code transformation, syllogism and overall intellectual level. The mean values indicate that the prospective teachers with OC community background have more intellectual level (28.80), followed by the prospective teachers with BC community background (27.40) and prospective teachers with SC and ST community background (26.69).

Hence, the formulated hypothesis, "There exists into significant difference in intellectual level of prospective teachers due to variation in community" is accepted for word meaning, analogy, classification, number series, code transformation, syllogism and overall intellectual level.

From the table, it can be concluded that the variations in community have not brought any significant difference in intellectual level of prospective teachers with respect to word meaning, analogy classification, number series, code transformation, syllogism and overall intellectual level. As per mean values, prospective teachers with OC community background have more intellectual level, followed by prospective teachers with BC and SC&ST community background.

The obtained F-values with respect to analogy (0.208), classification (0.758), number series (2.068), code transformation (1.789), syllogism (0.737) and intellectual level (2.236) are not significant at both levels. It means parental income has not significantly influenced the intellectual level of prospective teachers with respect to analogy, classification, number series, code transformation, syllogism and overall intellectual level. Further, the mean values also reveal that the prospective teachers with parental income ₹30,000 above, have more intellectual level (30.30), followed by prospective teachers with parental income ₹15,000-30,000 (27.57) and prospective teachers with parental income ₹0-15,000 (26.95).

Contrary to this, the F-value with respect to word meaning (3.070) is significant at 0.05 level. It means parental income has significantly influenced the intellectual level of prospective teachers with respect to word meaning. Hence, the formulated hypothesis, "There exists no significant difference in intellectual level of prospective teachers due to variation in parental income" is accepted for analogy, classification, number series, code transformation, syllogism and intellectual level. From the above table, it can be concluded that parental income has not significantly influenced the analogy, classification, number series, code transformation, syllogism and intellectual level of prospective teaches; whereas the parental income has significantly influenced the word meaning ability of prospective teachers in TGT. Prospective teachers with parental income of₹30,000 above have more intellectual level than the prospective teachers with parental income ₹15,000-30,000 and prospective teachers with parental income ₹0-15,000.

Table 4.15 presents the mean and SD of intellectual level scores of prospective teachers' with regard to word meaning, analogy, classification, number series, code transformation, syllogism and intellectual level, based on parental education background community background and calculated F-values.

From table 4.15, it clear that the stated hypothesis, "There exists no significant difference in intellectual level of prospective teachers due to variation in parental education" is rejected with respect to analogy, number series, code transformation and overall intellectual level, as the obtained t-values for analogy (3.227), number series (3.231), code transformation (2.795) and overall intellectual level (4.114) are significant at 0.01 level. It implies that the parental education has significantly influenced the teaching aptitude with respect to analogy, number series, code transformation and overall intellectual level.

Table 4.15: Showing *t*-test values of Intellectual Level Scores of Prospective Teachers with Parental Education Background

	Parental Education				
	Literate (N=134)		*Illiterate (N=166)*		
Dimensions of Intellectual Level	*Mean*	*SD*	*Mean*	*SD*	*t-values*
1. Word meaning	2.627	1.495	2.512	1.728	0.617@
2. Analogy	4.634	1.895	3.916	1.946	3.227**
3. Classification	4.993	1.953	4.590	1.917	1.788@
4. Number series	6.328	2.479	5.337	2.830	3.231**
5. Code transformation	5.933	2.296	5.102	2.851	2.795**
6. Syllogism	4.612	1.606	4.566	1.870	0.227@
Intellectual Level	29.127	5.930	26.024	7.131	4.114**

Note: ** = Significant at 0.01 level, * = Significant at 0.05 level & @ = Not Significant

Contrary to this, the obtained t-values for word meaning (0.617), classification (1.788) and syllogism (0.227) are not significant at both levels. It means, prospective teachers have not differed in their word meaning, classification and syllogism due to variation in parental education. The mean value of prospective teachers with literate parents (29.127) is greater than the mean value of prospective teachers with illiterate parents (26.024). It implies that prospective teachers with literate parents have more intellectual level than the prospective teachers with illiterate parents.

It can be summed up that the prospective teachers' intellectual level with respect to analogy, number series, code transformation and overall intellectual level are significantly influenced by the parental education. On the other hand, the prospective teachers' intellectual level with respect to word meaning, classification and syllogism are not significantly influenced by the parental education. Further, it also implies that prospective teachers with literate parents have more intellectual level than the prospective teachers with illiterate parents.

The obtained t-values for word meaning (1.052), classification (0.381), number series (1.944), code transformation (0.890) and syllogism (1.869) are not significant at both levels. It means, marital status has not significantly influenced the word meaning, classification, number series, code transformation and syllogism.

On the contrary, the t-values for analogy (3.610) and intellectual level (2.925) are significant at 0.01 level. It means, marital status has significant influence on analogy and overall intellectual level. Further, it is observed through the mean values that the unmarried prospective teachers have more intellectual level (28.201) than the married prospective teachers (25.729). Thus, the stated hypothesis, "There exists no significant difference in intellectual level of prospective teachers due to variation in marital status" is rejected only for analogy and overall intellectual level.

From the above, it can be concluded that the prospective teachers' analogy and overall intellectual level have been significantly influenced by their marital status; where as, prospective teachers' word meaning, classification, number series, code transformation and syllogism have not been significantly influenced by their marital status. The unmarried prospective teachers have more intellectual level than the married prospective teachers.

Influence of Gender, Age, Type of Locality, Type of Management, Educational Qualification, Type of Group, Methods of Teaching-I, Methods of Teaching-II, Community, Parental Income, Parental Education and Marital Status on the morality of Prospective teachers.

One of the major objectives of the study was to find out the significant differences if any, in the prospective teachers' morality due to variations in their independent variables. To know the significant differences if any, in the teaching aptitude of prospective teachers due to variations in gender, age, type of locality, type of management, educational qualification, type of group, methods of teaching-I, methods of teaching-II, community, parental income, parental education and marital status, mean and SD have been calculated for each dimension of morality of each group in the variable. Based on the mean and SD, t-values were worked out to know the significant differences between the two groups in the variable, F-values were worked out to know the significant difference among three or more than three groups in the variable. The same procedure was adopted for intellectual level and teaching aptitude of prospective teachers.

The influence of Gender, Age, Type of Locality, Type of Management, Educational Qualification, Type of Group, Methods of Teaching I, Methods of Teaching II, Community, Parental Income, Parental Education and Marital Status on the morality of Prospective teachers has been tested and explained further here..

Table 4.16 reveals that the 't'-values with respect to helping nature (3.742) and morality (3.026) are significant at 0.01 level and 't' – values with respect to truthfulness (2.238) and honesty (2.273) are significant at 0.05 level. It denotes that male and female prospective teachers studying in Colleges of Education are significantly differed with respect to helping nature truthfulness, honesty and overall morality.

Contrary to this, the t- values with respect to dutifulness (1.877), good conduct (1.354) and self-control (1.895) are not significant at 0.01 level and 0.05 level. It indicates that there are no variations in dutifulness, good conduct and self-control. Hence, based on overall morality, the formulated hypothesis, "There exists no significant difference in Morality of prospective teachers due to variation in gender" is rejected. Further, the mean values of male and female prospective teachers reveal that female prospective teachers have more morality (156.052) than male prospective teachers (148.878).

From the above table, it is concluded that gender has significantly influenced the helping nature, truthfulness, honesty and overall morality of prospective teachers studying in Colleges of Education; whereas, it has not significantly

Table 4.16: Showing t-test values of Morality Scores of Male and Female Prospective teachers

Dimensions of Morality	*Gender*				*t- values*
	Male (N=147)		*Female (N=153)*		
	Mean	*SD*	*Mean*	*SD*	
1. Truthfulness	26.211	4.834	27.471	4.916	2.238*
2. Dutifulness	24.932	4.449	25.941	4.863	1.877@
3. Good Conduct	23.551	3.709	24.163	4.118	1.354@
4. Helping Nature	24.646	5.147	26.824	4.923	3.742**
5. Self-Control	23.612	4.013	24.484	3.948	1.895@
6. Honesty	25.925	4.626	27.170	4.859	2.273*
Morality	148.878	20.417	156.052	20.651	3.026**

Note:** = Significant at 0.01 level, * = Significant at 0.05 level & @ = Not Significant

Table 4.17: Showing F-test values of Morality Scores of Prospective Teachers with different Age Groups

Dimensions of Morality	*Age*						
	20-26 years (N=204)		*26-30 years (N=49)*		*30 years above (N=47)*		
	Mean	*SD*	*Mean*	*SD*	*Mean*	*SD*	*F-values*
1. Truthfulness	26.09	4.73	27.80	5.18	29.19	4.48	9.127**
2. Dutifulness	24.71	4.48	26.22	4.82	27.83	4.03	9.754**
3. Good Conduct	23.13	3.62	24.55	4.06	26.32	3.95	14.592**
4. Helping Nature	24.76	5.06	27.61	4.29	28.13	5.02	12.849**
5. Self-Control	23.52	4.11	24.45	3.48	25.98	3.33	7.8034**
6. Honesty	25.86	5.00	28.06	4.00	28.02	3.75	7.013**
Morality	148.08	19.71	158.69	19.86	165.47	19.54	17.537**

Note: ** = Significant at 0.01 level, * = Significant at 0.05 level & @ = Not Significant

influenced the dutifulness, Good conduct and self-control of prospective teachers in the Morality Attitude Scale (MAS). Female prospective teachers have more moral values than male prospective teachers who are studying in Colleges of Education.

The obtained F-values in the table 4.17 with respect to truthfulness (9.127), dutifulness (9.754), good conduct (14.592), helping nature (12.849), self-control (7.803), honesty (7.013) and morality are significant at 0.01 level. It means, the variations in age of prospective teachers has brought significant differences in their morality with respect to truthfulness, dutifulness, good conduct, helping nature, self-control, honesty and overall morality.

Hence, based on overall morality, the formulated hypothesis, "there exists no significant difference in morality of prospective teachers due to variation in age" is rejected. The mean values also reveal that the prospective teachers with 30 years above of age group have more morality (165.47), followed by prospective teachers with 26-30 years age group (158.69) and 20-26 years age group (148.08).

From the above table, it can be concluded that age has significantly influenced the truthfulness, dutifulness, good conduct, helping nature, self-control, honesty and overall morality of prospective teachers studying in Colleges of Education at B.Ed. level; whereas, age group of 30 years above have more morality than age group between 26-30 years and age group between 20-26 years.

The obtained t-values for truthfulness, dutifulness, good conduct, helping nature, self-control, honesty and overall morality are significant at 0.01 level. It means, the type of locality has significant impact on the truthfulness, dutifulness, good conduct, helping nature, self-control, honesty and overall morality. It is important to note from the mean values that the prospective teachers from rural background have more morality (156.637) than the prospective teachers from Urban background (143.823). This may be happened due to impact of environmental factors for developing the morality among rural prospective teachers. Thus, the stated hypothesis, "There exists no significant difference in morality of prospective teachers due to variation in type of locality is rejected with respect to truthfulness, dutifulness, good conduct, helping nature, self-control, honesty and overall morality.

From the data collected, it is concluded that the type of locality has significant difference on truthfulness, dutifulness, good conduct, helping nature, self-control, honesty and overall morality. Further, prospective teachers of rural background have more morality than the prospective teachers of urban background.

The obtained t-values with respect to truthfulness, dutifulness, good conduct, helping nature, self-control, honesty and overall morality are significant at 0.01 level. It means, the variations in prospective teachers from government and private management have brought significant differences in their morality with respect to truthfulness, dutifulness, good conduct, helping nature, self-control, honesty and overall morality.

Further, the mean values also revealed that prospective teachers from private management have more morality (161.462) than the prospective teachers from government management (146.669). Hence, based on overall morality, the formulated hypothesis, "There exists no significant difference in morality of prospective teachers due to variation in type of management" is rejected with respect to truthfulness, dutifulness, good conduct, helping nature, self-control, honesty and overall morality.

From the above table, it can be concluded that type of management has significantly influenced the truthfulness, dutifulness, good conduct, helping nature, self- control, honesty and overall morality. Further, prospective teachers from private management have more morality than the prospective teachers from government management.

Table 4.18 depicts the mean and SD of the morality scores of prospective teachers with graduation and post-graduation on truthfulness, dutifulness,

Table 4.18: Showing t-test values of Morality Scores of Prospective Teachers of Graduation and Post Graduation

Dimensions of Morality	*Educational Qualification*				
	Graduation (N=203)		*Post graduation (N=97)*		
	Mean	*SD*	*Mean*	*SD*	*t-values*
1.Truthfulness	25.990	4.874	28.660	4.497	4.679**
2. Dutifulness	24.547	4.403	27.330	4.718	4.882**
3.Good conduct	23.394	3.636	24.845	4.335	2.852**
4. Helping nature	24.951	5.088	27.443	4.863	4.090**
5. Self-control	23.655	3.795	24.897	4.287	2.433*
6. Honesty	26.246	4.676	27.216	4.918	1.617@
Morality	148.783	19.671	160.392	21.052	4.526**

Note: ** = Significant at 0.01 level, * = Significant at 0.05 level & @ =Not Significant

good conduct, helping nature, self-conduct, honesty and overall morality and calculated t-values.

The t-values of morality scores of prospective teachers, for truthfulness (4.679), dutifulness (4.882), good conduct (2.852), helping nature (4.090) and overall morality (4.526) are significant at 0.01 level and t-value for self-control is significant at 0.05 level. It indicates that the morality of prospective teachers vary due to variations in the educational qualification. It means, the variations in the educational qualification have brought significant difference in morality of prospective teachers for truthfulness, dutifulness, good conduct, helping nature, self-control and overall morality.

Further, it is evident from the mean values that the prospective teachers with post graduation have more morality (160.392) than the prospective teachers with graduation (148.783). On the other hand, t-values of morality scores of prospective teachers for honesty (1.617) is not significant at both levels. It means, the variations in the educational qualification have not brought any significant differences in morality of prospective teachers for honesty. Hence, the formulated hypothesis, "There exists no significant difference in morality of prospective teachers due to variations in educational qualifications" is rejected for truthfulness, dutifulness, good conduct, helping nature, self-control and overall morality.

From the table, it can be concluded that the variations in the educational qualification have brought significant difference in morality of prospective teachers for truthfulness, dutifulness, good conduct, helping nature, self-control and overall morality; whereas, the variations in the educational qualifications have not brought any significant difference in morality of prospective teachers for honesty only. Based on mean values, prospective teachers with post-graduation have more morality than the prospective teachers with graduation.

The obtained t- values for truthfulness (3.138), dutifulness (4.088), self-control (2.962), honesty (2.728) and overall morality (3.862) are significant at 0.01 level and t-values for good conduct (2.405) and helping nature (2.094) are significant at 0.05 level. It indicates that the variations in prospective teachers from Science and Arts group background have brought significant differences in their morality with respect to truthfulness, dutifulness, good conduct, helping nature, self-control and honesty.

Further, the mean values reveal that the prospective teachers from Science group background have more morality (157.185) than the counterpart (148.130). Hence, the formulated hypothesis, "There exists no significant difference in morality of prospective teachers due to variation in type of group" is rejected with respect to truthfulness, dutifulness, good conduct, helping nature, self-control and honesty.

It means that there is significant difference in morality between the prospective teachers of Science group background and the prospective teachers of Arts group background with respect to truthfulness, dutifulness, good conduct, helping nature, self-control and honesty.

Table 4.19: Showing F-test values of Morality Scores of Prospective Teachers with different Methods of Teaching-I

Dimensions of Morality	*Methods of Teaching - I*								
	Physical Science (N=40)		*Mathematics (N=52)*		*Biological Science (N=60)*		*Social Studies (N=148)*		
	Mean	*S.D*	*Mean*	*S.D*	*Mean*	*S.D*	*Mean*	*S.D.*	*F-values*
1. Truthful ness	26.90	5.073	27.42	4.737	26.72	4.594	26.70	5.045	0.297@
2. Dutifulness	25.55	4.759	25.62	4.373	26.08	4.627	25.10	4.776	0.660@
3. Good conduct	23.42	3.807	24.00	4.142	24.03	3.733	23.86	3.965	0.222@
4. Helping nature	25.15	6.263	26.10	5.499	24.92	4.551	26.14	4.855	1.066@
5. Self-control	24.08	5.164	24.17	4.182	24.58	3.288	23.80	3.817	0.564@
6. Honesty	26.58	6.008	26.33	5.254	26.70	3.685	26.58	4.632	0.059@
morality	151.68	26.088	153.63	20.835	153.03	17.516	152.18	20.477	0.095@

Note: ** = Significant at 0.01 level
* = Significant at 0.05 level
@ =Not Significant

It is concluded that the variations in type of group have brought significant differences in morality of prospective teacher with respect to truthfulness, dutifulness, good conduct, helping nature, self-control and honesty. Based on mean values, the prospective teachers from Science group have more morality than the prospective teachers from Arts group backgrounds.

From the table 4.19, it is clear that the obtained F – values with respect to truthfulness (0.297), dutifulness (0.660), good conduct (0.222), helping nature (1.066), self-control (0.564), honesty (0.059) and overall morality (0.095) are not significant at both levels. It means, the variations in prospective teachers with different methods of teaching I, i.e., Physical Science, Mathematics, Biological Science and Social Studies, have not brought any significant differences in their morality with respect to truthfulness, dutifulness, good conduct, helping nature, self-control, honesty and Morality.

Further, the mean values also indicate that the prospective teachers with methods of teaching I i.e., Mathematics, have more morality (153.63), followed by the prospective teachers with different methods of teaching I i.e., Biological Science (153.03), Social Studies (152.18) and physical Science (151.68). Hence, the formulated hypothesis, "There exists no significant difference in morality of prospective teachers due to variation in methods of teaching I" is accepted for truthfulness, dutifulness, good conduct, helping nature, self-control, honesty and overall morality.

From the table, it can be concluded that the variations in the methods of teaching-I have not brought any significant difference in morality of prospective teachers with respect to truthfulness, dutifulness, good conduct, helping nature,

Table 4.20: Showing t-test values of Morality Scores of Prospective Teachers with different Methods of Teaching-II

	Methods of Teaching - II				
	English (N=139)		*Telugu (N=161)*		
Dimensions of Morality	*Mean*	*SD*	*Mean*	*SD*	*t-values*
1. Truthfulness	27.381	4.728	26.398	5.029	1.745@
2. Dutifulness	25.669	4.596	25.255	4.764	0.766@
3. Good conduct	24.079	3.977	23.677	3.889	0.882@
4. Helping nature	25.791	5.398	25.727	4.926	0.108@
5. Self-control	24.324	4.034	23.826	3.962	1.074@
6. Honesty	26.532	4.747	26.584	4.820	0.093@
Morality	153.777	21.497	151.466	20.209	0.955@

Note: ** = Significant at 0.01 level, * = Significant at 0.05 level & @ =Not Significant

self-control, honesty and overall morality. Based on mean values, the prospective teachers with methods of teaching-I i.e., Mathematics, have more morality than the corresponding methods of teaching-I i.e., Biological Science, Physical Science and Social Studies chosen by prospective teachers.

Table 4.20 demonstrates the mean, SD of morality scores of prospective teachers with regard to truthfulness, dutifulness, good conduct, helping nature, self-control, honesty and morality, based on methods of teaching-II and calculated t – values. The formulated hypothesis, "There exists no significant difference in morality of prospective teachers due to variation in methods of teaching-II" is accepted with respect to truthfulness, dutifulness, good conduct, helping nature, self-control, honesty and morality, as the calculated t-values for truthfulness, dutifulness, good conduct, helping nature, self-control, honesty and morality (1.745, 0.766, 0.882, 0.108, 1.074, 0.093 and 0.955 respectively), based on their morality scores are not significant at both levels. It means, the morality of prospective teachers not influenced by the variations in the methods of teaching-II chosen by prospective teachers. Further, mean values indicate that the prospective teachers with methods of teaching-II i.e., English have more morality (153.777) than the prospective teachers with methods of teaching II i.e., Telugu (151.466).

From the table, it can be concluded that the variable methods of teaching II has not influenced the morality of prospective teachers with regard to truthfulness, dutifulness, good conduct, helping nature, self-control, honesty and morality. Based on mean values, the prospective teachers with methods of teaching-II i.e., English, have more morality than the prospective teachers with methods of teaching-II i.e., Telugu

The obtained F-values with respect to truthfulness (0.804), dutifulness (1.775), good conduct (0.683), helping nature (0.270), self-control (0.605), honesty (0.439) and overall morality (0.550) are not significant at both levels. It indicates that the variations in prospective teachers with community background have not brought any significant difference in their morality with respect to truthfulness, dutifulness, good conduct, helping nature self control, honesty and overall morality.

Further, the mean values indicate that the prospective teachers with BC community background have more morality (154.10), followed by prospective teachers with OC community background (151.08) and SC & ST community background (151.82). Hence, the formulated hypothesis, "There exists no significant difference in morality of prospective teachers due to variation in community" is accepted for truthfulness, dutifulness, good conduct, helping nature, self control, honesty and overall morality.

From the table, it is concluded that the variations in community background of prospective teachers have not brought any significant differences in morality of prospective teachers with respect to truthfulness, dutifulness, good conduct, helping nature, self-control and honesty. Based on mean values, the prospective teachers with BC community background have more morality, followed by prospective teachers with OC and SC & ST community backgrounds.

The obtained F-values with respect to truthfulness (0.165), dutifulness (0.449), good conduct (0.458), helping nature (0.034), self-control (0.146), honesty (0.710) and overall morality (0.158) are not significant at both levels. It means, parental income has not significantly influenced the intellectual level of prospective teachers with respect to truthfulness, dutifulness, good conduct, helping nature, self-control and honesty.

Further, the mean values indicate that the prospective teachers with parental income ₹30,000 above have more morality (154.60), followed by prospective teachers with parental income ₹15,000-₹30,000 (151.90) and prospective teachers with parental income ₹0-15,000 (152.73). Hence, the formulated hypothesis, "There exists no significant difference in morality of prospective teachers due to variation in parental income" is accepted for truthfulness, dutifulness, good conduct, helping nature, self control, honesty and overall morality.

From the table, it can be concluded that the parental income has not significantly influenced the truthfulness, dutifulness, good conduct, helping nature, self control, honesty and overall morality of prospective teachers in Morality Attitude Scale (MAS). Prospective teachers with Parental income of ₹30,000 above per annum have more morality than the prospective teachers with Parental income of ₹15,000-30,000 per annum and prospective teachers with parental income of ₹0-15,000 per annum.

The stated hypothesis, "There exists no significant difference in morality of prospective teachers due to variation in their parental education" is rejected with respect to truthfulness, dutifulness, good conduct and overall morality, as the obtained t-value for truthfulness (2.299), dutifulness (2.498) and good conduct (2.334) are significant at 0.05 level and also for overall morality (2.661) is significant at 0.01 level. It implies that the parental education has significantly influenced the morality with respect to truthfulness, dutifulness, good conduct and overall morality.

On the other hand, the obtained t-values for helping nature (1.748), self control (1.517) and honesty (1.708) are not significant at both levels. It means, prospective teachers have not differed in their helping nature, self-control and honesty due to variation in their parental education. The mean value of prospective teachers with literate parents (156.060) is greater than the mean value of prospective teachers with illiterate parents (149.693). It implies that prospective teachers with literate parents have more morality than the prospective teachers with illiterate parents.

It can be summed up that the prospective teachers' morality with respect to truthfulness, dutifulness, good conduct and overall morality are significantly influenced by the parental education. On the other hand, the prospective teachers' morality with respect to helping nature, self-control and honesty are not significantly influenced by the parental education. Further, it also implies that the prospective teachers with literate parents have more morality than the prospective teachers with illiterate parents.

The obtained t-values for truthfulness (2.842), dutifulness (2.874), good conduct (3.649), helping nature (3.567) and overall morality (3.854) are significant at 0.01 level and t-values for honesty (2.488) is significant at 0.01 level. It means, marital status has significant influence on truthfulness, dutifulness, good conduct, helping nature, honesty and overall morality. The mean values indicate that the unmarried prospective teachers have more morality (155.578) than the married prospective teachers (146.037). On the contrary, the t-values for self-control (1.794) is not significant at both levels. It means, marital status has not significantly influenced on self-control. Thus, the formulated hypothesis, "There exists no significant difference in morality of prospective teachers due to variation in marital status" is rejected for truthfulness, dutifulness, good conduct, helping nature, honesty and overall morality of prospective teachers.

From the above, it can be concluded that the prospective teachers' truthfulness, dutifulness, good conduct, helping nature, honesty and overall morality have been significantly influenced by their morality status; Whereas, the prospective teachers', self-control has not been significantly influenced by their marital status. The unmarried prospective teachers have more morality than the married prospective teachers.

Mean, SD and calculated t- values of teaching aptitude scores, intellectual level scores and morality scores of prospective teachers as whole, based on gender, type of locality, type of management, type of group, educational qualification, methods of teaching-II, parental education and marital status. And also, calculated F–values of teaching aptitude scores, intellectual level scores and morality scores of prospective teachers as whole, based on age, community, parental income and methods of teaching-II are shown briefly in table 4.21, table 4.22 and table 4.23.

Table 4.21: Showing t-test values of Teaching Aptitude Scores, Intellectual Scores and Morality Scores of Prospective Teachers as Whole, Based on Gender, Type of Locality Type of Management and Type of group.

		Dependent Variables								
		Teaching Aptitude			*Intellectual Level*			*Morality*		
Independent Variables	*Sub-variables*	*M*	*SD*	*t-value*	*M*	*SD*	*t-value*	*M*	*SD*	*t-value*
1. Gender	a) Male (147)	24.313	6.470	3.859**	28.612	6.750	3.047**	148.878	20.417	3.026**
	b) Female (153)	27.373	7.254		26.255	6.645		156.052	20.651	
2. Type of Locality	a) Rural (204)	26.907	6.789	3.731**	27.980	6.584	2.079*	156.637	19.842	5.146**
	b) Urban (96)	23.677	7.089		26.198	7.085		143.823	20.247	
3. Type of Management	a) Govt. (181)	25.083	6.976	2.418*	26.149	6.675	4.087**	146.669	19.305	6.370**
	b) Private (119)	27.076	6.990		29.328	6.533		161.462	19.920	
4. Type of Group	a) Science (146)	27.295	7.955	3.439**	28.596	6.798	2.983**	157.185	19.284	3.862**
	b) Arts (154)	24.526	5.750		26.286	6.606		148.130	21.312	

Note: ** = Significant at 0.01 level
* = Significant at 0.05 level
@ = Not Significant

Table 4.22: Showing t-test values of Teaching Aptitude Scores, Intellectual Level Scores and Morality Scores of Prospective Teachers as Whole, Based on Educational Qualification, Methods of Teaching – II, Parental Education and Marital Status.

Independent Variables	*Sub-variables*	*Dependent Variables*								
		Teaching Aptitude			*Intellectual Level*			*Morality*		
		M	*SD*	*t-value*	*M*	*SD*	*t-value*	*M*	*SD*	*t-value*
5. Educational	a) Graduation (203)	25.192	6.857	2.400*	26.517	6.529	3.274**	148.783	19.671	4.562**
Qualification	b) Post-graduation (97)	27.299	7.230		29.278	6.972		160.392	21.052	
6. Methods of	a) English (139)	26.237	7.480	0.825@	28.151	6.763	1.763@	153.777	21.497	0.955@
Teaching - II	b) Telugu (161)	25.559	6.639		26.770	6.765		151.466	20.209	
7. Parental Education	a) Literate (134)	27.828	7.141	4.417**	29.127	5.930	4.114**	156.060	20.598	2.661**
	b) Illiterate (166)	24.295	6.562		26.024	7.131		149.693	20.612	
8. Marital Status	a) Married (96)	23.156	6.947	4.694**	25.729	6.941	2.925**	146.031	19.777	3.854**
	b) Un-married (204)	27.152	6.727		28.201	6.585		155.598	20.635	

Note: ** = Significant at 0.01 level
* = Significant at 0.05 level
@ = Not Significant

Table 4.23: Showing F-test values of Teaching Aptitude Scores, Scores of Intellectual Level Scores and Morality Scores of Prospective Teachers as Whole, Based on Age, Methods of Teaching-I, Community and Parental Income.

Independent Variable	Sub-variables	Dependent Variable: Teaching Aptitude *M*	*SD*	*F-value*	Intellectual Level *M*	*SD*	*F-value*	Morality *M*	*SD*	*F-value*
1. Age	a) 21 – 26 years (204)	24.77	6.978	8.822**	26.37	6.521	14.439**	148.08	19.718	17.537**
	b) 26 – 30 years (49)	27.45	6.383		27.29	6.596		158.69	19.866	
	c) 30 above (47)	29.02	6.752		32.04	6.243		165.47	19.548	
2. Community	a) OC (64)	26.05	8.115	0.209@	28.80	6.129	2.025@	151.08	20.465	0.550@
	b) BC (115)	26.11	6.999		27.40	6.421		154.10	19.602	
	c) ST & ST (121)	25.55	6.453		26.69	7.350		151.82	22.065	
3. Methods of Teaching - I	a) Physical Science (40)	25.38	8.036	0.188@	27.02	6.732	4.088**	151.68	26.088	0.095@
	b) Mathematics (52)	25.46	7.836		28.19	7.338		153.63	20.835	
	c) Biological Science (60)	26.20	7.307		29.75	6.485		153.03	17.516	
	d) Social Studies (148)	26.02	6.313		26.29	6.462		152.18	20.477	
4. Parental Income	a) Rs.0-15,000 (165)	25.96	6.966	1.146@	26.95	6.952	2.236@	152.73	21.273	0.158@
	b) Rs.15,000-30,000 (115)	25.39	6.913		27.57	6.443		151.90	20.292	
	c) Rs.30,000 – above (20)	27.95	8.034		30.30	6.761		154.60	20.279	

Note: ** = Significant at 0.01 level, * = Significant at 0.05 level and @ = Not Significant

Influence of Each Independent Variable on Dependent Variables as Whole

From the table 4.21, 4.22 and 4.23, it is clear that the obtained t- values for teaching aptitude (3.859), intellectual level (3.047) and morality (3.026) with respect to gender are significant at 0.01 level. It means that the gender has significant impact on the teaching aptitude, intellectual level and morality. The calculated t-values for teaching aptitude (3.731) and morality (5.146) with respect to type of locality are significant at 0.01 level. The obtained t-value for intellectual level (2.079) with respect to type of locality is significant at 0.05 level. It means that the type of locality has significant influence on the teaching aptitude, intellectual level and morality of prospective teachers.

The obtained t-values for teaching aptitude (2.418), intellectual level (4.078) and morality (6.370) with respect to type of management are significant at both levels. It means that type of management has significantly influenced the teaching aptitude, intellectual level and morality of prospective teachers. The calculated t – values for teaching aptitude (3.439), intellectual level (2.983) and morality (3.862) with respect of type of group are significant at 0.01 level. It means that type of group has significantly influenced the teaching aptitude, intellectual level and morality of prospective teachers.

The obtained t-values for teaching aptitude (2.400), intellectual level (3.274) and morality (4.562) with respect to educational qualification are significant at both levels. It means that the educational qualification has significant impact on the teaching aptitude, intellectual level and morality. The calculated t-values for teaching aptitude (0.825), intellectual level (1.763) and morality (0.955) with respect to methods of teaching-II are not significant at both levels. It means that methods of teaching-II has not significantly influenced the teaching aptitude, intellectual level and morality of prospective teachers.

The calculated t-values for teaching aptitude (4.417), intellectual level (4.114) and morality (2.661) with respect to parental education are significant at 0.01 level. It means that parental education has significantly influenced teaching aptitude, intellectual level and morality of prospective teachers. The obtained t-values for teaching aptitude (4.694), intellectual level (2.925) and morality (3.854) with respect to marital status are significant at 0.01 level. It means that marital status has significantly influenced the teaching aptitude, intellectual level and morality of Prospective teachers.

The calculated F – values for teaching aptitude (8.822), intellectual level (14.439) and Morality (17.537) with respect to age are significant at 0.01 level. It means that the age has significantly influenced the teaching aptitude, intellectual level and morality of prospective teachers. The obtained F-values for teaching aptitude (0.209), intellectual level (2.025) and morality (0.550) with respect to community are not significant at both levels. It means that community has not significantly influenced the teaching aptitude, intellectual level and morality of prospective teachers.

The calculated F-values for teaching aptitude (0.188) and morality (0.095) with respect to methods of teaching –I are not significant at both levels. But, F-value for intellectual level (4.088) with respect to methods of teaching-II is significant at 0.01 level. It means that methods of teaching-I has significant impact on intellectual level and has no significant impact on teaching aptitude and morality of prospective teachers. The obtained F-values for teaching aptitude (1.146), intellectual level (2.236) and morality (0.158) with respect to parental income are not significant at both levels. It means that the parental income has not significantly influenced the teaching aptitude, intellectual level and morality of prospective teachers.

PART III: CORRELATION STUDIES

Correlation Among the Teaching Aptitude, Intellectual Level and Morality of Prospective Teachers

One of the objectives of the study is to find out the relationship among teaching aptitude, intellectual level and morality of prospective teachers studying in Colleges of Education at B.Ed. level. To realize this objective, Karl Pearson's Coefficient of Correlation is computed based on teaching aptitude, intellectual level and morality scores.

In this present study, 'Teaching Aptitude' consists of six dimensions namely, professional knowledge, attitude towards children, school related information, social aspects, educational aspects and communicative aspects; Intellectual level consists of six dimensions namely, word meaning, analogy, classification, number series, code transformation and syllogism; Morality consists of six dimensions namely, Truthfulness, dutifulness, good conduct, helping nature, self-control and honesty. Thus, the correlation studies are made to find out the relationship between teaching aptitude and its dimensions, overall intellectual level and its dimensions, overall morality and its dimensions, teaching aptitude and dimensions of intellectual level, teaching aptitude and dimensions of morality, intellectual level and dimensions of teaching aptitude, intellectual level and dimensions of morality, morality and dimensions of intellectual level, morality and dimensions of teaching aptitude have been worked out.

In this section, Stepwise Multiple Regression Analysis is applied to find out how far and to what extent the independent variables (gender, age, type of locality, type of management, educational qualification, type of group, methods of teaching-I, methods of teaching-II, community, parental income, parental education and marital status) influence the dependent variables (teaching aptitude, intellectual level and morality). This analysis is useful to predict the contribution of independent variables to the dependent variables.

To establish the relationship between teaching aptitude and its dimensions i.e., teaching aptitude and professional knowledge and teaching aptitude and attitude towards children, teaching aptitude and school related information and teaching aptitude and social aspects, teaching aptitude and educational aspect and teaching aptitude and communicative aspects, correlation studies are taken up and r-values are worked out.

From data obtained, it is clear that r-values for teaching aptitude and professional knowledge (0.772), teaching aptitude and attitude towards children (0.770), teaching aptitude and school related information (0.593), teaching aptitude and social aspects (0.735). Teaching aptitude and educational aspects (0.54) and teaching aptitude and communicative aspects (0.479) are significant at 0.01 levels. It indicates that there is significant positive relationship between teaching aptitude and its dimensions. It means, higher the teaching aptitude, higher the dimensions of teaching aptitude. Hence, the formulated hypothesis, "There exists no significant relationship between teaching aptitude and its dimensions such as professional knowledge, attitude towards children, school related information, social aspects, educational aspects and communicative aspects" is rejected.

It can be concluded that teaching aptitude has positive significant relationship with its dimensions such as professional knowledge, attitude towards children, school related information, social aspects, educational aspects and communicative aspects. It means higher the teaching aptitude, higher the dimensions of teaching aptitude.

To find out the relationship between teaching aptitude and word meaning, teaching aptitude and analogy, teaching aptitude and classification, teaching aptitude and number series, teaching aptitude and code transformation and teaching aptitude and syllogism, the correlation studies are conducted and r-values are worked out.

r-values for teaching aptitude and word meaning (0.022), teaching aptitude and analogy (0.107), teaching aptitude and classification, (0.056), teaching aptitude and number series (0.045) teaching aptitude and code transformation (-0.47) and teaching aptitude and syllogism (-0.58) are not significant at 0.05 level. It implies that there is no significant relationship between teaching aptitude and word meaning, teaching aptitude and analogy, teaching aptitude and classification, teaching aptitude and number series. Thus, the stated hypothesis, "There exists no significant relationship between teaching aptitude and dimensions of intellectual level such as word meaning, analogy, classification, number series, code transformation and syllogism" is accepted.

It can be concluded that teaching aptitude of prospective teachers has not significant relationship with word meaning, analogy, classification, number series, code transformation and syllogism.

To establish correlation between teaching aptitude and dimensions of morality i.e., teaching aptitude and truthfulness, teaching aptitude and dutifulness, teaching aptitude and good conduct, teaching aptitude and helping nature, teaching aptitude and self-control, teaching aptitude and honesty, correlation studies are taken up and r-values are worked out. The obtained r-values with their significant levels are presented in table 4.24.

Table 4.24: Correlation between Teaching Aptitude and Dimensions of Morality such as Truthfulness, Dutifulness, Good conduct, Helping nature, Self-Control and Honesty

S.No	*Relationship Between*	*Correlative r-value*	*Significant Level*
1.	Teaching aptitude Vs Truthfulness	0.347**	0.01
2.	Teaching aptitude Vs Dutifulness	0.353**	0.01
3.	Teaching aptitude Vs Good conduct	0.273**	0.01
4.	Teaching aptitude Vs Helping nature	0.435**	0.01
5.	Teaching aptitude Vs Self -control	0.327**	0.01
6.	Teaching aptitude Vs Honesty	0.350**	0.01

Note: ** = Significant at 0.01 level, * = Significant at 0.05 level and @ =Not Significant

From the table, it is clear that r-values for teaching aptitude and truthfulness (0.347), teaching aptitude and dutifulness (0.353), teaching aptitude and good conduct (0.273), teaching aptitude and helping nature (0.435), teaching aptitude and self-control (0.327) teaching aptitude and honesty (0.350) are significant at 0.01 level.

It reveals that there is significant positive relationship between teaching aptitude and dimensions of morality. It means, higher the teaching aptitude, higher the dimensions of morality. Hence, the formulated hypothesis, "There exists no significant relationship between teaching aptitude and dimensions of morality such as truthfulness, dutifulness, good conduct, helping nature, self-conduct and honesty" is rejected.

It can be concluded that teaching aptitude has positive significant relationship with dimensions of morality such as truthfulness, dutifulness, good conduct, helping nature, self-control, and honesty. It means, higher the teaching aptitude, higher the dimensions of morality.

To identify correlation between intellectual level and its dimensions i.e., intellectual level and word meaning, intellectual level and analogy, intellectual level and classification, intellectual level and number series, intellectual level and code transformation and intellectual level and syllogism, correlation studies are taken up and r-values are worked out.

From collected data, it is noted that r-values for intellectual level and word meaning (0.431), intellectual level and analogy (0.513), intellectual level and classification (0.430), intellectual level and number series (0.747), Intellectual level and code transformation (0.645) and intellectual level and syllogism (0.292) are significant at 0.01 levels.

It indicates that there is significant positive relationship between intellectual level and its dimensions. It means, higher the intellectual level, higher the dimensions of intellectual levels. Hence, the formulated hypothesis, "There exists no significant relationship between intellectual level and its dimensions such as word meaning, analogy, classification, number series, code transformation and syllogism" is rejected.

Table 4.25: Correlation between Intellectual Level and Dimensions of Teaching Aptitude such as Professional Knowledge, Attitude towards Children, School related Information, Social aspects, Educational aspects and Communicative aspects

S.No.	*Relationship Between*	*Correlative r– value*	*Significant Level*
1	Intellectual level Vs. Professional Knowledge	.022@	0.05
2	Intellectual level Vs. Attitude towards Children	.050@	0.05
3	Intellectual LevelVs. School related Information	-0.001@	0.05
4	Intellectual level Vs. Social aspects	.117*	0.05
5	Intellectual level Vs. Educational Aspects	-0.021@	0.05
6	Intellectual level Vs. Communicative Aspects	-0.058@	0.05

Note: ** = Significant at 0.01 level, * = Significant at 0.05 level & @ =Not Significant

It can be concluded that intellectual level has positive significant relationship with its dimensions such as word meaning, analogy, classification, number series, code transformation and syllogism. It means higher the intellectual level, higher the dimensions of intellectual level.

To find out the relationship between intellectual level and professional knowledge, intellectual level and attitude towards children, intellectual level and school related information, intellectual level and social aspects, intellectual level and educational aspects and intellectual level and communicative aspects, the correlation studies are carried out and r-values are worked out. The obtained r-values with their significant levels are presented in table 4.25.

From the table, it is clear that r-values for intellectual level and professional knowledge (0.022), intellectual level and attitude towards children (0.050) are not significant at 0.05 level. It implies that there is no significant relationship between intellectual level and professional knowledge and intellectual level and attitude towards children. The r-values for intellectual level and school related information (-0.001), intellectual level and educational aspects (-0.021), intellectual level and communicative aspects (0.058) are not significant at 0.05 level. The r-value for intellectual level and social aspects (0.117) is significant at 0.05 level. It indicates that there is significant relationship between intellectual level and social aspects. Thus, the stated hypothesis, "There exists no significant relationship between intellectual level and dimensions of teaching aptitude such as professional knowledge, attitude towards children, school related information, social aspects, educational aspects and communicative aspects" is accepted only for intellectual level and dimensions of teaching aptitude except social aspects.

It can be concluded that the intellectual level and social aspects has significant relationship. It is also known that there is no significant relationship between intellectual level and professional knowledge, intellectual level and attitude towards children, intellectual level and school related information, intellectual level and educational aspects and intellectual level and communicative aspects.

Table 4.26: Correlation between Intellectual Level and Dimensions of Morality such as Truthfulness, Dutifulness, Good conduct, Helping nature, Self-control and Honesty

S.No.	*Relationship Between*	*Correlative r– value*	*Significant Level*
1	Intellectual level Vs. Truthfulness	-0.028@	0.05
2	Intellectual level Vs. Dutifulness	0.293**	0.01
3	Intellectual level Vs. Good conduct	-0.010@	0.05
4	Intellectual level Vs. Helping nature	0.337**	0.01
5	Intellectual level Vs. Self-control	-0.022@	0.05
6	Intellectual level Vs. Honesty	+ 0.292	0.01

Note: ** = Significant at 0.01 level, * = Significant at 0.05 level and @ =Not Significant

To know correlation between intellectual level and dimensions of morality, i.e., intellectual level and truthfulness, intellectual level and dutifulness, intellectual level and good conduct, intellectual level and helping nature, intellectual level and self-control and intellectual level and honesty, correlation studies are carried out and r-values are worked out. The obtained r-values with their significant levels are presented in table 4.26.

From the table, it is noted that r-values for intellectual level and truthfulness (-0.028), intellectual level and good conduct (-0.010), and intellectual level and self- control (-0.002) are not significant at 0.05 level. It indicates the non-existence of significant relationship between intellectual level and truthfulness, intellectual level and good conduct, and intellectual level and self-control. Thus, the formulated hypothesis, "There exists no significant relationship between intellectual level and dimensions of morality such as truthfulness, dutifulness, good conduct, helping nature, self-control and honesty" is accepted for intellectual level and truthfulness, intellectual and good conduct and intellectual level and self-control.

On the other hand, r-values for intellectual level and dutifulness (0.293), intellectual level and helping nature (0.337) and intellectual level and honesty (0.292) are significant at 0.01 level. It reveals that there is significant positive correlation between intellectual level and dutifulness, intellectual level and helping nature and intellectual level and honesty.

It can be concluded that there is non-existence of significant relationship between intellectual level and truthfulness, intellectual level and good conduct and intellectual level and self-control and there is significant positive relationship between intellectual level and dutifulness, intellectual level and helping nature intellectual level and honesty. It means, the higher the intellectual level, the higher the dimensions of morality such as dutifulness, helping nature and hones

To establish correlation between morality and its dimensions, i.e., morality and truthfulness, morality and dutifulness, morality and good conduct, morality and helping nature, morality and self-control and morality and honesty, correlation studies are taken up and r-values are carried out. The r-values with their significant levels are presented in table 4.27.

Table 4.27: Correlation between Morality and its Dimension such as Truthfulness, Dutifulness, Good conduct, Helping nature, Self-control and Honesty.

S.No.	*Relationship between*	*Correlative r– value*	*Significant Level*
1	Morality Vs Truthfulness	.756**	0.01
2	Morality Vs Dutifulness	.779**	0.01
3	Morality Vs Good Conduct	.706**	0.01
4	Morality Vs Helping Nature	.814**	0.01
5	Morality Vs Self-control	.679**	0.01
6	Morality Vs Honesty	.791**	0.01

Note:** = Significant at 0.01 level, * = Significant at 0.05 level and @ =Not Significant

From the table, it is clear that r-values for morality and truthfulness (0.756), morality and dutifulness (0.779), morality and good conduct (0.706), morality and helping nature (0.814), morality and self-control (0.679) and morality and honesty (0.791) are significant at 0.01 level. It implies that there is positive significant relationship between morality and its dimensions. It means, higher the morality, higher the dimensions of morality.

Hence, the formulated hypothesis, "There exists no significant relationship between morality and dimensions of morality such as truthfulness, dutifulness, good conduct, helping nature, self-control and honesty" is rejected. It means that there is relationship between morality and dimensions of morality such as truthfulness, dutifulness, good conduct, helping nature, self-control and honesty, It also can be concluded that morality has positive significant relationship with its dimensions such as truthfulness, dutifulness, good conduct, helping nature, self-control and honesty. It means, higher the morality, higher the dimensions of morality.

To know correlation between morality and dimensions of teaching aptitude i.e., morality and professional knowledge, morality and attitude towards children, morality and school related information, morality and social aspects, morality and educational aspects and morality and communicative aspects, correlation studies have been taken up and r-values are worked out. The obtained r-value with their significant levels are presented in table 4.28.

Table 4.28: Correlation between Morality and Dimension of Teaching Aptitude Such as Professional Knowledge, Attitude towards Children, School related Information, Social aspects, Educational aspects and Communicative aspects

S. No.	*Relationship Between*	*Correlative r– value*	*Significant Level*
1	Morality Vs Professional Knowledge	.406**	0.01
s2	Morality Vs Attitude towards children	.428**	0.01
3	Morality Vs School related information	.375**	0.01
4	Morality Vs Social Aspects	.228**	0.01
5	Morality Vs Educational aspects	.172**	0.01
6	Morality Vs Communicative aspects	.164**	0.01

Note: ** = Significant at 0.01 level, * = Significant at 0.05 level and @ =Not Significant

From the table, it is noted that the r-values for morality and professional knowledge (0.406), morality and attitude towards children (0.428), morality and school related information (0.375), morality and educational aspects (0.172), morality and social aspects (0.228) and morality and communicative aspects (0.164) are significant at 0.01 level. It implies that there is significant positive relationship between morality and dimensions of teaching aptitude. It means, higher the morality, higher the dimensions of teaching aptitude. Hence, the formulated hypothesis, "There exists no significant relationship between morality and dimensions of teaching aptitude such as professional knowledge, attitude towards children, school related information, social aspects, educational aspects and communicative aspects" is rejected.

It can be concluded that morality has positive significant relationship with the dimensions of teaching aptitude such as professional knowledge, attitude towards children, school related information, social aspects, educational aspects and communicative aspects. It means, higher the morality, higher the dimensions of teaching aptitude.

To identify correlation between morality and dimensions of intellectual level i.e., morality and word meaning, morality and analogy, morality and classification, morality and number series, morality and code transformation and morality and syllogism, correlation studies have been taken up.

From the collected data, it is revealed that the r-values for morality and word meaning (-0.050), morality and code transformation (-0.039) and morality and syllogism (-0.033) are not significant at 0.05 level. It implies the non-existence of significant relationship between morality and word meaning, morality and code transformation, morality and syllogism. Thus, the formulated hypothesis, "There exists no significant relationship between morality and dimensions of intellectual level such as word meaning, analogy, classification, number series, code transformation and syllogism" is accepted for morality and word meaning, morality and code transformation and morality and syllogism.

On the other hand, r-values for morality and analogy (0.244), morality and classification (0.290), morality and number series (0.235) are significant at 0.01 level. It means, there is significant positive relation between morality and analogy, morality and classification and morality and number series.

It can be concluded that there is non-existence of significant relationship between morality and word meaning, morality and code transformation and morality and syllogism. And also, there is significant positive relationship between morality and analogy, morality and classification and morality and number series. It means, higher the morality, higher the dimensions of intellectual level such as analogy, classification and number series.

To establish correlation between teaching aptitude and intellectual level, intellectual level and morality and teaching aptitude and morality, correlation studies have been taken up and r-values are worked out. The obtained r-values are presented in table 4.29.

Table 4.29: Correlation between Teaching Aptitude and Intellectual Level, Intellectual Level and Morality and Teaching Aptitude and Morality of Prospective teachers

Correlation	*Teaching Aptitude*	*Intellectual Level*	*Morality*
1. Teaching Aptitude	1.00	0.038@	0.463**
2. Intellectual level	.038@	1.00	0.295**
3. Morality	.463**	0.295**	1.00

Note: ** = Significant at 0.01 level, * = Significant at 0.05 level and @ =Not Significant

From the table, it is evident that r-values for teaching aptitude and intellectual level (0.038) is not significant at 0.05 level. It indicates that there is no significant relationship between teaching aptitude and overall intellectual level of prospective teachers. Thus, the formulated hypothesis "There exists no significant relationship between teaching aptitude and intellectual level of prospective teachers" is accepted.

It is also evident that r-value for intellectual level and morality (0.295) is significant at 0.01 level. It indicates that there is significant positive relationship between overall intellectual level and overall morality of prospective teachers. It means, higher the intellectual level, higher the morality. Thus, the formulated hypothesis, "There exists no significant relationship between intellectual level and morality of prospective teachers studying in Colleges of Education at B.Ed. level" is rejected.

It is clear that r-value for morality and teaching aptitude (0.463) is significant at 0.01 levels. It indicates that there is significant positive relationship between overall morality and teaching aptitude of prospective teachers. It means, higher the morality, higher the teaching aptitude of prospective teachers. Thus, the formulated hypothesis, "There exists no significant relationship between morality and teaching aptitude of prospective teachers" is rejected.

It can be concluded that there is positive significant relationship between teaching aptitude and morality and intellectual level and morality; whereas there is no significant relationship between teaching aptitude and intellectual level of prospective teachers.

Stepwise Multiple Regression Analysis

Stepwise Multiple Regression Analysis is the procedure for analysis of the relative contribution or magnitude of the influence of each of the different independent variables to the dependent variable. The task of scientific evaluation involves in establishing how much and how well a set of independent variables, having a logical bearing on the dependent variables, facilitates accurate prediction. This can be accomplished by applying Stepwise Multiple Regression Analysis.

One of the objective of the present study is to know how far and to what extent the independent variables (gender, age, type of locality, type of management, educational qualification, type of group, methods of teaching I, methods of teaching II, community, parental education, parental income and marital status) influence the dependent variables (teaching aptitude, intellectual level and morality) of prospective teachers. For this, Stepwise Multiple Regression Analysis is applied to predict the contribution of independent variables to the dependent variable.

In this analysis, the variables – teaching aptitude (R1), Intellectual level (R2) and morality (R_3) are treated as dependent variables. The independent variables in the study are expressed as gender (V_1), age (V_2), type of locality (V_3), type of management (V_4), educational qualification (V_5), type of group (V_6), methods of teaching –I (V_7), methods of teaching – II (V_8), community (V_9), parental Income (V_{10}), Parental education (V_{11}) and Marital status (V_{12}) to predict their influence on the dependent variable. Stepwise Multiple Regression has been carried out for each dependent variable and is presented in the form of tables.

To identify how far and to what extent the independent variables contribute to the dependent variable, i.e. teaching aptitude of prospective teachers (R_1), Stepwise Multiple Regression Analysis has been carried out. In this process, the independent variables V_1, V_2, V_3, V_6, V_{11} and V_{12} have emerged respectively.

$$R = a + B_1X_1 + B_2X_2 + B_3X_3 + \text{---}\ BzXz$$

The above multiple regression equation is used to explain the contribution of the independent variables to the unit increasing in the dependent variable (teaching aptitude –R_1). Here 'a' is constant, R is a predicted score on the dependent variable. B_1, B_2, B_3---- Bz are partial regression coefficients and X_1, X_2, X_3 ---Xz are scores on different independent variables.

$$R1 = 24.13 + 3.1314\,(V_1) + 1.4429\,(V_2) + [-2.1454\,(V3)] + [-2.0513(V6)] + [-2.2689(V_{11})] + 2.5862\,(V_{12})\text{(Partial Regression Coefficient)}$$

$$24.13 + 0.2221(V_1) + 0.1536(V_2) + [-0.1420(V_3)] + [-0.1454(V_6)] + [-0.1600(V_{11})] + 0.1711\,(V_{12})\text{ (B-Coefficient)}$$

Based on this stepwise multiple regression equation, partial regression coefficient, β-coefficient, the individual contribution of the variable and percentage wise individual contribution of the independent variables is presented in table 4.30.

Table 4.30: Summary of the Stepwise Multiple Regression Analysis for Teaching Aptitude Scores of Prospective Teachers – R1

Dependent Variable	*Independent Variable*	*Partial Regression Coefficient*	*β-coefficient*	*Individual Contribution of the Variable*	*Percentagewise Individual Contribution of the Variable*
Teaching Aptitude	Gender (V1)	3.1314	0.2221	0.0481	4%
	Age (V2)	1.4429	0.1536	0.0361	3%
	Type of locality (V3)	-2.1454	-0.1420	0.0303	3%
	Type of group (V6)	-2.0513	-0.1454	0.0285	2%
	Parental Education (V11)	-2.2689	-0.1600	0.0398	3%
	Marital status (V12)	2.5862	0.1711	0.0452	4%

The independent variables, gender (V_1) and martial status (V_{12}) contributed a high of 4 per cent each to teaching aptitude of prospective teachers studying College of Education at B.Ed. level. The other independent variables, age (V_2), Type of locality (V_3) and parental education (V11) contribute 3 per cent each to the dependent variable i.e. teaching aptitude.

The others independent variable, type of group (V_6) contributes 2 per cent to dependent variable: teaching aptitude.sssIt means, 4 per cent of dependent variable, teaching aptitude is influenced by the gender. Again 4 per cent the teaching aptitude is influenced by martial status. 3 per cent contribution by their age, 3 per cent contribution by their type of locality 3 per cent contribution by their parental education and 2 per cent contribution by their type of group.

From the above, it is concluded that the gender and marital status, followed by age, type of locality and parental education are the fore most predictors to the teaching aptitude of prospective teachers like wise, type of group is also predictor to teaching aptitude of prospective teachers, even though, its contribution is less than the contribution of gender, marital status, age, of locality and parental education.

In order to know how the extent of the influence of independent variables to the dependent variable, intellectual level (R2), stepwise multiple regression analysis has been worked out. In this process, the independent variables V_1, V_2, V_4, V_5, V_6 and V_{11} have emerged respectively.

The multiple regression equation, $R = a+B_1X_1 + B_2X_2 + B_3X_3 + \text{----} BzXz$ is used to explain the contribution of the independent variables to the unit increasing in the dependent variable (Intellectual level – R_2). Here 'a' is constant; R is a predicted score on the dependent variable. B_1, B_2, B_3 ---- B_z are partial regression coefficients, X_1, X_2, X_3....Xz are scores on different independent variables

$$R_2 = 29.77 + [-2.812(V_1)] + 1.3677\,(V_2) + 2.6101\,(V_4)\ \text{(partial regression coefficients)}$$

$$29.77 + [-0.2068(V_1)] + 0.1509\,(V_2) + 0.1878\,(V_4) + 0.1232\,(V_5) + (-0.1114(V_6) + (-0.1817\,(V_{11})]\ (\beta\text{-Coefficient})$$

Based on this Stepwise Multiple Regression Equation, Partial Coefficient, β-Coefficient, the individual contribution of the variable and percentage wise individual contribution of the independent variable is presented in table 4.31.

The independent variables, age (V2), type of management (V_4) and parental education (V_{11}) contribute a high of 4 per cent each to intellectual level of prospective teachers. The other independent variable, gender (V_1) contributes 3 per cent to the dependent variable; intellectual level. The other independent variable, Educational qualification (V_5) contributes 2 per cent to the dependent variable: intellectual level. The other independent variable, type of group (V_6) contributes only 1 per cent to the dependent variable: intellectual level.

Table 4.31: Summary of the Stepwise Multiple Regression Analysis for Intellectual Level Scores of Prospective Teachers – R_2

Dependent Variable	*Independent Variable*	*Partial Regression Coefficient*	*β-coefficient*	*Individual Contribution of the Variable*	*Percentage wise Individual Contribution of the Variable*
Intellectual level	Gender (V1)	-2.8124	-0.2068	0.0358	3%
	Age (V2)	1.3677	0.1509	0.0423	4%
	Type of Management (V4)	2.6101	0.1878	0.0429	4%
	Education Qualification (V5)	1.7908	0.1232	0.0234	2%
	Type of Group (V6)	-1.5150	-0.1114	0.0189	1%
	Parental Education (V11)	-2.4854	-0.1817	0.0412	4%

From the above, it is summed that the independent variables – age, type of management and parental education are the fore most predictors (4% contribution each) to the intellectual level of prospective teachers, followed by gender (3% contribution). The variable educational qualification (V_5) is entered as the predictor (2% contribution) to the intellectual level of prospective teachers. Even though contribution of variable – type of group is less (1% contribution), it has emerged as the predictor to the intellectual level of prospective teachers.

To establish how for and to what extent the independent variables contribute to the dependent variable – Morality (R3), Stepwise Multiple Regression Analysis has been worked out. In this process, the independent variables V1, V2, V3, V4, V5, V6, and V12 have emerged respectively.

The multiple regression equation

$R = a + B1\ X1, + B_2X_2 + B_3X_3$ +-----BzXz is used to explain the contribution of the independent variables to the unit increasing in the dependent variable (morality – R_3).

$$\text{Here, } R_3 = 126.817 + 6.0466\ (V_1) + 5.7318\ (V_2) + [-8.4061\ (V_3)] + 9.1949\ (V_4) + 5.9069\ (V_5) + [-5.8893\ (V_6)] + 4.4494\ (V12)$$

(Partial Regression coefficient)

$$126.817 + 0.1450\ (V_1) + 0.2063\ (V_2) + [-0.1881\ (V_3)] + 0.2158\ (V_4) + 0.1325\ (V_5) + [-0.1412\ (V_6)] + (0.0996\ (V_{12})]$$

(β-Coefficient)

Based on this Stepwise Multiple Regression Equation, Partial Coefficient, β-Coefficient, the individual contribution of the variable and percentage wise individual contribution of the independent variables is presented in table 4.32.

The independent variable-type of management (V4) contributes a high of 4 per cent to dependent variable – morality. Hence, the type of management is the

Table 4.32: Summary of the Stepwise Regression Analysis for Morality Scores of Prospective Teachers – R_3

Dependent Variable	*Independent Variable*	*Partial Regression Coefficient*	*β-Coefficient*	*Individual Contribution of the Variable*	*Percentage Wise Individual Contribution of the Variable*
Morality	Gender(V1)	6.0466	0.1450	0.0249	2%
	Age (V2)	5.7318	0.2063	0.0667	6%
	Type of locality (V3)	-8.4061	-0.1881	0.0539	5%
	Type of Management (V4)	9.1949	0.2158	0.0749	7%
	Educational Qualification (V_5)	5.9069	0.1325	0.0345	3%
	Parental Education (V_6)	-5.8893	-0.1412	0.0306	3%
	Martial Status (V_{12})	4.4494	0.0996	0.0213	2%

forerunner in influencing the morality of prospective teachers. The variable 'age' shares 6 per cent contribution, followed by 5 per cent contribution of 'type of locality'. Educational qualification and type of group contribute 3 per cent each to the dependent variable, morality. The other independent variables; gender and marital status contribute 2 per cent each to the dependent variable-morality.

To sum up, the type of management is the major predictor contributing more to morality of prospective teachers, whereas 'age' and 'type of locality' are also predictors of morality of prospective teachers. The variables, educational qualification and type of group have emerged as predictors (3% contribution each) to morality of prospective teachers. The other independent variables gender and marital status have also emerged as predictors (2% contribution each) to the morality of prospective teachers studying in Colleges of Education at B.Ed. level.

5

Findings, Educational Implications and the Way Ahead

In any educational system, teacher is a pivot for the transmission of intellectual traditions and moral values from one generation to another generation. The roles of teacher as planner, decision maker, implementer, dispenser of information, task master, communicator, organizer, psychologist, philosopher, friend, guide, surrogate parent, facilitator of learning, disciplinarian, midwife, motivator, evangelist evaluator etc., are significant in teaching-learning process. For fulfilling these roles, he/she needs sufficient intellectual abilities, moral qualities and teaching aptitude in the profession.

Findings of the Study

Part I

1. The mean of teaching aptitude scores of prospective teachers on six dimensions of Teaching Aptitude Test (TAT) is 25.873. The values of median and mode are 26.000 and 28.000. The mean and median are almost equal and therefore, it may be concluded that the distribution is normal. The standard deviation of the teaching aptitude scores is 7.061. This shows that there is normal dispersion in the teaching aptitude of prospective teachers with respect to the dimensions, namely, Professional Knowledge, Attitude towards the Children, School related Information, Educational Aspects, Social Aspects and Communicative Aspects. The value of Skewness is 0.201. It states that the scores are more or less normally distributed. The kurtosis value is -0.002. It indicates peakedness or flatness of a frequency distribution as compared with the normal distribution.
2. According to the classification in the teaching aptitude test, out of the sample of 300 prospective teachers, there are 15 or 5% of prospective teachers in the classification of 'Excellent', 36 or 12% of prospective teachers in the classification of 'Good', 105 or 35% of prospective teachers in the classification of 'Average', 120 or 40% of prospective teachers in the classification of 'Low' and 24 or 8% of prospective teachers in the classification of 'Poor'. By observing these values, it is clear that there are more prospective teachers in the category of low (40%) and there are less prospective teachers come under the category of excellent (5%).
3. The mean of intellectual level scores of prospective teachers on different dimensions of Test of General Intelligence (TGI) is 27.410. The values of

median and mode are 28.000 and 20.000. The mean and median are almost equal and therefore, it may be concluded that the distribution is normal. The standard deviation of intellectual level scores is 6.811. This shows that there is a normal dispersion in the intellectual level of prospective teachers with respect to the dimensions, namely, Word Meaning, Analogy, Classification, Number Series, Code Transformation and Syllogism. In this distribution, mean and median fall at different points. So, the distribution is said to be skewed. The value of Skewness is 0.067. Thus, the distribution is said to be positively skewed. The value of Kurtosis is -0.227. This value is less than the value of 0.263. So, the distribution is Lepto Kurtic.

4. According to the classification in the test of general intelligence, out of the sample of 300 prospective teachers, there are 3 or 1% of prospective teachers in the classification of 'Gifted', 30 or 10% of prospective teachers in the classification of 'Above Average', 132 or 44% of prospective teachers in the category of 'Average', 90 or 30% of prospective teachers in the category of 'Below Average' and 45 or 15% of prospective teachers in the category of 'Poor'. By observing these values, it is evident that there are more prospective teachers in the classification of 'Average' (44%) and less prospective teachers in the classification of 'Gifted' (1%).
5. The mean of morality scores of prospective teachers on different dimensions in Morality Attitude Scale (MAS) is 152.537. The values of median and mode are 150.500 and 135.00. The standard deviation of morality scores is 20.882. This shows that there is a normal dispersion in the morality of prospective teachers with respect to the dimensions, namely, Truthfulness, Dutifulness, Good conduct, Helping nature, Self-control and Honesty. In this distribution, mean and median fall at different points. So, distribution is said to be skewed. The value of Skewness is -0.204. This value is less than the value of 0.263. So, the distribution is Lepto Kurtic.
6. According to the classification in the morality attitude scale, out of the sample of 300 prospective teachers, there are 24 or 8% of prospective teachers in the classification of 'Excellent', 81 or 27% of prospective teachers in the classification of 'Good', 90 or 30% of prospective teachers in the classification of 'Average', 99 or 33% of prospective teachers in the category of 'Low' and 6 or 2% of prospective teachers in the classification of 'Poor'. By observing these values, it is clear that there are more prospective teachers in the category of 'Low' (33%) and there are less prospective teachers come under the category of 'Poor' (2%).

Part II

1. Gender has significantly influenced the professional knowledge (t-value:3.592), attitude towards children (t-value:2.824), school related information (t-value:3.138), educational aspects (t- value:2.613) and overall teaching aptitude (t-value:3.859) of prospective teachers studying

in Colleges of Education; whereas, it has not significantly influenced the social aspects (t- value:1.185) and communicative aspects (t- value:1.588) of prospective teachers in Teaching Aptitude Test (TAT). Female prospective teachers have more teaching aptitude (Mean value: 27.373) than male prospective teachers (Mean value: 24.313).

2. Age has significantly influenced the professional knowledge (F-value: 4.906), attitude towards children (F-value: 8.380), school related information (F-value: 3.626), social aspects (F-value: 5.323) and overall teaching aptitude (F-value: 8.822) of prospective teachers studying in colleges of education at B.Ed level; whereas age has not influenced the educational aspects (F-value: 2.024) and communicative aspects (F-value:1.44) of prospective teachers in Teaching Aptitude Test (TAT). Age group of 30 years above have more teaching aptitude (Mean value: 29.02) than age group between 26-30 years (Mean value: 27.45) and age group between 20-26 years (Mean value: 24.77).
3. Type of locality has a significant influence on professional knowledge (t-value: 2.094), attitude towards children (t-value: 3.665), school related information (t-value: 4.664), social aspects (t-value: 2.811) and overall teaching aptitude (t-value: 3.731). And, type of locality has not caused significant difference in educational aspects (t-value: 1.745) and communicative aspects (t-value: 0.315). Further, prospective teachers of rural background have more teaching aptitude (Mean value: 26.905) than the prospective teachers of urban background (Mean value: 23.677).
4. Type of management has significantly influenced the professional knowledge (t-value: 2.185), attitude towards children (t-value: 2.171), social aspects (t-value: 2.067) and overall teaching aptitude (t-value: 2.418); whereas type of management has not significantly influenced the school related information (t-value: 1.347), educational aspects (t-value: 1.538) and communicative aspects (t-value: 0.448). Further, prospective teachers from private management have more teaching aptitude (Mean value: 27.076) than the prospective teachers from government management (Mean value: 25.083).
5. Educational qualification has significant impact on professional knowledge (t- value: 3.157), attitude towards children (t-value: 2.608) and overall teaching aptitude (t-value: 2.400); whereas the variations in the educational qualification have not brought any significant differences in teaching aptitude of prospective teachers with respect to school related information (t-value: 0.046), social aspects (t-value: 0.046), educational aspects (t-value: 0.842) and communicative aspects(t-value: 0.760). Based on mean values, prospective teachers with post- graduation have more teaching aptitude (Mean value: 27.299) than prospective teachers with graduation (Mean value: 25.192).
6. Type of group has brought significant difference in teaching aptitude of prospective teachers with respect to professional knowledge (t-value: 2.077),

attitude towards children (t-value: 2.806), social aspects (t-value: 2.079), educational aspects (t-value: 2.360), communicative aspects (t-value: 2.997) and overall teaching aptitude (t-value: 3.439); where as the variations in the type of group have not brought significant difference in teaching aptitude of prospective teachers with respect to school related information. Based on mean values, the prospective teachers from Science group background have more teaching aptitude (Mean value: 27.295) than the prospective teachers from Arts group background (Mean value: 24.526).

7. Methods of teaching I have not brought any significant difference in teaching aptitude of prospective teachers with respect to professional knowledge (F-value: 0.095), Attitude towards children (F-value: 0.043), school related information (F-value: 0.461), social aspects(F-value: 0.960), educational aspects (F-value: 0.947), communications aspects (F-value: 0.509) and overall teaching aptitude (F-value: 0.188). Based on mean values, the prospective teachers with methods of teaching I i.e, Biological Science have more teaching aptitude (Mean value: 26.20) than the corresponding methods of teaching I i.e (Mean value: 25.16), Physical Science (Mean value: 25.38) and Social Studies (Mean value: 26.02) chosen by prospective teachers.
8. Methods of teaching II has not influenced the teaching aptitude of prospective teachers with respect to professional knowledge (t-value: 0.946), attitude towards children (t-value: 1.015), school related information (t-value: 1.145), social aspects (t-value: 0.174), educational aspects (t-value: 0.549), communicative aspects (t-value: 0.263) and overall teaching aptitude (t-value: 0.825). Based on mean values, the prospective teachers with methods of teaching II i.e., English have more teaching aptitude (Mean value: 26.237) than the prospective teachers with methods of teaching II i.e., Telugu (Mean value: 25.559).
9. Community have not brought significant difference in teaching aptitude of prospective teachers with respect to professional knowledge (F-value: 0.401), attitude towards children (F-value: 1.641), school related information (F-value: 0.980), social aspects (F-value: 0.737), educational aspects (F-value: 0.144), communicative aspects (F-value: 0.292) and overall teaching aptitude (F-value: 0.209). As per the mean values, the prospective teachers with OC and BC community backgrounds are approximately similar in their teaching aptitude. The prospective teachers with BC community background have more teaching aptitude (Mean value: 26.11) than the prospective teachers with SC & ST community background (Mean value: 25.55).
10. Parental Income has not significantly influenced the professional knowledge (F-value: 0.122), attitude towards children (F-value: 0.236), school related information (F-value: 1.848), social aspects (F-value: 0.578), educational aspects (F-value: 0.845) and overall teaching aptitude

(F-value: 1.146); whereas parental Income has significantly influenced the communicative aspects (F-value: 4.878) of prospective teachers in TAT. Prospective teachers with parental income of ₹30, 000 above/annum have more teaching aptitude (Mean value: 27.95) than the prospective teachers with Parental income ₹15, 000-30,000 (Mean value: 25.39) and prospective teachers with parental income ₹0-15,000 (Mean value: 25.96).

11. Teaching aptitude with respect to attitude towards children (t-value: 4.723), social aspects (t-value: 5.088), educational aspects (t-value: 2.305) and overall teaching aptitude (t-value: 4.417) are significantly influenced by the parental education. On the other hand, the prospective teachers' teaching aptitude with respect to professional knowledge (t-value: 1.937), school related information (t-value: 1.784) and communicative aspects (t-value: 1.157) are not significantly influenced by the parental education. Further, it also implies that prospective teachers with literate parents have more teaching aptitude (Mean value: 27.878) than the prospective teachers with illiterate parents (Mean value: 24.295).
12. Prospective teachers' professional knowledge (t-value: 4.384), attitude towards children (t-value: 3.975), school related information (t-value: 4.311), social aspects (t-value: 4.311) and overall teaching aptitude (t-value: 4.694) have been significantly influenced by their marital status, where as, prospective teachers' educational aspects and communicative aspects (t-value: 1.074) have not been significantly influenced by their marital status. The unmarried prospective teachers have more teaching aptitude (Mean value: 27.152) than the married prospective teachers (Mean value: 23.156).
13. Gender has significantly influenced the ability of analogy (3.442), syllogism (2.843), number series (2.020) and overall intellectual level (3.047) of prospective teachers studying in colleges of education; where as, gender has not significantly influenced the ability of word meaning (0.581), classification (0.011) and code transformation (0.933) of prospective teachers in Test of General Intelligence (TGI). Male prospective teachers (28.612) have more intellectual level than female prospective teachers (26.255).
14. Age has significantly influenced the ability in analogy (t-value:8.773), number series (t-value:9.928), classification (t-value:3.394), code transformation (t-value:3.638) and overall intellectual level (t-value:14.439), of prospective teachers studying in Colleges of Education at B.Ed level; where as, age has not influenced the ability in word meaning (t-value:1.340) and syllogism (t-value:0.862) of prospective teachers in Test of General Intelligence (TGI). Age group of 30 years above has more intellectual level (Mean value:32.04), than age group between 26-30 years (Mean value:27.29) and age group between 20-26 years (Mean value:26.37).

15. Type of locality has a significant influence on analogy (t-value: 3.721) and overall intellectual level (t-value: 2.079). And, type of locality has not caused significant difference in word meaning (t-value: 0.156), classification (t-value: 0.056), number series (`0.866), code transformation (1.669) and syllogism (0.228). Further prospective teachers of rural background have more intellectual level (Mean value: 27.980) than the prospective teachers of urban back ground (Mean value: 23.677).
16. Type of management has significantly influenced the analogy (2.319), number series, (t-value:3.212) code transformation, (t-value: 2.801), syllogism (t-value: 2.197) and overall intellectual level (t-value:4.087); whereas type of management has not significantly influenced the word meaning (t-value:0.934) and classification (t-value:0.628). Further, prospective teachers from private management have more intellectual level (Mean value: 29.238) than the prospective teachers from government management (Mean value: 26.149).
17. The variations in the educational qualification have brought significant difference in intellectual level of prospective teachers for word meaning (t-value:2.844), number series(t-value:2.65) and overall intellectual level t-value:3.274); where as the variations in the educational qualification have not brought any significant difference in intellectual level of prospective teachers with respect to analogy (t-value:1.763), classification (t-value:1.838), code transformation(t-value:1.109) and syllogism(t-value:0.283). Based on mean values, prospective teachers with post graduation have more intellectual level(Mean value:29.278) than the prospective teachers with graduation (Mean value:26.517).
18. The variations in the type of group have brought significant difference in intellectual level of prospective teachers with respect to analogy (t-value:1.984), number series (t-value:4.10), code transformation(t-value:2.198), syllogism (t-value:2.164) and overall intellectual level(t-value:2.983); whereas the variations in the type of group have not brought any significant difference in intellectual level of prospective teachers with respect to word meaning (t-value:0.407) and classification (t-value:1.349). Based on mean values, the prospective teachers from Science group background have more intellectual level (Mean value:28.596) than the prospective teachers from Arts group background (Mean value:26.286).
19. The variations in the methods of teaching I have brought significant difference in intellectual level of prospective teachers with respect to analogy (F-value:2.963), number series (F-value:3.913), code transformation (F-value:4.454) and overall intellectual level(F-value:4.088); whereas the variations in the methods of teaching I have not brought any significant difference in intellectual level of prospective teachers with respect to word meaning (F-value:0.569), classification (F-value:0.993) and

syllogism(F-value:1.272). Based on mean values, the prospective teachers with methods of teaching I i.e., Biological science have more intellectual level(Mean value:29.75) than the corresponding methods of teaching I i.e., Mathematics(Mean value: 28.19), Physical Science (Mean value: 27.02) and Social Studies (Mean value: 26.29) chosen by prospective teachers.

20. The variable: methods of teaching II has influenced the intellectual level of prospective teachers with respect to analogy(t-value:3.592), number series (t-value:2.000) and syllogism(t-value:2.825); whereas the variable: methods of teaching II has not influenced the intellectual level of prospective teachers with regard to word meaning (t-value:0.958), classification (t-value:1.120), code transformation (t-value:1.457) and overall intellectual level(t-value:1.763). As per the mean values, the prospective teachers with English as methods of teaching II, have more intellectual level(Mean value:28.151) than the prospective teachers with Telugu as methods of teaching II(Mean value: 26.770).
21. The variations in community have not brought any significant difference in intellectual level of prospective teachers with respect to word meaning (F-value:0.833), analogy (F-value:1.143), classification (F-value:0.298), number series (F-value:2.789), code transformation(F-value:0.451), syllogism (F-value:2.295) and overall intellectual level(F-value:2.025). As per mean values, prospective teachers with OC community background have more intellectual level (Mean value:28.80), followed by prospective teachers with BC (Mean value:27.40) and SC&ST community background(Mean value:26.69).
22. Parental income has not significantly influenced the analogy (F-value:0.208), classification (F-value:0.758), number series (F-value:2.068), code transformation (F-value:1.789), syllogism (F-value:0.737) and overall intellectual level (F-value:2.236) of prospective teaches; whereas the parental income has significantly influenced the word meaning(F-value:3.070) ability of prospective teachers in Test of General Intelligence (TGT). Prospective teachers with parental Income of ₹30,000 above have more intellectual level (Mean value: 30.30) than the prospective teachers with parental income ₹15,000-30,000 (Mean value: 27.57) and prospective teachers with parental income ₹0-15,000 (Mean value: 26.95).
23. The prospective teachers' intellectual level with respect to analogy (t-value:3.227), number series(t-value:3.231), code transformation(t-value:2.795) and overall intellectual level(t-value:4.114) are significantly influenced by the parental education. On the other hand, the prospective teachers' intellectual level with respect to word meaning, classification and syllogism are not significantly influenced by the parental education. Further, it also implies that prospective teachers with literate parents have more intellectual level(Mean value:29.127) than the prospective teachers with illiterate parents(Mean value:26.024).

24. The prospective teachers' analogy and overall intellectual level have been significantly influenced by their marital status; whereas, prospective teachers' word meaning(t-value:1.052), classification(t-value:0.381), number series(t-value:1.944), code transformation(t-value:0.890) and syllogism(t-value:1.869) have not been significantly influenced by their marital status. The unmarried prospective teachers have more intellectual level (Mean value: 28.201) than the married prospective teachers (Mean value: 25.729).
25. Gender has significantly influenced the helping nature (t-value: 3.742), truthfulness (t-value: 2.238), honesty (t-value: 2.273) and overall morality (t-value: 3.026) of prospective teachers studying in Colleges of Education; whereas, it has not significantly influenced the dutifulness (t-value: 1.877), Good conduct (t-value: 1.354) and self-control (t-value: 1.895) of prospective teachers in the Morality Attitude Scale (MAS). Female prospective teachers have more moral values (Mean value: 156.052) than male prospective teachers (Mean value: 148.878) who are studying in Colleges of Education.
26. Age has significantly influenced the truthfulness (F-value: 9.127), dutifulness (F-value: 9.754), good conduct (F-value: 14.593), helping nature (F-value: 12.849), self-control (F-value: 7.803), honesty (F-value: 7.013) and overall morality (F-value: 17.537) of prospective teachers studying in Colleges of Education at B.Ed. level; whereas, age group of 30 years above have more morality (Mean value: 165.47) than age group between 26-30 years (Mean value: 158.69) and age group between 20-26 years(Mean value: 148.08).
27. The type of locality has significant difference on truthfulness (t-value: 5.270), dutifulness (t-value: 2.670), good conduct (t-value: 3.075), helping nature (t-value: 4.116), self-control (t-value: 3.631), honesty (t-value: 3.976) and overall morality (t-value: 5.146). Further, prospective teachers of rural background have more morality (Mean value: 156.637) than the prospective teachers of urban background (Mean value: 143.823).
28. The type of management has significantly influenced the truthfulness (t-value: 5.047), dutifulness (t-value: 4.879), good conduct (t-value: 3.901), helping nature (t-value: 5.481), self-control (t-value: 3.933), honesty (t-value: 4.544) and overall morality (t-value: 6.370). Further, prospective teachers from private management have more morality (Mean value: 161.462) than the prospective teachers from government management (Mean value: 146.669).
29. The variations in the educational qualification have brought significant difference in morality of prospective teachers for truthfulness (t-value: 4.679), dutifulness (t-value: 4.882), good conduct (t-value: 2.852), helping nature (t-value: 4.090), self-control (t-value: 2.433) and overall morality (t-value: 4.526); whereas, the variations in the educational qualification have not brought any significant difference in morality of prospective teachers for honesty (t-value: 1.617) only. Based on mean values, prospective

teachers with post graduation have more morality (Mean value: 160.392) than the prospective teachers with graduation (Mean value: 148.783).

30. The variations in type of group have brought significant differences in morality of prospective teacher with respect to truthfulness (t-value: 3.138), dutifulness (t-value: 4.088), good conduct (t-value: 2.405), helping nature (t-value: 2.094), self-control (t-value: 2.962) and honesty (t-value: 2.728). Based on mean values, the prospective teachers from Science group have more morality (Mean value: 157.85) than the prospective teachers from Arts group backgrounds (Mean value: 148.130.
31. The variations in the methods of teaching I have not brought any significant difference in morality of prospective teachers with respect to truthfulness (F-value: 0.297), dutifulness (F-value: 0.660), good conduct (F-value: 0.222), helping nature (F-value: 1.066), self-control (F-value: 0.564), honesty (F-value: 0.059) and overall morality (F-value: 0.095). Based on mean values, the prospective teachers with methods of teaching I i.e., Mathematics, have more morality (Mean value: 153.63) than the corresponding methods of teaching I i.e., Biological Science (Mean value: 153.03), Physical Science (Mean value: 151.68) and Social Studies (F-value: 152.18) chosen by prospective teachers.
32. The variable, methods of teaching II has not influenced the morality of prospective teachers with regard to truthfulness (t-value: 1.745), dutifulness (t-value: 0.766), good conduct (t-value: 0.882), helping nature (t-value: 0.108), self-control (t-value: 1.074), honesty (t-value: 0.093) and overall morality (t-value: 0.944). Based on mean values, the prospective teachers with methods of teaching II i.e., English, have more morality (Mean value: 153.777) than the prospective teachers with methods of teaching II i.e., Telugu (Mean value: 151.466).
33. The parental income has not significantly influenced the truthfulness (F-value: 0.165), dutifulness (F-value: 0.449), good conduct (F-value: 0.458), helping nature (F-value: 0.034), self-control (F-value: 0.146), honesty (F-value: 0.718) and overall morality (F-value: 0.158) of prospective teachers in Morality Attitude Scale (MAS). Prospective teachers with Parental income of ₹30,000 above per annum have more morality (154.60) than the prospective teachers with Parental income of ₹15,000-30,000 per annum (151.90) and prospective teachers with parental income of ₹0-15,000 per annum (152.73).
34. The prospective teachers' morality with respect to truthfulness (t-value: 2.299), dutifulness (t-value: 2.498), good conduct (t-value: 2.334) and overall morality (t-value: 2.661) are significantly influenced by the parental education. On the other hand, the prospective teachers' morality with respect to helping nature (t-value: 1.748), self-control (t-value: 1.517) and honesty (t-value: 1.708) are not significantly influenced by the parental education. Further, it also implies that the prospective teachers with literate

parents have more morality (Mean value: 156.060) than the prospective teachers with illiterate parents (Mean value: 149.693).

35. The prospective teachers' truthfulness (t-value: 2.842), dutifulness (t-value: 2.974), good conduct (t-value: 3.649), helping nature (t-value: 3.567), honesty (t-value: 2.488) and overall morality (t-value: 3.854) have been significantly influenced by their morality status; whereas, the prospective teachers', self-control (t-value: 1.794) has not been significantly influenced by their marital status. The unmarried prospective teachers have more morality (Mean value: 155.578) than the married prospective teachers (Mean value: 146.037).

PART III

1. Teaching aptitude has positive significant relationship with its dimensions such as professional knowledge (r-value: 0.772), attitude towards children (r-value: 0.770), school related information (r-value: 0.593), social aspects (r-value: 0.735), educational aspects (r-value: 0.544) and communicative aspects (r-value: 0.479). It means higher the teaching aptitude, higher the dimensions of teaching aptitude.
2. Teaching aptitude of prospective teachers has not significant relationship with word meaning (r-value: 0.022), analogy (r-value: 0.107), classification (r-value: 0.056), number series (r-value: 0.045), code transformation (r-value: -0.44) and syllogism (r-value: -0.58).
3. Teaching aptitude has positive significant relationship with dimensions of morality such as truthfulness (r-value: 0.347), dutifulness (r-value: 0.353), good conduct (r-value: 0.273), helping nature (r-value: 0.435), self-control (r-value: 0.327), and honesty (r-value: 0.350). It means, higher the teaching aptitude, higher the dimensions of morality.
4. Intellectual level has positive significant relationship with its dimensions such as word meaning (r-value: 0.431), analogy (r-value: 0.513), classification (r-value: 0.430), number series (r-value: 0.747), code transformation (r-value: 0.645) and syllogism (r-value: 0.292). It means, higher the intellectual level, higher the dimensions of intellectual level.
5. The intellectual level and social aspects (r-value: 0.117) has significant relationship. It is also known that there is no significant relationship between intellectual level and professional knowledge (r-value: 0.022), intellectual level and attitude towards children (r-value: 0.050), intellectual level and school related information (r-value: -0.001), intellectual level and educational aspects (r-value: -0.021) and intellectual level and communicative aspects (r-value: -0.058).
6. There is non-existence of significant relationship between intellectual level and truthfulness (r-value: -0.028), intellectual level and good conduct (r-value: -0.010) and intellectual level and self-control (r-value: -0.022) and there is significant positive relationship between intellectual level and

dutifulness (r-value: 0.293), intellectual level and helping nature (r-value: 0.337), intellectual level and honesty (r-value: 0.292). It means, the higher the intellectual level, the higher the dimensions of morality such as dutifulness, helping nature and honesty.

7. Morality has positive significant relationship with its dimensions such as truthfulness (r-value: 0.756), dutifulness (r-value: 0.779), good conduct (r-value: 0.706), helping nature (r-value: 0.814), self-control (r-value: 0.679) and honesty (0.791). It means, higher the morality, higher the dimensions of morality.
8. Morality has positive significant relationship with the dimensions of teaching aptitude such as professional knowledge (r-value: 0.406), attitude towards children (r-value: 0.428), school related information (r-value: 0.375), social aspects (r-value: 0.228), educational aspects (r-value: 0.172) and communicative aspects (r-value: 0.164). It means, higher the morality, higher the dimensions of teaching aptitude.
9. There is non-existence of significant relationship between morality and word meaning (r-value: -0.050), morality and code transformation (r-value: -0.039) and morality and syllogism (r-value: -0.033). And also, there is significant positive relationship between morality and analogy (r-value: 0.244), morality and classification (r-value: 0.290) and morality and number series (r-value: 0.235). It means, higher the morality, higher the dimensions of intellectual level such as analogy, classification and number series.
10. There is positive significant relationship between teaching aptitude and morality (r-value: 0.463) and intellectual level and morality (r-value: 0.295); whereas there is no significant relationship between teaching aptitude and intellectual level of prospective teachers (r-value: 0.038).
11. The gender and marital status, followed by age, type of locality and parental education are the fore most predictors to the teaching aptitude of prospective teachers like wise, type of group is also predictor to teaching aptitude of prospective teachers, even though, its contribution is less than the contribution of gender, marital status, age, of locality and parental education.
12. The independent variables – age, type of management and parental education are the fore most predictors (4% contribution each) to the intellectual level of prospective teachers, followed by gender (3% contribution). The variable educational qualification (V_5) is entered as the predictor (2% contribution) to the intellectual level of prospective teachers. Even though contribution of variable – type of group is less (1% contribution), it has emerged as the predictor to the intellectual level of prospective teachers.

13 The type of management is the major predictor contributing more to morality of prospective teachers; whereas 'age' and 'type of locality' are also predictors of morality of prospective teachers. The variables, educational qualification and type of group have emerged as predictors

(3% contribution each) to morality of prospective teachers. The other independent variables gender and marital status have also emerged as predictors (2% contribution each) to the morality of prospective teachers studying in Colleges of Education at B.Ed. level.

Educational Implications

Psychologists, researchers and curriculum practitioners are in an agreement that one of the most important factors in teaching-learning process is that of the teachers. Prospective teachers, who are getting training at pre-service teacher education institutions, are the pivotal agents in transforming intellectual traditions and moral values. They have a powerful and abiding influence in providing quality education when they become real teachers. Thus, primarily, they should have aptitude in teaching, sufficient intellectual level and morality. If they have these essential components, they may shape the child into the thing of beauty, proportion and balance. And also, they can shape the child's behaviour in desirable manner. With the help of the previous studies, it is evident that teaching aptitude, intellectual level and morality are essential variables in the field of teaching. Hence, the investigation has paid attention on studying the teaching aptitude, intellectual level and morality of prospective teachers.

On the basis of the results of this investigation the following implications and recommendations are made.

1. Applied research in the area of teacher education in connection with psychological, philosophical and sociological components, is required for bringing out intellectual trainees and for making moralistic ones in real life situations and classroom situations. The research findings can be effectively used in the process of identifying and selecting the prospective teachers into the training institutions and detecting intellectual prospective teachers who have real aptitude in teaching profession.
2. Teaching is considered to be noble profession which confers special privileges and obligations on those who practice it. It plays significant role in affecting the work performance of the teacher. Therefore, the teaching profession ought to attract candidates, who are professionally sound, have keen interest, capabilities and commitment to the profession. Prospective teachers with good teaching aptitude may be encouraged to take up the teaching profession.
3. Teaching aptitude of prospective teachers reflects the specicity, unitary composition, facilitation of learning, constancy, probability of success in teaching profession and required potentialities in the teaching-learning process. It also reflects the duty, integrity, teacher behaviour, and teacher effectiveness, teacher performance, willingness to improve professionality, interest in profession, reading and love for children.
4. Prospective teachers and teachers working at primary and secondary levels should have teaching aptitude in terms of professional knowledge, mental

abilities, attitude towards children, social and educational aspects, moral and spiritual aspects, communicative and leadership aspects. Quality and competency of any educational institutional is determined by the role played by its teachers. Therefore, it is a must for the University and concerned authority to be impartial in recruiting the faculty on purely merit basis. There is need to plan organize orientation and refresher courses for school teachers.

5. The existing training program has partially failed to provide adequate opportunity to prospective teachers to develop competency to face the varied types of situations in their real teaching life. It seems that the entire teacher education programme in our country lacks professional aptitude which is extremely essential for a sound programming of teacher education. This study may also be helpful in constructing test material for selection of candidates for administration into the teacher education programme.
6. Intellectual level of prospective teachers reflects in terms of variety of considerations: being well adopted, being flexible, versatile, quick, effective, efficient, being able to make duteous to reach a certain goal, coping successfully with an environment, being able to deal with new situations and being able to look ahead. Hence, the teacher education programme should attract the intellectual candidates into the teaching field.
7. Intelligent prospective teacher is expected to exhibit intelligent behaviour in terms of sensing-thinking-acting cycles. They function the activities well even though activities are associated with difficulty, complexity, abstraction and economy. They have habits if mind that lead them to actively use the tool kit of analysis, skills and the various strategies for acquiring information.
8. Intelligent prospective teachers and teachers are viewed as quick-witted, acute, keen, sharp, canny, astute, bright and brilliant in real classroom situations. They may early solve the classroom problems, acquire the knowledge and apply the knowledge in suitable circumstances. They may understand concrete and abstract concepts and relationships among objects and ideas.
9. Morality is an essential component for teachers and prospective teachers. Because, it is connected with manners, customs, habits, traditions and values. It is also characterized by conventional virtues like sincerity, simplicity, gentleness, modesty, compassion, humility, courtesy, self-reliance, self-control, truthfulness, dutifulness, good conduct, helping-nature, honesty, decency, respectability, correctness high mindedness, purity, conscience etc.
10. Selecting quality trainees in teacher education has become a prerequisite to quality improvement in education at any level when they become real teachers. Here, quality is associated with cognitive abilities, moral virtues and righteous aptitude in teaching. Having these essential things, prospective teachers are expected to be more efficient, more dynamic and more humane in teaching-learning process.

Suggestions for Further Research

1. This study may be extended to regions of the Andhra Pradesh state i.e., Rayalaseema, Andhra and Telangana and other states of the country.
2. Similar studies may be undertaken on the prospective teachers of D.Ed. colleges.
3. Attempts can be made to assess the teaching aptitude, intellectual level and morality of primary school teachers.
4. Studies can be attempted to assess the teaching aptitude, intellectual level and morality of secondary school teachers.
5. Studies can be made to assess the teaching aptitude, intellectual level and morality of teachers working in special schools and integrated setup.
6. Similar studies may be undertaken on the teacher educators working in Colleges of Education and DIET colleges.
7. Attempts can be made to assess the teaching aptitude, intellectual level and morality of heads of the general schools and special schools.
8. Correlation studies can be made in relation to personality, self-concept, role-taking abilities, adjustment, teachers' effectiveness, teachers' performance, study habits and level of aspiration.
9. The present study is focused on dependent and independent variables pertaining to the student teachers. The future researchers may also add psycho-socio variables of the subjects involved.
10. The future researchers may take up studies in the field of teacher education covering many psychological, philosophical and sociological components such as personality, morality, sociability etc.

Select Bibliography

Abebe, B. (1991). *Principle of curriculum: A teaching material for the course principle of curriculum inquiry*. Addisababa: Department of Curriculum and Instruction, Faculty of Education.

Abron, S. R., & Irwin, D. M. (1975). Role-taking and moral judgment in five and seven years olds. *Developmental Psychology*, II, 102.

Acharya Ramamurthi Committee. (1992). *Report on Moral and Religious Instruction.* New Delhi: MHRD.

Adaval, S. D. (1973). *Quality of teacher*. Allahabad: Amitab Prakashan.

Aboral, D. N. (1977). A *study of achievement motivation in relation to intelligence, vocational interests, achievement, sex and socio-economic status*. Unpublished doctoral dissertation, Delhi University, Delhi, India.

Adaval, S. B. (1952). A*n investigation into the qualities of teachers under training.* Unpublished doctoral dissertation, Agra University, Agra, India.

Aggarwal, Y. P. (1980). *Motivational factors in the choice of teaching as a profession and its relationships with some other variables.* Unpublished doctoral dissertation, Rajasthan University, Rajasthan, India.

Ajwani, J. K. (1979). *Problem solving behaviour in relation to personality intelligence and age.* Unpublished doctoral dissertation, RS University, New Delhi

Anand, K.K. (1961). S*election of Men School Teachers (Assessment of Teachers' qualities) through projective techniques.* Unpublished doctoral dissertation, Patna University, Patna, India.

Avanija, K.K. (1987). *Moral judgment and personality adjustment of teacher trainees at T.CH. level: An investigation*, Unpublished M.Ed. dissertation, University of Mysore, Mysore, India.

Aggarwal, J. C. (1969). T*eacher and education in a developing society*. New Delhi: Vikas Publishing House Pvt. Ltd.

Ahmad, J., & Salma, K. (2010). Teaching aptitude of prospective teachers in relation to their Acadamic Back Ground. *Edutracks,* February 2010.

Aiken, Lewis R. (1980). *Psychological Testing and Assessment: 7th ed,* Boston: Allyn and Bacon.

Al-Deenhala, F. (1991). Moral judgment in mentally retarded children. D*erasat-Nafsevah,* Vol. I (14), pp. 553-570.

Allport, G.W. (1929). The composition of political attitudes, *American Journal of Sociology,* 35, pp. 220-228

Anand, S.P. (1989). Teachers' accountability: An analysis, *Journal of Higher Education* (UGC), Vol. 14.

Anastasi, Anne. C. (1957). *Psychological Testing, 6th Ed.* London and New York: Macmillan.

Anderson, H. (1999). The measurement of domination and socially interactive behaviour in teachers' contacts with children, *Child Development*, Vol.10, pp. 73-89

Anderson, M. (1992). *Intelligence and development: A Cognitive theory,* Oxford: Blackwell.

Arons, F. J. (1971). The nature of variety and social patterning of moral responses to transgression, *Journal of Abnormal and Social Psychology,* 63, pp. 223-241.

Banerji, N. K. (1956). A *study of specific ability and attainment in the teaching profession in junior high and higher secondary school.* Allahabad: GCPI.

Bhagavathy, G. P. K. (1977). A*nalytical study on the personality, intelligence, values and problems of adolescent's girls.* Unpublished doctoral dissertation, Agra University, Agra, India.

Bhattacharya., & Shah. (1967). *Tryout and standardization of teacher efficiency inventory.* Baroda:CASE.

Bhullar. (1976). *The attitude of university students towards physical activity in relation to academic performance, intelligence, socio-economic status and personality characteristics.* Unpublished doctoral dissertation, Patna University, Patna, India.

Benniga, J. (Ed). (1991). *Moral character and civil education in the elementary school,* New York: Teachers College Press.

Berg-Cross, L. G. (1975). Intentionality, degree of damage and moral judgment. C*hild Development*, 46, 970-974.

Best, J. W., & khan. (1989). *Research in education.* New Delhi: Prentice Hall of India.

Bhatt, C. (1966). A *study of gifted children.* New Delhi: NCERT.

Bhushan, A. (1977). Values as a function of population density and mode of community relationship in rural and urban areas. *Avagahana,* 1(2):1:3, October.

Binet, A. (1905). The development of intelligence in children. In Shipley, T. (ed.). (1961). *Classics in Psychology*, New York: Philosophical Library.

Binet, A. & Simon, T. (1905). The development of intelligence in children. In Shipley, T. (ed.). (1961), *Classics in Psychology*, New York: Philosophical Library.

Bird. (1940). *Social psychology.* New York: Appleton-Century-Crofts.

Boehm, L. (1962). The development of conscience: A comparison of American children of different mental and socio-economic levels. *Child Development,* 33, 575-590(a).

Brown, A. L., Bransford, J. D., Ferrara, R. A., & Campione, J. C. (1983). Learning, remembering, and understanding. In J. Flavell & E. M. Markman (eds.), *Handbook of Child Psychology,* New York: Widey.

Brubacher, J. S. (1966). *Modern philosophies of education*, New Delhi: Tata McGraw-Hill Publishing Company Limited.

Bruner, J. S. (1962). T*he processes of education.* Cambridge: Harvard University Press.

Buch, M. B. (1960). T*est of social intelligence: Construction and standardization.* Baroda: MSU.

Budhisagar, M., & Sansanwal. (1991). Achievement of B.Ed students effect in relation to intelligence, aptitude towards teaching and their interactions. *Indian Educational Review,* Vol. 27 (4), 47-65.

Buros, O. K. (Ed.). (1972). *The Mental Measurement.* Hightand Park and N.J: Gryphon Press.

Burt, C. (1955). The evidence for the concept of intelligence. *Educational Psychology,* 25, 158-177.

Burton, W. H. (1961). *Guidance of learning activities.* New York: Application century crofts.

Byrant, B. K., & Crockenberg, S. B. (1980). Correlation and dimension or pro-social behaviour: A study of female siblings with their mother. *Child Development,* 51, pp. 529-544.

Carroll, J. B. (1997). Factors of Verbal achievement. In A. Anastasi (ed.), *Testing Problems in Perspective,* Washington, DC: American Council on Education.

Cattell, R. B. (1971). Theory of fluid and crystallised intelligence: A critical experiment. *Journal of Educational Psychology*, 54, 1-22.

Chakrabarthi Mohit. (2005). *Teacher education- modern trends* (2nd Ed). New Delhi: Kanishka publication.

Chatterji, R. S. (1998). *A comparative study of personality, intelligence and academic motivation of students in different academic groups*. Unpublished doctoral dissertation, Patna University, Patna, India.

Chaudhary. (1971). *Relationship between achievement motivation and anxiety, intelligence, sex, social class and vocational aspirations*. Unpublished doctoral dissertation, Patna University, Patna, India

Child, D. (1970). *The essentials of Factor Analysis*. London: Holt, Rinehart and Winston.

Committee on plan project. (1964). *A report on teacher training*. New Delhi: MHRD.

Crittenden, B. (1972). *Content in moral education.* Toronto: Ontario Institute for Studies in Education.

Cronbach, Lee J. (1990). *Essentials of Psychological Testing.* New York and London: Harper.

Dahiya & Singh. (2004). *Teaching aptitude test.* Baglore: Psychtronics.

Das, R. C. (1997). Teacher education: Present and future. In Panda, B. N. & Tewari, A. D. (Ed.), *Teacher education,* New Delhi: A.P.H. publishing carporation.

Deb, K. (2004). The changing scenario of teacher education. In Singh, M.S. (Ed.), *Quality impact in teacher education* New Delhi: Adhyayan Publishers and Distributors.

Deese, J. (1993). Human abilities versus intelligence, *Intelligence* 17, 107-116.

Dennett, D. C. (1979). *Brainstroms: Philosophical essays on mind and psychology.* Hassocks, Esses: Harvest press.

DeSouza, A. (1969). *The human factor in education.* New Delhi: Orient Longmans.

Dewey, J. (1959). *Moral principles in education.* New York: Philosophical library Inc.

Dhanavel. (2000). Importance of value-based teachers. *University News,* Vol. 38, No. 18, p.1.

Dhar, T. N. (Ed.). (1996). *Professional status of teachers.* New Delhi: NCERT.

Dosajh, N. L. (1956). *Imagination and maturity as factors indicative of success in teaching.* Unpublished doctoral dissertation, Punjab University, Punjab, India.

Durkheim, E. (1925). *Moral education.* New York: The Free Press of Glencoe Inc.

Eysenck, H. J. (1976). The biology of morality. In Lickona, T. (ed.), *Moral development and behaviour: Theory, Research and Social Issues*. New York: Holt, Rinehart and Winston.

Eysenck, H. J. (1988). The concept of intelligence: Useful or useless? *Intelligence,* 12, pp. 1-16.

Feather, N. T. (1998). Moral judgement and human values. *British Journal of Social Psychology*, Vol. 27 (3), pp. 239-246.

Fraenkel, J. R. (1988). *How to teach about values: An analytical approach,* NJ: Prentice-Hall, Englewood Cliffs.

Francis, E. (1978). *Man for himself,* London: Routledge and Kegan Paul.

Freeman, F. S. (1965). Tests of values. *Theory and practice of psychological testing, 35,* pp. 487-488.

Freud, S. (1933). *The ego and the id.* London: Hogarth.

Ganguly. (1965). An *experimental study of the intellectual factors in the students of the pre-school leaving class under different systems of secondary education.* Unpublished doctoral dissertation, Pune University, Pune, India.

Gowrishankar, H. (1999). *Sri Sathya Sai Baba of education: Theory and practice.* Unpublished doctoral dissertation, Utkal University, Utkal, India.

Gardner, H. (1983). On some paradoxes in moral education. *Journal of Philosophy of Education*, Vol. 15, No. 1.

Gardner, H. (1993). *Multiple intelligence: the theory in Practice*. New York: Basic Books.

Gewirth, A. (1994). Cultural pluralism relevant to moral knowledge. *Social Philosophy and Policy,* 11(1), 22-43.

Ghisehi, E. E. (1981). *Measurement theory for the Behavioral Sciences*. San Francisco: W.H. Free man.

Gnanaguru, A. S. (2005). Empowering the teacher education for the globalization of education. In Talwar, M.S. (Ed.), *Teacher education and globalization.* Bangalore: Cauvery prakasana.

Goldsmith. S. P. N. (1929) Personality, ego development, and moral reasoning differences between feminists and non-feminists. *Dissertation Abstracts International,* 39, 6096-6097-B.

Gongre. (1981). A study of moral judgement using the defining issues test for 3 ethnic groups at bacon college. *Dissertation abstract International*, November, Vol. 42, No. 5, p. 1986-A.

Good, C. V. (Ed.). (1959). *Dictionary of education.* New York: Tata McGraw Hill Book Company. Inc.

Good & Cartwright. (1998). The development of moral judgement among undergraduate university students. *College-student Journal,* June, Vol. 32 (2), pp. 270-276.

Goodnow, J. J. (1990). Using sociology to extend psychological accounts of cognitive development. *Human Development*, 33, 81-107.

Green. (2000). *The activities of teaching.* New York: Tata McGraw-Hill.

Green., & Wood, G. E. (1984). Relationship between teacher morale and teacher behaviour. *Journal of Educational Psychology*, 64, pp. 105-108.

Grinder, R. E. (1962). Parental child rearing practices conscience & resistance to temptation to 6th grade children. *Child Development*, 33, pp. 803-820.

Guilford, J. P. (1967). *The nature of human Intelligence.* New York: McGraw-Hill.

Gupta, M. (1963). *Moral development in school children.* Gurgaon: The Academic press.

Gupta, A. K. (1980). *A factorial study of verbal and non-creativity intelligence and socio-economic status.* Jammu: Model Institute of Education and Research.

Gururaja, Sreelakshmi. (1978). *Development of moral concepts in Indian children.* Accepted for presentation at International Conference of Cross-Culture, Psychology, Munich.

Gutman, A. (1947). *Democratic education,* NJ:Princeton University Press.

Harris, D., Mussen, K., & Rutherford. L. (1976). Group differences in the values within a university. *Journal of Abnormal and Social Psychology,* Vol. XXIII, No. 2, p. 72.

Harrshorne, H. (1928). *Studies in the nature of character, Vol. I-III,* New York: Macmillan.

Hawkridge David. (1995). A short walk to 2000 AD: what's to be done? *British Journal of educational technology*, Vol 26, No. 3, pp. 216-217.

Hilton. (1978). The relationship between the level of moral judgement of high school students and their levels of interpersonal trust, socio-economic status and intelligence. *Dissertation abstract international*, Vol. 39, No. 6, p. 3375-A.

Hoffman, S. (1977). Intelligence and the development of moral judgement in children. *Journal of Genetic Psychology*, 130, 27-34.

Hogan, R. (1975). Moral development and the structure of personality. In Depalma, D. J. & Feley J. M. (eds.), *Moral development: Current theory and research.* New Jersey: Lawrence Eribaum Association.

Hood, J. (1976). *The humanistic frame*, New York: Harper Press.

Holstein, C. B. (1976). Irreversible stepwise sequence in the development of moral judgement: A longitudinal study of males and females. *Child Development,* 47, 51-61.

International Commission on Education. (1978). *Learning to Be,* UNESCO, New Delhi: Sterling Publications.

Ismail, M. A. (1977). A cross cultural study of moral judgement: the relationship between American, Saudi Arabian University students on the DIT. *Dissertation Abstracts International*, 37, 5702-5703.

Jai Prakash., & Srivastava. (1965). *Teaching aptitude test.* Agra: NPC.

Jain, B. A. (1982). *A study of classroom behaviour patterns of teachers in relation to their attitude towards profession, morale and values*. Unpublished Ph.D. thesis, Education, Jamelia Islamia University, India.

Jain, S. (1983). *Concept formation as a function of verbal intelligence and achievement motivation.* Unpublished doctoral dissertation. Rajasthan University, Rajasthan, India.

James, W. (1983). *Principles of psychology.* Stanford: Harvard Currency Press.

Johnson, R. C. (1962). Early studies of children's moral judgement. *Child Development*, 33, 603-605.

Johri, P. K. (2007). *Educational psychology.* New Delhi: SBS Publishers and Distributors Pvt Ltd.

Joshi, Kireet. (1984). *Can values be taught*? New Delhi: NCERT.

Kant, I. (1987). *The moral law*, London: Hutchinson University Press Library.

Kantner, J. E. (1976). The relationship between moral judgement and personality variables in adult offenders. *Dissertation Abstracts International,* 36, 5262-5263.

Kauser, F. (1982). *Children's curiosity and its relationship to intelligence, creativity and personality.* Unpublished doctoral dissertation Madras University, Chennai, India.

Kulanclaivel, K., & Rao, T.R.S. (1968). *Qualities of a good teacher and a good student.* Coimbatore: R.K. mission vidyalaya.

Kumar, D. (1981). *A psychological study of intelligence and intellectual stimulation received by the students studying in different types of junior high schools.* Unpublished doctoral dissertation. Pune University, Pune, India.

Kumar, P. C. (1980). *Leadership traits as perceived by peers*. Unpublished doctoral dissertation, Benaras Hindu University, Benaras, India.

Kumari Sudha. (1982). A study of intelligence, achievement, adjustment and socio-economic patterns of different socio-metric groups of adolescents, unpublished doctoral dissertation, Punjab University, Punjab, India.

Kay William. (1975). *Moral education.* London: Allen and Unwin Ltd.

Keasey, C. B. (1973). Experimentally induced change in moral opinions and reasoning. *Journal of personality and social psychology*, 26, 30-38.

Kline, P. (1991). *Psychological testing: The measurement of intelligence, ability and persolity.* London: Malaby.

Kohlberg, L. (1968). *Moral development*. New York: MacMillan and Free Press.

Krishnaji. (1996). Responsibilities and rights of teachers, In T. N. Dhar. (Ed.), *professional status of teachers*, New Delhi: NCTE.

Kulanclaivel, K., & Rao, T.R.S. (1968). *Qualities of a good teacher and a good student.* Coimbatore : R.K. mission vidyalaya.

Kulkarni, S. S. (1968). *Introduction to educational technology,* New Delhi: Oxford and IBH publications

Kundu, C. L. (1996). Ideal teachers' association. In T. Dhar (Ed.), *Professional status of teachers,* New Delhi: NCTE.

Lele, T. P., Theker, R. S., Bhagatwale, J. A., Kotwal, S., Desai, D. B. & Patel, J. (1957). *Group test of intelligence.* Baroda: MSU.

Levine, B. B. (1964). Punishment Technique and the Development of conscience. In M. L. Hoffman, & L. W. Hoffman (Eds.), Review *of Child Development Research.* Vol. 1, New York: Russel and Sage Publications.

Lickona, Thomas. (1976). *Research on Piagets' theory of moral development, behaviour, theory, research, and social issues.* New York: Rinehart and Winston.

Lickona, T. (1991). *Educating for character: How our school can teach respect and responsibility.* New York: Britain.

Likert. (1932). A technique for the measurement of attitudes. *Journal of applied psychology,* 35(5), pp. 307-311.

Loevinger, J., & Wechsler, R. (1970). *Measuring Ego Development: Volume 1.* San Francisco: Jossey-Bass Inc.

Longstreth, L. E. (1971). Values in the social studies: Implication, explicit or ignored. *Social education,* Vol. 35, No. 4, p. 42.

Mahender, R. S. (Ed.). (2006). *Quality improvement in teacher education.* New Delhi: Sarup and Sons Publications.

Mann, S. S. (1980). *Some correlates of success in teaching of secondary school teachers.* Unpublished doctoral dissertation, Punjab University, Punjab, India.

Mathew. (1965). The *relation between the social attitudes and intelligence of the child delinquents among waifs and strays.* Unpublished doctoral dissertation, Michegon University, Michegon.

Mehta, P. (1958). *A study of intelligence of rajasthan children of age group 12-14 years reading in school grades vii and above.* Unpublished doctoral dissertation, Rajastan University, Rajastan, India.

Menon, P. N. (1982). *Performance of students at polytechnics in relation to their academic achievement, intelligence, differential aptitude, adjustment and aspiration level.* Unpublished doctoral dissertation, MS. University, Baroada, India.

Muddu. (1980). *A study of some personality correlation of intelligence and creative abilities among high school students in Andhra Pradesh.* Unpublished doctoral dissertation, Osmania University, Hyderabad, India.

McDougall, W. (1908). *An introduction to social psychology.* London: Methuen University Paper backs.

Mefarland, D., & Bossier, T. (1993). *Intelligent behaviour in animals and robots.* Cambridge, MA: MIT press.

Ministry of Education. (1966). *Education and national development,* New Delhi: NCERT.

Misra, B. (2003). *Problems and methods of teacher training.* New Delhi: Mohit Publications.

Mohanty, J. (2007). *Teacher Education.* New Delhi: Deep and Deep Publications.

Morgan. (1934). *keeping a social mind,* New York: Mac Millan.

Morris, C. (1956). *Varieties of Human value.* Chicago: University of Chicago Press.

Murphy, M., & Gilligan, C. (1980). Moral development in late adolescence and adulthood. *Human Development,* 23, 77-104.

Naik, C. (2000). Higher education and values. *University News.* April, 10.

Nagar. (1990). Reinforcement and inculcation of values, *Journal of Indian Education,* September, pp. 33-37.

Nayar, P. R. (1988). *Social intelligence test.* Mysore: Mysore University.

Nayar, P. R. (1996). Responsibilities and rights of teachers and teacher educators, In T. N. Dhar (Ed.), *Professional status of teachers*, New Delhi: NCTE.

NCERT. (1990). *Documents on social, moral and spiritual values in education.* New Delhi: NCERT.

NCTE. (1998). *Curriculum framework for quality teacher education.* New Delhi: NCTE.

NCTE. (2003). *Envisioning teacher education*, New Delhi: NCTE.

NCTE. (2004). *Discussion document, some specific issues and concerns of teacher education.* New Delhi: NCTE.

Nelson, E. (1980). A values' profile in education. *Dissertation abstract*, Vol. 31A, No. 10.

Newell, A., & Simon, H. A. (1981). Computer science as empirical inquiry: Symbols and search. In J. Haugeland (Ed.), *Mind design, philosophy, psychology and artificial intelligence.* Montgomery, VT: Bradford Book.

NPE (1986). *A report of ministry of human resource development,* New Delhi, India.

Page, R. A. (1981). Longitudinal evidence for the sequentiality of Kohlberg's stages of moral judgement in adolescent males. *Journal of genetic psychology,* 139, pp. 3-9.

Pandey, A. A. (1976). Comparative study of values between intellectually bright and average high school Indian adolescents. *India psychological review*, 15, pp. 35-37.

Pandey, M. M. (1980). *Mathematical aptitude in relation to intelligence and achievement among the rural and urban secondary school students of Bihar.* Unpublished doctoral dissertation, Patna University, Patna, India.

Patel. (1980). *Teaching aptitude test: construction and standardisation.* Unpublished doctoral dissertation, Gujarat University, Gujarat, India.

Patil, G. G. (1984). *A differential study of intelligence, interest and attitude of the B.Ed college students as contributory factors towards theory achievements in the compulsory subjects.* Unpublished doctoral dissertation, Nagpur University, Nagpur, India.

Patric. (1979). Analysing aptitudes for learning. In R. Glaser (Ed), *Advances in instructional psychology,* Vol.2, pp.41-59.

Pradhan, & Pandey. (1996). Moral judgement of tribal secondary school children in relation to their sex. *Indian journal of psychometry and education*, January, Vol. 27 (1), pp. 21-25.

Prasad, M. (1970). *Evaluation of professional efficiency of primary school teacher in service.* Unpublished doctoral dissertation, Ahmadabad University, Ahmadabad, India.

Prahallada, N. N. (1982). *An investigation of the moral judgement of junior college students and their relationship with the socio-economic status, intelligence and personality adjustment.* Unpublished doctoral dissertation, Mysore University, Mysore, India.

Passi, B. K. (1995). Need of values in Education. *University News.* September 13.

Pyle, D. W. (1979). *Intelligence: An Introduction.* London: Routledge and Kegqan Paul.

Rai, V. K. (1999). *Professional education and teacher training: A study.* Allahabad: Chugh Publications.

Rajput, J. S. (1999). *Education in the changing world: Fallacies and forces.* New Delhi: Vikas Publishing House.

Rama Rao, K. (1994). *Moral education: A practical approach.* Mysore: RIMSE.

Rao, A. C. (1992). *Accountability in education*, New Delhi: *Progressive Educational Herald*, Vol. 16. No. 3.

Rao, V. K. (2004). *Teacher education.* New Delhi: APH Publishing Corporation.

Report of the Committee on Religious and moral instruction. (1959). Ministry of Education, Government of India, New Delhi.

Report of the Indian Education Commission. (1964-66). Ministry of Education, Government of India, New Delhi.

Report of the Review Committee on National Policy of Education. (1991). Ministry of Human Resource Development, Government of India, New Delhi.

Report of the Secondary Education Commission. (1952-53). Ministry of Education, Government of India, New Delhi.

Sawyer, J. C. (1977). A factor analytical study of the dimensional structure within stages of moral development and that structures relationship to specific personality traits. *Dissertation Abstracts International*, 38, 2009-A.

Schruner Greeta. (1976). Sex difference and personality variable in the moral reasoning of young adults. *Dissertation abstract international,* January 1977, Vol. 7, p. 4244-A.

Searle, J. (1980). Minds, brains, and programs. *Behavioral and Brain Sciences* 3, 413-457.

Singh, C. (1996). Teacher education for professional development: Issues and implications, In T. N. Dhar (Ed.), *Professional status of teachers*, New Delhi: NCTE.

Singh, H. (2004). Self financing Vs commercialization of teacher education. In M.S. Singh (Ed), *Quality impact in teacher education.* New Delhi: Adhyayan Publishers and Distributors.

Sinha, D., & Verma, M. (1972). Knowledge of moral values in children. *Psychological Studies*, 17, 1-6.

Shah, M. M. (1962). *An aptitude test for secondary school teachers: Construction and standardization.* Unpublished Ph.D. thesis, MS University, Baroda, India.

Sen Gupta, M. (1972). *Intellective and non-intellective factors associated with engineering creativity*. Unpublished Ph.D. thesis, Meerut University, Meerut India.

Sharma. (1978). An *investigation into the influence of age and intelligence on the problems encountered by adolescent boys of Gorakpur District.* Unpublished Ph.D. thesis, Gorakhpur University, Gorakhpur, India.

Sharma S. N. (1969). *A teaching aptitude tests of elementary school teachers*. Unpublished Ph.D. thesis, Patna University, Patna, India.

Sherry G. P. (1964). A *battery of psychological tests for prediction of success in teaching.* Unpublished Ph.D. thesis, Agra University, Agra, India.

Solso L. R. (2001). *Cognitive Psychology*. New Delhi: Pearson Publications

Srikanth, G. S. (1996). Innovate and revolutionise teacher preparations or perish. In Dhar. (Ed.). *Professional Status of Teachers*. New Delhi: NCERT.

Srivastava, P. K. (2005). Quality concern in teacher education. In Talwar, M.S. (Ed.). *Teacher education and collaboration*, Bangalore: Cauvery Prakasana.

Sternberg, Robert. J. (1986). *Intelligence Applied: Understanding and Increasing Your Intellectual Skills.* Orlando, Fla: Harcourt Brace Jovanovich.

Sternberg, Robert J. (1988). *The Triarchic Mind.* New York: Viking Press.

Stinnett, T. M. (1968). *The profession of the teaching,* New Delhi: Prentice-Hall of India.

Storfer, Miles D. (1990). *Intelligence and Giftedness*: *The Contributions of Heredity and Early Environmen.,* San Francisco: Jossey Bass.

Stremberg, R. J. (1977). *Intelligence, information processing, and analogical reasoning.* New York: Viking Press.

Sullivan, E. V. (1977). A study of Kohlberg's structural theory of moral development: A critique of liberal social science ideology. *Human Development*, 20, 352-376.

Terman, L. M. (1916). *The measurement of Intelligence*. Boston: Houghton Mifflin.

Thakur, S., & Kang. (2002). Moral values and judgement as a function of Age and Sex. *Indian psychological review*, Vol. 58, No. 1, pp. 8-13.

Thomsan, E., & Carr, S. G. (1966). *Values of High School students.* California: The University of California.

Thorndike, E. L. (1926). *Measurement of Intelligence.* New York: Teacher College, Columbia University.

Thurston L. L. (1938) *Primary mental abilities.* California: Psychometric monographs.

Tiwari, G., etal. (1981). A study of family background, intellectuality ability of educationally disadvantaged Vs. advantaged groups. *Asian Journal of psychology and education,* 7(1), pp. 40-43.

Tripathi., & Gurishwar. (1982). Development of moral judgement among indian children. *Indian psychological abstracts,* Vol. 18, No. 1, p. 193.

Tripati, K. M. and Mishra, G. (1979). Development of moral judgement. *India Children psychology,* 22, pp. 164-169.

Turiel, E. (1966). An experimental test of the sequentiality of developmental stages in child's moral judgment. *Journal of personality and social psychology,* 611-618.

Tyler, Leona Elizabeth. (1979). *Tests and Measurements.* Englewood cliffs, N.J: Prentiee-Hall.

Uberoi, N. K.(1996). Responsibilities and rights of teachers, In Dhar, T.N. (Ed.), *Professional status of teachers,* New Delhi: NCTE.

Varma, M. (1971). *Moral judgment test for children.* National Psychological corporation, Agra.

Vernon, P. E. (1960). *Intelligence and attainment Test.* London: University of London Press.

Vetta, A. (1980). Concepts and issues in the IQ debate, *Psychological society,* 33, 241-243.

Walker, L. J. (1982). *Sex differences in the development of moral reasoning: a critical review of the literature.* Montreal: Canadian psychological association.

Walsh, W. Bruce, and Nancy E. Betz. (1995). *Tests and Assessment.* Englewood Cliffs, N.J: Prentice-Hall,

Wark., & Krebs. (1996, 2000). Gender and dillemma differences in real life moral judgement. *Developmental psychology,* march, Vol. 32 (2), pp. 22-230.

Weiner, P., & Peter, N. (1973). A cognitive developmental analysis of achievement and moral judgment. *Developmental Psychology,* 9, 290-309.

Whitehead, A. N. (1979). *The aims of Education and other essays,* New York: MacMillan Co.

Williams. (1985). *Ethics and the limits of philosophy.* London: Fontana.

Williams, B. (1981). *Moral luck.* Cambridge: Cambridge University Press.

Willson. (1998). *Moral thinking.* New York: Routledge.

Wiseman. S. (Ed.). (1967). *Intelligence and ability,* New Jersey: Penguin and Harmondsworth.

Wolman, B. B. (1982). *Handbook of developmental psychology.* New Jersey: Prentice Hall Inc.

Yadava., Sharma., &Gandhi. (2001). Aggression and moral disengagement. *Inter-personality and clinical studies.* September, Vol. 17 (2), pp. 95-99.

Zupancic & Horvat (1990). The role of moral judgment in child's school functioning. *Psychologiche-beifraege,* Vol. 32 (1-2), pp. 111-118.